Lesson Plan Book

Great Source Education Group
a Houghton Mifflin Company
Wilmington, Massachusetts

www.greatsource.com

AUTHORS

Laura Robb
Author
Powhatan School, Boyce, Virginia
Laura Robb, author of *Reading Strategies That Work* and *Teaching Reading in Middle School*, has taught language arts at Powhatan School in Boyce, Virginia, for more than 30 years. She is a co-author of the *Reading and Writing Sourcebooks* for grades 3–5 and the *Summer: Success Reading* program. Robb also mentors and coaches teachers in Virginia public schools and speaks at conferences throughout the country on reading and writing.

Ron Klemp
Contributing Author
Los Angeles Unified School District, Los Angeles, California
Ron Klemp is the Coordinator of Reading for the Los Angeles Unified School District. He has taught Reading, English, and Social Studies and was a middle school Dean of Discipline. He is also coordinator/facilitator at the Secondary Practitioner Center, a professional development program in the Los Angeles Unified School District. He has been teaching at California State University, Cal Lutheran University, and National University.

Wendell Schwartz
Contributing Author
Adlai Stevenson High School, Lincolnshire, Illinois
Wendell Schwartz has been a teacher of English for 36 years. For the last 24 years he also has served as the Director of Communication Arts at Adlai Stevenson High School. He has taught gifted middle school students for the last 12 years, as well as teaching graduate level courses for National-Louis University in Evanston, Illinois.

Editorial: Developed by Nieman, Inc.
Design: Ronan Design: Christine Ronan, Sean O'Neill, and Maria Mariottini
Illustrations: Mike McConnell

Printed in the United States of America
International Standard Book Number: 0-669-48859-3
1 2 3 4 5 6 7 8 9—MZ—08 07 06 05 04 03 02

READERS AND REVIEWERS

Jay Amberg
Glenbrook High School
Glenview, Illinois

Mary Baker
Beach Middle School
Chelsea, Michigan

Marlene Beirle
Westerville City Schools
Westerville, Ohio

Ann Bender
Guoin Creek Middle School
Speedway, Indiana

Martha Clarke
Roosevelt Center-Dayton
Public Schools
Dayton, Ohio

Cindy Crandall
Suttons Bay Middle School
Suttons Bay, Michigan

Janet Crews
Wydown Middle School
Clayton, Missouri

Marilyn Crow
Wilmette Public Schools
Wilmette, Illinois

Deanna Day
Tucson, Arizona

Demetra Disotuar
Martin Luther King
Lab School
Evanston, Illinois

Pam Embler
Allen Jay Middle School
High Point, North Carolina

Julie Engstrom
Hillside Junior High School
Boise, Idaho

Shelly Fabozzi
Holmes Middle School
Colorado Springs, Colorado

Aimee Freed
Perry Middle School
Worthington, Ohio

Patricia Fry
Templeton Middle School
Sussex, Wisconsin

Barb Furrer
Templeton Middle School
Sussex, Wisconsin

Lorraine Gerhart
Crivitz, Wisconsin

Laurie Goodman
Pioneer Middle School
Hanford, California

Jane Goodson
Brunswick, Georgia

Pam Grabman
Center Middle School
Youngstown, Ohio

Bianca Griffin
Audubon Middle School
Milwaukee, Wisconsin

Dorsey Hammond
Oakland University
Rochester, Michigan

Cheryl Harry
Southfield, Michigan

Jeff Hicks
Whitford Middle School
Beaverton, Oregon

Claire Hiller
Timber Ridge Magnet School
Skokie, Illinois

Terri Huck
John Bullen Accelerated
Middle School
Kenosha, Wisconsin

Ralph Huhn, Jr.
Key West, Florida

Dana Humphrey
F. Zumwalt North
Middle School
O'Fallon, Missouri

Dennis Jackson
Danvers Public Schools
Danvers, Massachusetts

Jean Lifford
Dedham High School
Dedham, Massachusetts

Linda Maloney
Ridgewood Junior
High School
Arnold, Missouri

Nancy McEvoy
Anderson Middle School
Berkley, Michigan

Mary McHugh
Franklin School
Belleville, Illinois

Catherine McNary
Proviso West High School
Hillside, Illinois

Marsha Nadasky
Western Reserve
Middle School
Berlin Center, Ohio

Cheryl Nuciforo
City School District of Troy
Troy, New York

Lucretia Pannozzo
John Jay Middle School
Katonah, New York

Brenda Peterson
Templeton Middle School
Sussex, Wisconsin

Evelyn Price
Grand Avenue Middle School
Milwaukee, Wisconsin

Richard Santeusanio
Danvers School District
Danvers, Massachusetts

Jennifer Sellenriek
Wydown Middle School
Clayton, Missouri

Jill Vavrek
Proviso West High School
Hillside, Illinois

Dave Wendelin
Educational Service Center
Golden, Colorado

Michel Wendell
Archdiocese of St. Louis
Cathedral School
St. Louis, Missouri

Roberta Williams
Traverse City East Junior
High School
Traverse City, Michigan

Sharon Williams
Bay Point Middle School
St. Petersburg, Florida

Table of Contents

Lesson Plan Book Overview

The *Lesson Plan Book* includes a suggested reading curriculum for each grade level, weekly and daily lesson plans, and professional articles.

Week at a Glance

Shows **daily lessons** for the week.

Summary notes can be used to teach mini-lessons.

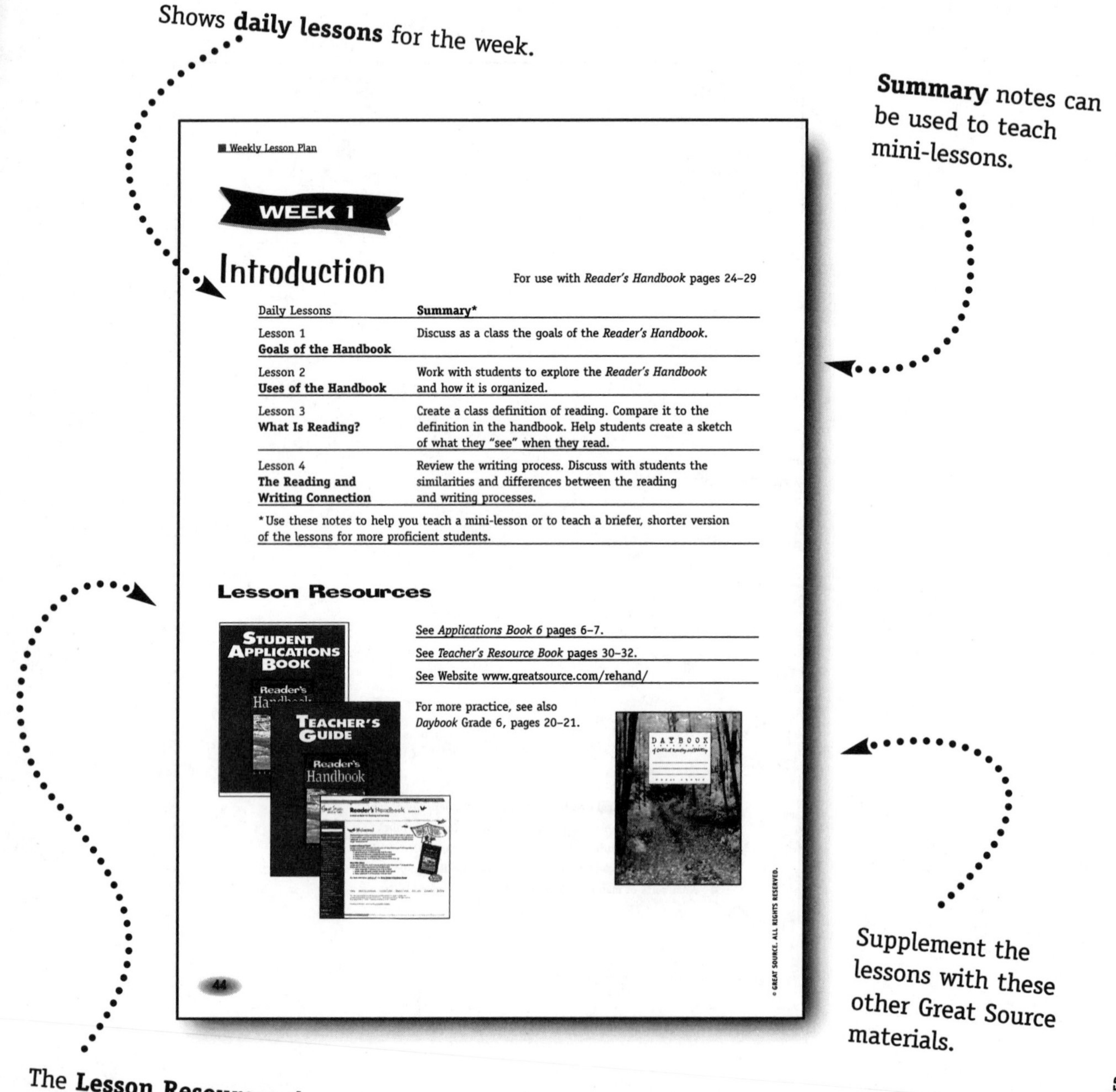

■ Weekly Lesson Plan

WEEK 1

Introduction

For use with *Reader's Handbook* pages 24–29

Daily Lessons	Summary*
Lesson 1 **Goals of the Handbook**	Discuss as a class the goals of the *Reader's Handbook*.
Lesson 2 **Uses of the Handbook**	Work with students to explore the *Reader's Handbook* and how it is organized.
Lesson 3 **What Is Reading?**	Create a class definition of reading. Compare it to the definition in the handbook. Help students create a sketch of what they "see" when they read.
Lesson 4 **The Reading and Writing Connection**	Review the writing process. Discuss with students the similarities and differences between the reading and writing processes.

* Use these notes to help you teach a mini-lesson or to teach a briefer, shorter version of the lessons for more proficient students.

Lesson Resources

See *Applications Book 6* pages 6–7.

See *Teacher's Resource Book* pages 30–32.

See Website www.greatsource.com/rehand/

For more practice, see also *Daybook* Grade 6, pages 20–21.

44

Supplement the lessons with these other Great Source materials.

The **Lesson Resources** show all of the other materials that accompany the lesson.

Lesson Plans

The **Teaching Focus** section gives background along with key instruction.

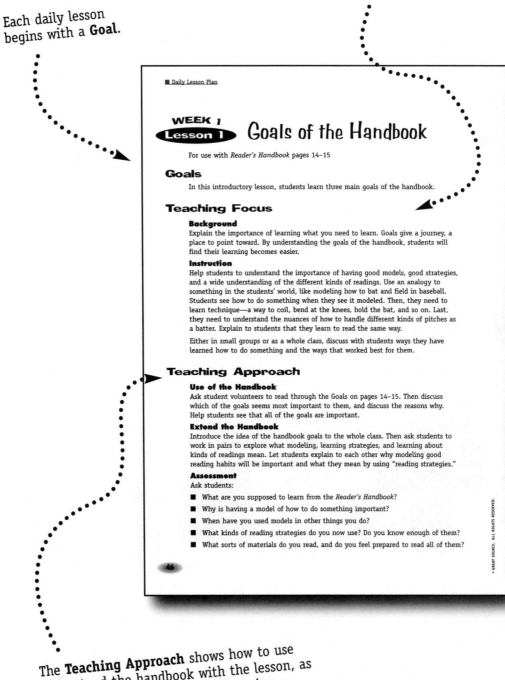

Each daily lesson begins with a **Goal**.

Daily Lesson Plan

WEEK 1
Lesson 1

Goals of the Handbook

For use with *Reader's Handbook* pages 14–15

Goals

In this introductory lesson, students learn three main goals of the handbook.

Teaching Focus

Background

Explain the importance of learning what you need to learn. Goals give a journey, a place to point toward. By understanding the goals of the handbook, students will find their learning becomes easier.

Instruction

Help students to understand the importance of having good models, good strategies, and a wide understanding of the different kinds of readings. Use an analogy to something in the students' world, like modeling how to bat and field in baseball. Students see how to do something when they see it modeled. Then, they need to learn technique—a way to coil, bend at the knees, hold the bat, and so on. Last, they need to understand the nuances of how to handle different kinds of pitches as a batter. Explain to students that they learn to read the same way.

Either in small groups or as a whole class, discuss with students ways they have learned how to do something and the ways that worked best for them.

Teaching Approach

Use of the Handbook

Ask student volunteers to read through the Goals on pages 14–15. Then discuss which of the goals seems most important to them, and discuss the reasons why. Help students see that all of the goals are important.

Extend the Handbook

Introduce the idea of the handbook goals to the whole class. Then ask students to work in pairs to explore what modeling, learning strategies, and learning about kinds of readings mean. Let students explain to each other why modeling good reading habits will be important and what they mean by using "reading strategies."

Assessment

Ask students:

- What are you supposed to learn from the *Reader's Handbook*?
- Why is having a model of how to do something important?
- When have you used models in other things you do?
- What kinds of reading strategies do you now use? Do you know enough of them?
- What sorts of materials do you read, and do you feel prepared to read all of them?

46

The **Teaching Approach** shows how to use and extend the handbook with the lesson, as well as ways to assess student learning.

Frequently Asked Questions

How did you define what a reading strategy is, and how did you choose which ones to use in the handbook?

In the *Reader's Handbook*, a **strategy** is defined as having a broad application across different genres. A strategy can serve a number of purposes. For example, you can *outline* or *find cause and effect* with fiction or nonfiction, a textbook, or a test. But some skills, such as *drawing conclusions* or *comparing and contrasting,* are so fundamental that they underlie almost everything. That's why these skills are called **"reading know-how."** The handbook also refers to **"reading tools,"** which are more specialized and have a specific use or purpose. The Almanac lists 36 key reading tools used throughout the handbook. A K-W-L chart, for example, is used with nonfiction texts; Story Strings work specifically with fiction; Two Per Line is most appropriate for poetry. These distinctions between strategies, know-how, and tools are an attempt to use terms consistently in the absence of any consensus, and an attempt to create a set of terms teachers can use within a school to create a shared, common language.

How did you decide on these specific steps of the reading process, and why are they in the order they are?

Reading is almost infinitely complex. It—like writing—hardly follows any single process or, for that matter, works in any single direction. But students need specifics on what to do. They need a good model, and they need to develop good habits. So, rather than presenting reading in all its complex splendor, the handbook organizes reading around an easy-to-remember process, explaining what students need to do Before, During, and After Reading. It breaks down the process into brief, easy steps. As with the writing process, students may sometimes skip a step, go backward occasionally, or spend a long time on one of the steps. That's OK. The reading process will help students make the decisions they need in order to be effective readers.

What kind of students is the handbook for?

The *Reader's Handbook* is for all students. Different students will take away different things from the handbook. Good readers will refine the strategies they use and learn some new reading tools they can apply, and perhaps even learn more about how different kinds of texts are organized. Average readers will add to the reading strategies and tools they use, and they'll develop a stronger understanding of the reading process. And students who struggle will acquire some good strategies, tools, and understanding of the process of reading.

Where should I begin as a teacher?

For help in teaching the handbook, start with the *Teacher's Guide* and *Overhead Transparencies*. To develop a curriculum or daily lesson plans, start with the *Lesson Plan Book* for your grade. To see if students can apply the strategies, use the *Student Applications Book* for your grade.

For more Frequently Asked Questions, see the website at: www.greatsource.com/rehand/

Reading Curriculum

Each *Lesson Plan Book* suggests a reading curriculum for teachers to implement in their classrooms. This curriculum was designed for a 36-week school year, and it shows what a teacher can reasonably cover in a single year. For convenience, the *Lesson Plan Book* organized lesson plans in two-week segments, so you can see at a glance all of the daily lessons and resources for a genre.

To customize a curriculum for your students, see pages 12–15.

Grade 6 Curriculum

Week	Unit	Week	Unit
1	Introduction	19	Reading a Novel
2	The Reading Process	20	Reading a Novel
3	Essential Reading Skills	21	Elements of Fiction
4	Reading Actively	22	Elements of Fiction
5	Reading Know-how: Reading Paragraphs	23	Reading a Poem
6	Reading Know-how: Reading Paragraphs	24	Elements of Poetry
7	Reading Geography	25	Reading a Play
8	Reading Geography	26	Focus on Language
9	Elements of Textbooks	27	Reading a Website
10	Elements of Nonfiction	28	Elements of the Internet
11	Reading Biographies and Autobiographies	29	Reading a Graphic
12	Reading Biographies and Autobiographies	30	Elements of Graphics
13	Reading a Newspaper Article	31	Reading a Test and Test Questions
14	Focus on Persuasive Writing	32	Reading a Test and Test Questions
15	Reading a Short Story	33	Improving Vocabulary
16	Focus on Plot	34	Improving Vocabulary
17	Focus on Characters	35	Strategy Handbook
18	Focus on Setting	36	Reading Tools

Grade 7 Curriculum

Week	Unit
1	Introduction
2	The Reading Process
3	Reading Know-how
4	Reading Paragraphs
5	Reading History
6	Reading History
7	Reading Math
8	Focus on Word Problems
9	Elements of Textbooks
10	Elements of Nonfiction
11	Reading an Essay
12	Reading an Essay
13	Reading a Magazine Article
14	Focus on Speeches
15	Reading a Short Story
16	Reading a Novel
17	Focus on Dialogue
18	Focus on Theme

Week	Unit
19	Elements of Fiction
20	Elements of Poetry
21	Reading a Poem
22	Focus on Language
23	Reading a Play
24	Elements of Drama
25	Reading a Website
26	Elements of the Internet
27	Reading a Graphic
28	Elements of Graphics
29	Reading a Test and Test Questions
30	Focus on Essay Tests
31	Focus on Math Tests
32	Focus on Science Tests
33	Improving Vocabulary
34	Improving Vocabulary
35	The Reader's Almanac
36	The Reader's Almanac

Grade 8 Curriculum

Week	Unit
1	Introduction
2	The Reading Process
3	Reading Know-how
4	Reading History
5	Reading Science
6	Reading Science
7	Reading Math
8	Elements of Textbooks
9	Reading an Essay
10	Reading Biographies and Autobiographies
11	Reading a Magazine Article
12	Focus on Persuasive Writing
13	Focus on Real-World Writing
14	Elements of Nonfiction
15	Reading a Short Story
16	Reading a Novel
17	Focus on Plot and Theme
18	Focus on Comparing and Contrasting
19	Elements of Fiction
20	Elements of Poetry
21	Reading a Poem
22	Focus on Meaning, Sound, & Structure
23	Reading a Play
24	Focus on Theme and Language
25	Reading a Website
26	Reading a Graphic
27	Reading a Test and Test Questions
28	Focus on Essay Tests
29	Focus on Vocabulary Tests
30	Focus on Social Studies Tests
31	Focus on Math Tests
32	Focus on Science Tests
33	Improving Vocabulary
34	Improving Vocabulary
35	The Reader's Almanac
36	The Reader's Almanac

Build Your Own Curriculum

The lesson plans in the *Lesson Plan Book* are adaptable to fit any curriculum. You can pick and choose lessons to teach with a specific emphasis. You can also use lesson plans from other grade levels, which are available from the website (www.greatsource.com/rehand/). See the examples below and on the next page for suggestions to design your own curriculum.

Example

Use the year-long Curriculum Plan to map out which chapters to teach in each quarter. The example below shows a model that emphasizes teaching reading across the curriculum.

Reading Across the Curriculum Focus

Quarter 1	Quarter 2
Reading Process Reading Know-how Reading Textbooks	Reading Textbooks Reading Nonfiction
Quarter 3	**Quarter 4**
Reading Fiction Reading Poetry Reading Graphics	Reading Drama Reading on the Internet Reading for Tests Improving Vocabulary

Quarter 1 Plan

Week 1	Reading Process
Week 2	Reading Know-how
Week 3	Reading Know-how
Week 4	Elements of Textbooks
Week 5	Reading History
Week 6	Reading Geography
Week 7	Reading Science
Week 8	Reading Science
Week 9	Reading History

Once a Curriculum Plan is set for the year, create a Quarter Plan to focus on which lessons to teach week-by-week during each quarter.

Other Year-long Curriculum Plan Examples

Vocabulary and Language Focus

Quarter 1	Quarter 2
Reading Process Reading Know-how Improving Vocabulary Reading Textbooks	Reading Fiction Reading Poetry Reading Nonfiction Reading for Tests
Quarter 3	**Quarter 4**
Reading Textbooks Reading Nonfiction Reading Poetry Improving Vocabulary	Reading Graphics Reading Drama Improving Vocabulary Reading for Tests

Literature Focus

Quarter 1	Quarter 2
Reading Process Reading Know-how Improving Vocabulary Reading Fiction	Reading Fiction Reading Poetry Improving Vocabulary Reading for Tests
Quarter 3	**Quarter 4**
Reading Textbooks Reading Nonfiction Reading Drama Reading Poetry	Reading Nonfiction Reading Graphics Reading on the Internet Reading for Tests

Test-Success Focus

Quarter 1	Quarter 2
Reading Process Reading Know-how Improving Vocabulary Reading for Tests	Reading Textbooks Reading Graphics Reading Nonfiction Reading for Tests
Quarter 3	**Quarter 4**
Reading Fiction Reading Poetry Improving Vocabulary Reading for Tests	Reading Drama Reading on the Internet Reading Textbooks Reading for Tests

Build Your Own Curriculum

CURRICULUM: ______________________________

1st Quarter	2nd Quarter

3rd Quarter	4th Quarter

Build Your Own Curriculum

QUARTER::____

Week 1

Week 2

Week 3

Week 4

Week 5

Week 6

Week 7

Week 8

Week 9

Reading Strategy Overview

Reading Lesson	Selection	Reading Strategy	Rereading Strategy
Reading History	"Indian Wars"	Note-taking	Outlining
Reading Geography	"Population"	Using Graphic Organizers	Note-taking
Reading Science	"Exploring the Ocean"	Note-taking	Skimming
Reading Math	"Connections to Algebra"	Visualizing and Thinking Aloud	Note-taking
Reading an Essay	"America the Not-so-Beautiful"	Outlining	Questioning the Author
Reading a Biography	*Harriet Tubman: Conductor on the Underground Railroad*	Looking for Cause and Effect	Outlining
Reading an Autobiography	*Up from Slavery*	Synthesizing	Looking for Cause and Effect
Reading a Newspaper Article	"Robots get ready to rumble"	Reading Critically	Summarizing
Reading a Magazine Article	"A Killer Gets Some Respect"	Questioning the Author	Reading Critically
Reading a Short Story	"Charles"	Using Graphic Organizers	Close Reading
Reading a Novel	*Roll of Thunder, Hear My Cry*	Synthesizing	Using Graphic Organizers
Reading a Poem	"Winter Poem"	Close Reading	Paraphrasing
Reading a Play	*The Diary of Anne Frank*	Summarizing	Visualizing and Thinking Aloud
Reading a Website	"The International Dyslexia Association Website"	Reading Critically	Skimming
Reading a Graphic	"Gallup Survey on Crime"	Paraphrasing	Reading Critically
Reading a Test and Test Questions	*Geronimo: His Own Story*	Skimming	Visualizing and Thinking Aloud

Focus Lesson	Selection	Reading Strategy
Focus on Science Concepts	"Cell Growth and Division"	Using Graphic Organizers
Focus on Word Problems	Math Problems	Visualizing and Thinking Aloud
Focus on Persuasive Writing	"Parents, Not Cash Can Enrich a School"	Reading Critically
Focus on Speeches	"The future doesn't belong to the fainthearted"	Reading Critically
Focus on Real-world Writing	School Conduct Handbook Computer Game Instructions Train Schedule	Skimming
Focus on Characters	*The Cay*	Using Graphic Organizers
Focus on Setting	*Shiloh*	Close Reading
Focus on Dialogue	*Roll of Thunder, Hear My Cry*	Close Reading
Focus on Plot	"Last Cover"	Using Graphic Organizers
Focus on Theme	*Roll of Thunder, Hear My Cry*	
Focus on Comparing and Contrasting	Greek Myth of King Midas and *A Christmas Carol*	Using Graphic Organizers
Focus on Language	"Words"	Close Reading
Focus on Meaning	"Those Winter Sundays"	Close Reading
Focus on Sound and Structure	"The Sloth"	Close Reading
Focus on Theme	*The Diary of Anne Frank*	
Focus on Language	*The Diary of Anne Frank*	
Focus on Essay Tests	Sample Essay Questions	
Focus on Vocabulary Tests	Sample Vocabulary Questions	
Focus on Social Studies Tests	Sample Social Studies Questions	
Focus on Math Tests	Sample Math Questions	
Focus on Science Tests	Sample Science Questions	

Guide to the *Reader's Handbook*

Reading Lessons

Reading lessons model how to read different kinds of materials using the reading process. The reading process has three steps: Before Reading, During Reading, and After Reading.

Before Reading

Before Reading consists of setting a purpose, previewing a reading, and planning a reading strategy.

The Goals box shows **what students will learn** from the lesson.

Goals

Here you'll learn how to:

- ✔ read **history**
- ✔ use the strategy of **note-taking**
- ✔ see **the way history textbooks are often organized**

The Setting a Purpose box suggests one or more **questions that students can attempt to answer as they read.**

Setting a Purpose

- **What** were the Indian Wars?
- **When** did they take place?
- **Who** was involved in these wars?
- **Where** did they take place?
- **Why** did they occur?

The Preview Checklist lists what to look for when **previewing a reading.**

Preview Checklist

- ✔ *the title and any section guides or goals boxes*
- ✔ *the first and last paragraphs*
- ✔ *the headings*
- ✔ *any names, dates, words, or terms set in boldface or that are repeated*

The Reading Strategy helps students **use a reading strategy** for a specific type of reading.

Reading Strategy: Note-taking

So, here's your purpose—to gather general, basic information about the Indian Wars. One excellent strategy to use to collect that information is **note-taking.**

The During Reading step includes reading actively, looking for information that fits the reading purpose, and creating a personal connection to the text.

Reading Tools are suggested to help students understand the reading and **look for information that fits their reading purpose.**

1. Summary Notes

Learn something from each page or section of your textbook. Take notes about the most important information. Look for key facts or names and any terms or ideas in boldface or headings.

Page 559	1800—Indians lived in peace. 1840—Reservations began. Indians and whites clashed on Plains.
Page 560	1860s—Treaties were broken. Settlers went through Indian lands and killed buffalo. Indians raided white settlements.
Page 561	1876—Sitting Bull and Crazy Horse attacked Gen. Custer. Massacre was last major Indian victory.

The How Texts Are Organized **looks at how different kinds of reading are organized** so students can understand them better.

How History Textbooks Are Organized

Active readers can create more understanding than readers who simply turn the pages. Understanding a passage takes time and effort, and it helps to know what to look for.

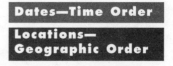

Dates—Time Order

Locations—Geographic Order

Look back for a moment at the history text on pages 69–72. If you follow the highlighting in the example, you will notice that the reader marked many of the names, dates, and locations.

In the Connect step, students **create a personal connection to the text.**

Connect

The idea that you are responsible for your own reading is one of the most important ideas in this handbook. You need to take charge and grab the information you need.

The After Reading step includes pausing, reflecting, and looking back to see if students accomplished their reading purpose. It also shows students a rereading strategy to find out information they may have missed the first time around. The last part is Remember, a final step that suggests ways students can remember what they've learned.

The Looking Back checklist asks students to monitor their reading. This helps students see if they've **accomplished their reading purpose.**

Looking Back

- **Can I answer the *who, what, where, when,* and *why* questions?**
- **Can I summarize 2–3 important ideas in my own words?**
- **Do my notes cover the whole chapter, and do I understand them?**

A Rereading Strategy is suggested so students can **find out information they may have missed the first time through.**

Reading Strategy: Outlining

When you reread, try a new reading strategy. **Outlining** is a good way to review the key information in a chapter. Remember when you previewed the headings? They can help you create a quick, effective Topic or Sentence Outline. Textbooks are usually carefully organized.

The Remember step shows one or more ways students can **remember what they've learned.**

INDIAN WARS

I. Government Policy
  A. 1840s—white settlement
  B. mid-1800s—changing policy

II. Clash of Cultures
  A. settlers farming and hunting on the land
  B. Indians using what they needed to live on

III. Fighting Begins
  A. raids on settlements
  B. led by Red Cloud, a Sioux chief

IV. Little Bighorn
  A. miners' invasion of Indian lands in Black Hills
  B. ambush of Gen. Custer

Focus Lessons

Focus lessons take a closer look at one type of reading or specific element, such as theme, setting, essay tests, and so on. They are shorter lessons that zero in on a single subject. A combination of reading tools, reading strategies, and tips are suggested to help students better understand the subject.

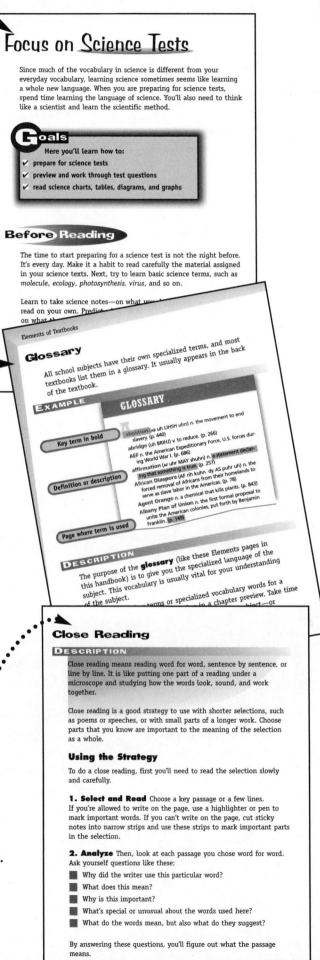

Focus on Science Tests

Since much of the vocabulary in science is different from your everyday vocabulary, learning science sometimes seems like learning a whole new language. When you are preparing for science tests, spend time learning the language of science. You'll also need to think like a scientist and learn the scientific method.

Goals

Here you'll learn how to:

- ✔ prepare for science tests
- ✔ preview and work through test questions
- ✔ read science charts, tables, diagrams, and graphs

Before Reading

The time to start preparing for a science test is not the night before. It's every day. Make it a habit to read carefully the material assigned in your science texts. Next, try to learn basic science terms, such as *molecule, ecology, photosynthesis, virus,* and so on.

Learn to take science notes—on what ...
read on your own. Predict...
on what ...

Elements Lessons

Elements lessons explain key terms related to the genre. Each lesson starts off with an **example,** so students see how the term is used. Next, students read a **description** about the term in the example. The lesson ends with a clear **definition**.

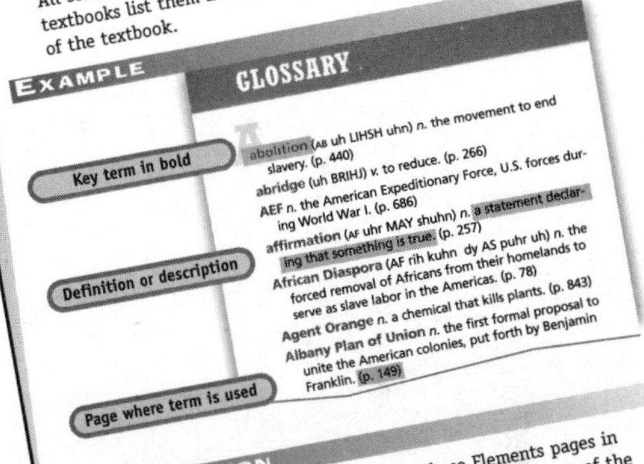
Elements of Textbooks

Glossary

All school subjects have their own specialized terms, and most textbooks list them in a glossary. It usually appears in the back of the textbook.

EXAMPLE

Key term in bold
Definition or description
Page where term is used
GLOSSARY
abolition (AB uh LIHSH uhn) n. the movement to end slavery. (p. 440)
abridge (uh BRIHJ) v. to reduce. (p. 266)
AEF n. the American Expeditionary Force, U.S. forces during World War I. (p. 686)
affirmation (AF uhr MAY shuhn) n. a statement declaring that something is true. (p. 257)
African Diaspora (AF rih kuhn dy AS puhr uh) n. the forced removal of Africans from their homelands to serve as slave labor in the Americas. (p. 78)
Agent Orange n. a chemical that kills plants. (p. 843)
Albany Plan of Union n. the first formal proposal to unite the American colonies, put forth by Benjamin Franklin. (p. 149)

DESCRIPTION

The purpose of the **glossary** (like these Elements pages in this handbook) is to give you the specialized language of the subject. This vocabulary is usually vital for your understanding of the subject.

... terms or specialized vocabulary words for a ... in a chapter preview. Take time ... bject—or

Reader's Almanac

The Reader's Almanac is a reference guide.

The **Strategy Handbook** describes in detail each of the 12 main reading strategies.

The **Reading Tools** section describes and gives examples of the 36 main reading tools.

Last, **Word Parts** gives a list of Greek and Latin roots, prefixes, and suffixes.

Close Reading

DESCRIPTION

Close reading means reading word for word, sentence by sentence, or line by line. It is like putting one part of a reading under a microscope and studying how the words look, sound, and work together.

Close reading is a good strategy to use with shorter selections, such as poems or speeches, or with small parts of a longer work. Choose parts that you know are important to the meaning of the selection as a whole.

Using the Strategy

To do a close reading, first you'll need to read the selection slowly and carefully.

1. Select and Read Choose a key passage or a few lines. If you're allowed to write on the page, use a highlighter or pen to mark important words. If you can't write on the page, cut sticky notes into narrow strips and use these strips to mark important parts in the selection.

2. Analyze Then, look at each passage you chose word for word. Ask yourself questions like these:

- Why did the writer use this particular word?
- What does this mean?
- Why is this important?
- What's special or unusual about the words used here?
- What do the words mean, but also what do they suggest?

By answering these questions, you'll figure out what the passage means.

Correlations

Overview

The *Reader's Handbook* is a multifaceted guide to reading, and it easily supplements several other Great Source reading and writing products. Use the correlations charts that follow to see how to complement lessons with different materials.

1. *Daybooks of Critical Reading and Writing*, grade 7

Like the *Reader's Handbook*, the *Daybooks* show students how to become active readers. The *Daybooks* complement the *Reader's Handbook* by offering further opportunities to practice using reading strategies and tools, as well as the reading process and reading know-how. The *Daybooks* have been correlated to the *Reader's Handbook* through the genre of the selections. In other words, nonfiction selections from the *Daybook* are suggested for the Reading Nonfiction chapter in the handbook; poetry selections with Reading Poetry, and so on.

Reader's Handbook Chapter	*Daybook*, grade 7	Pages
I. Introduction	from *A Summer Life*	10
II. Reading Process	"Seventh Grade"	11–18
III. Reading Know-how	from "A Sea Worry"	142-143
IV. Reading Textbooks	from *Volcano*	130-134
V. Reading Nonfiction	from *Living Up the Street*	24-25
	from *The Diary of Latoya Hunter*	28-29
	"Playgrounds of the Future"	32-33
	"Hero on the Ball Field"	54-56
	from *I Never Had It Made*	58-59
	from *Stealing Home*	62-63
	from *Don't Sweat the Small Stuff*	84-85
	from "The Eternal Frontier"	89-90
	"Ain't I a Woman?"	92-93
	from *The Invisible Thread*	102-103
	from *Desert Exile*	108
	from *On the Road with Charles Kuralt*	136-138
	"Our Juvenile Curfew Is Working"	190-191
	"Homeless"	198-201
	Introduction to *S Is for Space*	216-217

***Reader's Handbook* Chapter**	***Daybook*, grade 7**	**Pages**
VI. Reading Fiction	from "Seventh Grade"	11-18
	from *The Adventures of Tom Sawyer*	40-44
	from *So Far from the Bamboo Grove*	45-46
	"The Dinner Party"	48-49
	"Birthday Box"	77-80
	from "The Princess of Light"	98-100
	"Shells"	146-151
	"Appointment in Baghdad"	153
	from "Ta-NA-E-Ka"	155-156
	from *Dragonwings*	158-159
	from *The Call of the Wild*	162-163
	from *Island of the Blue Dolphin*	163
	from "Uncle Einar"	204-205
	from *The Martian Chronicles*	206-207
	"Fever Dream"	208-214
VII. Reading Poetry	"A Time to Talk"	36
	"Jackie Robinson"	65
	"knoxville, tennessee"	70
	"Graduation Morning"	73
	"Mother to Son"	75
	"Chinese Hot Pot"	166
	"Direction"	172
	"The Funeral"	176
	"There's This That I Like About Hockey, My Lad"	178
	"Annabel Lee"	180-181
	"Cynthia in the Snow"	183
	"Chrysalis Diary"	185-186
VIII. Reading Drama	*The Inspector-General*	168-171
XII. Improving Vocabulary	from *Journey Home*	105
	from *"Titanic"*	195-196

2. Reading and Writing Sourcebooks, grade 7

One way the *Reader's Handbook* can be used is to help struggling readers. The *Sourcebooks* focus on struggling readers, teach a reading process and reading tools, and encourage students to become active readers. In these three ways, the *Sourcebooks* complement the *Reader's Handbook*. To facilitate using both programs, each *Sourcebook* selection has been correlated to an appropriate chapter in the *Reader's Handbook*.

***Reader's Handbook* Chapter**	***Sourcebook*, grade 7**	**Pages**
II. The Reading Process	"Mrs. Olinski" from *The View from Saturday*	12-20
III. Reading Know-how	"The Day It Rained Cockroaches" from *The Pigman and Me*	21-31
	"Hanging Out" from *Rumble Fish*	70-74
IV. Reading Textbooks	"Lexington and Concord"	40-49
	"Taken in Slavery" from *Slavery in the United States*	204-210
	"Misery Days" and "A Child's Pain"	211-218
V. Reading Nonfiction	"Eyewitness to the Boston Tea Party"	32-39
	"On the Red Man's Trail"	93-102
	"The Washwoman" from *In My Father's Court*	104–110
	"The Washwoman" from *In My Father's Court*	111-121
	"Migrant Family Life"	151-160
	"Fear" from *Living Up the Street*	193-202
VI. Reading Fiction	"Ready" from *Johnny Tremain*	50-58
	"It's Tonight" from *Johnny Tremain*	59-66
	"Being Fourteen" from *Can You Sue Your Parents for Malpractice?*	75-82
	"Attack" from *The Girl Who Chased Away Shadows*	84-92
	"Louie Hirshfield" from *The Zodiacs*	122-130
	"George Santini" from *The Zodiacs*	131-140
	"You Can't Swallow Me Up," from . . . *And the Earth Did Not Devour Him*	142-150
	"September 3, 1919" from *Letters from Rifka*	162-169
	"October 5, 1919" from *Letters from Rifka*	170-178
	"Escape" from *A Girl*	180-192
XII. Improving Vocabulary	"Born into Slavery" from *I, Juan de Pareja*	220-229
	"My Master" from *I, Juan de Pareja*	230-238

3. Write Source 2000

The main goal of the *Reader's Handbook* is to teach all students how to become better readers. *Write Source 2000* directly complements the handbook through its teaching of a writing process and how types of writing are organized. To teach both programs side by side, the correlation below shows which parts of *Write Source 2000* best complement individual chapters in the *Reader's Handbook*.

***Reader's Handbook* Chapter**	**Correlation**	***Write Source 2000* ©1999**
I. Introduction	understanding writing	3–8
II. The Reading Process	writing process	5–18
III. Reading Know-how	writing paragraphs	56, 110, 310–311, 377
IV. Reading Textbooks	word problems note-taking	281, 301–306, 466–482, 491–506, 528
V. Reading Nonfiction	essays	56, 103, 115–122, 170–173, 263
VI. Reading Fiction	novels stories	176, 184, 277, 294, 342, 343–344
VII. Reading Poetry	writing a poem	193–207, 342
VIII. Reading Drama	writing a play	342
IX. Reading on the Internet	using the Internet	43, 265–272
X. Reading Graphics	using graphs	56, 302–303
XI. Reading for Tests	test-taking skills	375–380
XII. Improving Vocabulary	improving vocabulary	323–340

The Place of Reading in Middle School

by Jolene Borgese and Wendell Schwartz

Why teach reading in middle school?

For many of us, the teaching of reading beyond the third or fourth grade seems like the mythical Gordian knot. As teachers, all too often we are not sure where to begin. Oddly enough, when confronting an obviously struggling reader, teachers may have numerous resources, such as remedial reading classes, reading specialists, or even tutors available. However, as the reader's abilities improve and decoding is no longer a problem, the issues become more subtle and the solutions to the student's needs are less obvious. As teachers, we all know that reading is a skill that continues to grow and mature all through our lives and that our students, even the successful ones, can become more efficient and effective readers only if we better understand how we can help them grow.

How well can students read?

A popular rallying cry in recent years has been that "All teachers are teachers of reading." But, especially in middle school and high school, where teachers are often subject area specialists, that simply is not true; we are teachers of science, of math, of literature, of history. Most of us do not define ourselves as teachers of reading; if we do at all, it is usually a secondary role. According to Ruth Schoenbach in *Reading for Understanding*, "Many middle school teachers and most high school teachers see their primary responsibility as teaching the important knowledge base of their disciplines—the content. Filling in orally what students are either not able or not willing to learn from the course texts is a natural response for any dedicated teacher. . . . Teachers may read to students, talk through the book, or show a related video." Rather than helping our students to read the text, we find ways to work around the reading act in an effort to help our students learn the content. This points to the clear need for a reading program that is rooted in the various content areas of the middle school curriculum and that has as its goal the improved learning and achievement of the students in each subject area. We all know that our students need to be effective readers in order to succeed in our classrooms and, in fact, long after that.

Very often it seems that we understand what to do at the beginning of the reading process. For example, beginning a piece of fiction for most students is like the prewriting activities we ask them to do before they write. This is usually the fun part— previewing, predicting, and building interest. These are usually activities students can do without much stress. Teachers have a long history of knowing how to check for comprehension Short quizzes, extensive essay exams, classroom discussions, book reports, oral presentations, and objective tests all are tools we use to check for understanding after the reading is completed.

However, so many of these post-reading assessments reveal that students' reading has been ineffective. Something has gone wrong during the reading process, and we now find ourselves at a loss on what to do. While a teacher can look at an early draft of a student's writing and understand what happened during the writing process, the during reading step of the reading process cannot be seen. It is at this point that we as teachers should see the need to teach more reading skills and strategies that will help our students monitor their own understanding and to take these skills and transfer them to other reading experiences.

What are the characteristics of the middle school reader?

Think about the students who fill your classrooms every day, year after year. Chances are good that they will fall into at least a few broad, general classifications. There will be those who clearly are struggling to keep up with their peers. These students may put forth effort and read the assignments we give them, but all too often we hear from them the familiar refrain, "I read it, but I didn't get it." This is probably true in many, many cases. They know the words, but they don't really know how to read in the truest sense of the word.

According to Ruth Schoenbach in *Reading for Understanding*, "Most adolescents whom teachers might initially describe as 'not even able to get the words off the page' are far less likely to have problems with decoding than with comprehension, unfamiliar vocabulary, insufficient background knowledge, reading fluency, or engagement."

At the opposite end of the spectrum are those students who are skillful readers. They interact with the text, often without realizing it. They ask themselves questions as they read, monitor their comprehension, and make adjustments along the way. They anticipate what may happen next in a story or what the author's intent or purpose in an article may be. They have strategies for integrating new knowledge into what they already understand, and when that does not happen, they know what questions to ask.

For example, in *Reading Reminders*, Jim Burke writes about teaching his students to ask themselves questions not only after they read, but while they read as well. This leads to what Burke calls "dense" questions that help them to relate what they have read to other things they have read, to other things in their experience, and to what they may already know about the topic. These students read with insight and with understanding. They have a general sense, sometimes almost innate, of the reading process. And, they read with a purpose.

What if my students can already read?

But most students probably fall somewhere between these two extremes. They read some texts more successfully than others, often because they have a limited number of techniques or strategies, and they tend to read all texts the same way. A short story is approached in much the same way a chapter in a science book is approached. They do not monitor their own comprehension during the actual act of reading, deciding—when it's too late—that they didn't understand important elements of the text but not knowing what to do about it "after the fact." They may have a sense of the reading process, but it is only vaguely defined for them. They may understand what to do at the beginning of a reading task, but they do not know what to do as they are reading or what to do after they have finished.

Many of us would define these students as "about average" readers, when in fact they are not really readers at all. They often find ways to compensate for limited reading skills and for barely finishing their reading assignments (if at all). They may be good listeners in class; they may be good at studying for tests, even though they understood only some of what they read along the way. These students present us, as teachers, with the greatest challenges because they are not usually thought of as students with "reading problems," yet when asked to read and comprehend on their own, their success is limited.

What's the current state of middle school reading programs?

In recent years, the specific reading curriculum—that is, a coherent, sequenced series of competencies and skills embedded in a meaningful context—has slipped away. Teachers are exhorted to make their students better readers, but given little support, inservice, or materials to help them achieve this goal. Teachers find themselves left to their own resources to try to figure out "what works," and that usually is some variation of what has worked for them over the years. There are few, if any, formal reading programs currently in place for use in the middle school. Generally, reading programs are seen as appropriate for the lower elementary grades, and as long as students know how to decode the words in front of them, "reading" is taking place as best it can with our older students.

In most middle schools, the reading of various forms of literature takes the place of actual reading instruction. Teachers may try to help students in these "reading" classes, but most often the goal is to help students understand the story, essay, or poem, not to consciously employ reading strategies that will help them later when they encounter challenging texts on their own. Where formal reading programs do exist, they are usually created with the weak or struggling reader in mind. Thus, the direct teaching of reading at the middle or high school level becomes a "remedial" issue, where poor students are "fixed" in hopes that their learning will eventually improve. Reading programs for successful or even moderately able students do not exist in most places. As Ruth Schoenbach says in *Reading for Understanding,* "The idea that at age eleven, fourteen, or seventeen it is too late to become a strong and independent reader of academic texts is both insidious and self-perpetuating. . . . The assumption that children who have not become good readers in the early grades will never catch up is both incorrect and destructive."

How can you teach reading?

For many of us in the classroom, the direct teaching of reading was not part of our teacher training. We were taught how to encourage, how to coach, how to support students as they try to master our various content areas. We were not taught, however, how to demonstrate, model, and present specific reading techniques and strategies that would help all of our students, the weak readers as well as the strong ones, to become better students and to achieve at higher levels.

What's the *Reader's Handbook* solution?

The *Reader's Handbook* is designed to be used by students at all these levels of reading proficiency. It will be useful for struggling readers by introducing them to the reading process, the central concept of all effective reading. It will help them to set a purpose for their reading beyond simply finishing it. The *Reader's Handbook* will help them to learn how to answer questions as they read, not only after they have finished. It will help them learn how to reflect on what they have read and decide what to do next. As most teachers know, these are skills that struggling readers simply do not have. There are also strategies and tools for dealing with vocabulary issues, for taking notes, and for using graphic organizers. The *Reader's Handbook* also contains dozens of other comprehension aids that struggling or reluctant readers either know nothing at all about or are seldom called upon to use.

Just as important, the *Reader's Handbook* can help proficient and highly skillful readers become even better. Reading is a skill for which there is really no "ceiling," and the *Reader's Handbook* can help these readers address issues of academic literacy that will increase their levels of achievement in all content areas. The handbook includes suggestions for learning how to synthesize information that is often presented in different formats—for example, traditional text combined with graphs or illustrations. The *Reader's Handbook* presents many ways for self-monitoring of comprehension during the act of reading itself. Specific approaches to the reading of various genres of literature, as well as textbooks and other types of nonfiction, are also addressed.

For the more skillful readers, the handbook discusses typical text structures they can expect to encounter and how to deal with them effectively and efficiently. A conscious understanding of the most prevalent text structures and how information is embedded within them is a sophisticated skill that good middle school readers seldom can articulate. Reading non-traditional material, such as websites and graphics, is also thoroughly covered. Even tailoring how one reads various kinds of tests is presented.

In short, the *Reader's Handbook* is not simply a "remedial" book for struggling readers. It is a book that can and does introduce weak readers to critical strategies and tools that will help them improve their comprehension. But it can also assist proficient readers to become more purposeful in their approach to a multitude of reading tasks and become more successful in all areas of the curriculum as a result.

How would I use the *Reader's Handbook*?

From a teacher's perspective, the *Reader's Handbook* can be used in several ways. Perhaps the single most important issue to understand is that it is intended to be useful and supportive for teachers in all content areas, not only reading. The *Reader's Handbook* needs to be viewed as a resource to be used by students in all of their classes. As the table of contents reveals, there are very specific sections of the handbook dedicated to reading strategies in specific areas of the middle school curriculum, from literature in its various forms, to reading in math class, social studies, science, and more. In some schools, the *Reader's Handbook* may become the backbone of a school-wide reading program covering grades 6–8. Together with its enrichment materials, it is extensive and versatile enough to provide instructional units for all levels of readers over a period of years.

In other cases, the *Reader's Handbook* may be seen as exactly that, a handbook. A teacher can use it contextually and as an integral part of preparing his or her students for an important upcoming reading task. For example, at the beginning of the school year, the social studies teacher will want to use the handbook as a guide for showing his or her students how to most effectively deal with the many elements of the typical history textbook. Later in the school year, that same teacher may call on the handbook again for lessons on how to read graphs, charts, and illustrations. Finally, before the students are asked to go the library to gather information, the unit on reading a website would be of great help.

Teachers may rely on the *Reader's Handbook* to provide them not only with the skeleton of a coherent reading program, but also with enough material to flesh out the program as well. Others may see it primarily as a book a teacher "dips into" to troubleshoot reading issues as they are identified to prepare his or her students for a challenging or new kind of reading. The *Reader's Handbook* is a resource for teachers and students that has many uses, the chief of which is to make students better readers.

REFERENCES

Burke, J. (2000). *Reading reminders: tools, tips, and techniques.* Portsmouth: Boynton/Cook Heinemann.

Robb, L. (2000). *Teaching reading in middle school.* New York: Scholastic.

Schoenbach, R., et al. (1999). *Reading for understanding.* San Francisco: Jossey-Bass.

Teaching a Reading and Writing Workshop

by Laura Robb

"I like all the different things we do in workshop—read, discuss, write, work with a partner or our teacher. And most of the time I'm liking what we do." These words, spoken by a sixth-grade boy, say a great deal about the varied learning experiences in a reading workshop. Within a block of time, a workshop approach to reading enables you to model reading strategies, then support individuals and small groups, while the rest of the class completes independent reading, discusses a text, or writes about their reading.

The Benefits of a Reading/Writing Workshop

- **Independence** Middle school students can develop the independence they crave during choice time when students work alone, in pairs, or in small groups.
- **Guided Practice** The blocks of time available during a workshop allow students to practice and apply strategies and skills to new materials under the expert guidance of you, the teacher.
- **Social Aspects of Learning** Talking to and hanging out with friends is what middle schoolers enjoy. Workshops build on students' social natures by fostering focused talk about reading.
- **Flexible Grouping** Because students learn to work independently, teachers can meet with individuals or small groups to support strategic reading and the interpretation of various literary genres.

Establish Workshop Routines

Reflect on the kinds of independent work you want students to complete during the workshop. Here's the list a seventh-grade teacher compiled: independent reading; reviewing specific genres in the *Reader's Handbook*; applying reading methods such as marking the text, finding the main idea, using a graphic organizer to figure out theme in their independent reading books; or completing a lesson in the *Daybook* or *Sourcebook* that relates to what's being studied in the *Reader's Handbook*.

Allow five to six weeks to teach routines and have students practice them, as well as understand what the behavior expectations are. The time you invest in helping students understand the different levels of workshop learning is directly related to the level of organization and productivity in your class.

Four Workshop Elements

The graphic organizer on page 34 will help you visualize these workshop elements.

1. Teach It By planning a mini-lesson, you can demonstrate how a reading or writing strategy works for you by modeling your process and thinking aloud to share your anxieties, frustrations, and ideas. The *Reader's Handbook* offers a wealth of mini-lesson ideas. Start the year by presenting these mini-lessons from the *Reader's Handbook*: "The Reading Process" and "Reading Know-how." You'll also want to design and present these mini-lessons: "Reading Nonfiction," "Reading Fiction," "Reading Poetry," "Reading Drama," "Reading for Tests," and "Improving Vocabulary." One possible curriculum to follow is laid out in the *Lesson Plan Book*. Use it as a model to construct your own, or follow it as a plan for your school.

2. Practice It During this block of time, you can work with groups who need support with applying strategies to different materials. While you work with a small group, student-led groups or partners can discuss literature, write about their reading, read independently, or study and review specific pages in the *Reader's Handbook*. For example, if you've had two to three mini-lessons on the short story, you might want students to check the Reader's Almanac in their handbook for a refresher on Character Maps or Plot Diagrams.

3. Apply It Here students have multiple opportunities to work independently, with a partner or in a small group, to apply what they have learned and practiced to new material. You'll also be able to carve out some time during this block to support struggling readers or students who missed a lesson.

Once students have worked through the lesson on the novel in the *Reader's Handbook*, they can apply some of the strategies to a free-choice book at their independent reading level. Ask students to keep written work in their journals so that they have a record of their thinking and learning.

4. Evaluate It Student journals, independent work done in the *Student Applications Books*, and student's writing about literature are all potential assessments. Independently completed work in the *Daybooks* and *Sourcebooks* are also good assessments that you can use to evaluate students' progress.

While students complete work, you can block out some time to hold brief meetings with those who still need more guidance to improve their reading and writing skills.

Basic Workshop Experiences

The experiences that follow offer choices that enable you to interact with students and monitor their progress.

Teacher Read-Aloud Teachers read aloud from genres that relate to those the class is studying.

Paired Questioning Partners read passages and question one another.

Complete a Journal Entry See suggestions in the *Reader's Handbook* and *Student Applications Book*.

Practice a Strategy Students, solo or in small groups, use books at their independent reading level to cement their understanding of a strategy.

Peer Conferences Pairs or small groups discuss how they apply a reading strategy and/or share journal entries that explain a strategy. The *Teacher's Guide* offers a wealth of independent reading suggestions as well.

Student-led Book Discussions Organize heterogeneous groupings, mixing ability levels and gender. The *Reader's Handbook* offers many possible discussion topics: the structure of a genre and supporting examples from a text, finding themes, character analysis, cause and effect, close readings, inferences, and so on.

Teacher-led Strategic Reading Groups These are homogeneous pairs or small groups that require additional instruction on how to apply a reading strategy, complete a graphic organizer, or transfer their knowledge of a specific genre to students' independent reading.

Integrating the *Reader's Handbook* into Your Reading Workshop

Here are some suggestions for constructing strategy lessons and reading and writing experiences using the *Reader's Handbook*, the *Teacher's Guide,* and the *Student Applications Book*. As you integrate the *Reader's Handbook* into your workshop, you will discover dozens of additional learning experiences and strategy lessons to bring to your students.

Possible Mini-lessons

- Setting a purpose
- Reading autobiographies, biographies, essays, geography textbooks, history textbooks, magazine articles, math textbooks, newspaper articles, novels, science textbooks, short stories
- Previewing a text
- Making a reading plan
- Using graphic organizers
- Making connections
- Inferring ideas
- Understanding the structure of short stories, novels, poems
- Understanding the structure of nonfiction books, essays, newspapers

Guided Practice

- Use the *Student Applications Book* and offer opportunities to apply your mini-lessons during workshop time called "Practice It."
- Create reading and writing experiences from the *Reader's Handbook* and your *Lesson Plan Book,* such as taking notes, building vocabulary, and making personal connections.

Gathering Written Work for Evaluation

- Evaluate students' progress based on their journal writing.
- Collect work students complete in the *Student Applications Book,* and evaluate whether they understand a skill, tool, or strategy.

Independent Reading

- Reserve time for students to read books at their independent level.
- Invite students to choose books that relate to the genres you're teaching.

Sourcebooks and *Daybooks*

- Use *Sourcebooks* and *Daybooks* to engage students in practice and reinforcement at students' instructional levels. This means that in an eighth-grade class you might have students in a sixth-grade *Sourcebook* because they are reading at that level, students reading on grade level in an eighth-grade *Daybook*, and several in ninth- or tenth-grade *Daybooks* because they are proficient readers.
- If your class has many struggling readers, consider using the *Sourcebooks* to meet their needs. In such a sixth-grade class, most students will be in a fourth- or fifth-grade *Sourcebook*. Those reading on grade level will use a sixth-grade *Daybook*.

Closing Thoughts

As an indispensable resource for you and your students, the *Reader's Handbook* and support materials will quickly become the foundation for your workshop. By using these materials, you can organize a workshop that meets the needs of each child and reaches all reading levels.

REFERENCE

Robb, L. (2000). *Teaching reading in middle school.* New York: Scholastic.

Workshop Approach

Teach It

Model a strategy.
(10–20 minutes)

- Mini-lesson with *Reader's Handbook*
- At start, in middle
- Reading and/or writing strategy

Practice It

Students use; teacher supports.
(20–40 minutes)

- Discussion groups
- Strategic reading
- Groups—student and teacher led
- Writing
- Independent work

Reading/Writing Workshop

Apply It

Students refine reading and writing.
(15–30 minutes)

- Whole group, small group, independent
- Work with students who need extra help.
- Work with *Daybooks*, or *Sourcebooks*.

Evaluate It

Students show what they can do.
(15–30 minutes)

- Complete work independently.
- Write about reading and writing strategies.
- Teacher support for those who need help

Academic Literacy: Making Students Content Learners

by Ron Klemp

One of the challenges facing today's middle schools is the demand for rigorous demonstrations of competency across the curriculum. High-stakes testing has opened discussion surrounding middle school students' ability to successfully negotiate the demands of texts used in classrooms across every district in the United States. In order to accomplish deeper understanding across subject areas, teachers and students alike are having to gear up to the demands of academic literacy.

Academic literacy can be defined as a continuing developmental process of knowing how to navigate through different forms of text. Becoming academically literate means that a learner has an inventory of effective strategies to meet the demands of different forms of text. As students encounter graphics, attend to text structure, and handle new and somewhat perplexing vocabulary, they will need to use strategies that may not be a part of their past reading experiences. In addition, the emphasis on integration of a language arts curriculum across and through all disciplines has challenged secondary teachers to "think differently about the role of literacy in understanding content" (Irvin, 1998). Essentially, the challenge for teachers is to devise ways to support students' emergence into becoming academically literate.

A recent NAEP report (Campbell, et al., 1998) noted that many middle school students fail to understand texts beyond a literal level. On the surface, this report may be startling. But on a deeper level this revelation is not surprising. Many teachers and older students reveal that in their middle school experiences they were rarely asked to do more than report what was read in the text or what was said during the teacher's lecture. Most adults admit to their own middle school student careers being the same. The teacher lectured and students took notes or read chapters and then reported the information back to the teacher in the form of a test, quiz, or essay. The need for academic literacy did not extend very far. In addition, the report noted that most middle school students do not use effective strategies. To get beyond the literal level, students will have to engage a type of reading that will foster deeper thought and analysis. In other words, they will need to attain academic literacy.

To understand the interactive role of literacy across disciplines, it is important to paint a picture of literacy at the secondary level. According to a joint publication by the Northwest Regional Laboratory, National Council of Teachers of English, and the International Reading Association, levels of literacy can be described as (but not limited to):

Basic Literacy—refers to the ability to decode, recognize, and comprehend printed signs, symbols, and words.
Proficient Literacy—refers to the ability to extend ideas, make inferences, draw conclusions, and make connections to personal experiences from printed texts.
Advanced Literacy—refers to the ability to use language to solve problems and to extend cognitive development. New understandings within and across texts and the ability to

summarize, evaluate, and apply strategies to text and construct meaning from various perspectives also describe someone at an advanced level of literacy.
While these levels appear to be clear demarcations of ability, it is feasible that students could move between the various levels depending on prior knowledge of topics, language ability, and other variables that render the lines a little shaggy. A reader who may be at an advanced level could conceivably be faced with text that he or she can decode but not comprehend. In short, the academic literacy demands placed on students require functioning at all three levels. Students who have not acquired agility with academic literacy need concrete examples and continuous support to "mentally map" ways of meeting these demands. What some students lack is the insight that successful readers use when they shift approaches from narrative to expository or subject area text.

Here is an example of the type of reading demanded by one state's sixth-grade history-social studies content standards: "Students analyze the causes and effects of the vast expansion and ultimate disintegration of the Roman Empire." Within this standard, students are also asked to study the strengths and contributions of Rome, including Roman law, architecture, engineering, philosophy, and geographic borders, as well as learn about the Byzantine Empire and Constantinople. Subsequent to this content standard, students explore Mesopotamia, Ancient Egypt, Ancient Greece, and the Hebrews (California Department of Education, 1999). In order to meet the demands of these standards, students will have to do a fair amount of reading, but not a recreational kind of reading.

For middle school teachers and students, the important factors for content-based academic literacy include the following:

- Knowing what to do when they encounter unusual or irregular words that make up so much content-specific vocabulary
- Understanding the organization of the text, which helps set the purpose for reading (that is, cause and effect, problem and solution, sequence, and so forth)
- Maintaining an inventory of effective strategies, including ways of prereading, close reading, re-inspecting, summarizing, and reflecting or reviewing

Today, the role of content-area teachers is to "encourage the thinking processes essential to understanding, i.e., to facilitate learning with text" (Readance, 2000). Teachers who see themselves as facilitators of learning will "apprentice" students to a variety of strategies based upon students' understanding of the organization of text, a purpose for reading the text, and a variety of strategies to engage them in the reading of text. Inherent in this call is the necessity for all teachers to understand that literacy extends to all subject areas.

To become more successful in facilitating content instruction though academic literacy, teachers will need to approach their content though a process focus. Cognitive strategies serve as subtext to the curriculum. Content teachers may be "content rich, but process poor." In other words, they are well versed in the content, but they might not have a command of strategies needed to enhance students' comprehension of text. To become "process rich," teachers will need to have "topical knowledge," an inventory of different reading strategies, and knowledge of when to use a particular strategy. Teachers will also need to explore ways of sharing strategies among the disciplines. The missing ingredient in middle school literacy efforts has been the lack of continuity across the disciplines. Rather than allowing strategies to remain covert and internal, content teachers will need to externalize and guide students in a way that embeds in academic literacy into a school-wide curriculum. The *Reader's Handbook* allows teachers to do that. The *Reader's Handbook* becomes a vehicle for sharing an inventory of strategies across the entire middle school. Not only do the teachers become "process rich," but the students also begin to understand that there are different types of reading strategies that have distinct uses and some that cross over disciplines.

Through this overt approach to "unpacking" text, students will have topical knowledge of the strategies and also conditional knowledge, in which they know when to use a particular strategy depending on the text they are reading. Through effective teacher modeling with the *Reader's Handbook*, students will improve their ability to shift approaches to reading various forms of text. Students will become more effective learners, and teachers will bring a new dimension to their instructional practice that will allow access to the curriculum for all students.

REFERENCES

Braunger, J. & Lewis, J. (1998). *Building a knowledge base in reading*. Portland: Northwest Regional Education Laboratory.

California Department of Education. (1999). *Reading/language arts framework for California public schools*. Sacramento: CDE Press.

Campbell, J., et al. (1998). *NAEP 1998 Reading Report Card for the Nation and the States*. Washington, D.C.: U.S. Department of Education.

Irvin, J. (1998). *Reading and the middle school student: strategies to enhance literacy*. Boston: Allyn & Bacon.

Readance, J., Bean, T., & Baldwin, S. (2000). *Content area literacy: an integrated approach*. Dubuque: Kendall Hunt.

Creating a Middle School Reading Initiative

by Dennis Jackson and Richard P. Santeusanio

Our goal in writing this article is to identify the seven building blocks required to implement a successful middle school reading initiative. We begin by sharing three fictitious—but common—scenarios that illustrate how some educators with good intentions and good ideas fail to make a difference in a middle school reading program.

The Top Down Approach

Superintendent Dr. Ralph Sullivan of the Top Down City School District doesn't like what he sees as he reviews his middle school's state assessment scores. "Things are going to change around here," he says to himself. "Our kids deserve better than what we are providing for them." So Dr. Sullivan, in his opening day remarks to his staff in the fall, declares that one of the district goals is to improve reading scores, with particular emphasis on the middle school. At the end of the year, the scores from the middle school arrive. There is no improvement. Why?

While it can be argued that it takes more than a year to improve test scores, Dr. Sullivan himself contributed to the stagnant scores because he merely announced reading at the middle school was a priority. He had what Fullan (1999) calls "moral purpose"; he wanted to do what was right for the middle school in his district. But he had no plan to develop a comprehensive middle school program.

The Autonomous Approach

Seventh-grade teacher Marsha Jones at the Independence School wants her students to be good readers, and she knows what to do. "It is time for me to put my master's in reading to work," she tells a friend over a Saturday afternoon lunch.

Marsha does indeed do the job. When the scores for her language arts classes are reported at the end of the school year, significant progress is documented. Her students move on to grade eight to a team of teachers who do not have the same focus on reading Marsha had with her students. The gains made at the end of seventh grade are lost at the end of grade 8. Why?

The simple answer is that while most schools can point to pockets of success and innovation, real and permanent school improvement occurs when teachers work collaboratively and "buy in" to a school-wide reading initiative.

The Commodity Approach

Principal Wayne Mackin of the Materials Middle School wants his students to be the best readers in the state. "We're above average now," he tells his assistant principal, "and we're going to get to the top. We can do it if we can just get the right materials in the hands of our teachers and students."

Wayne does indeed get many new, attractive language arts books into the Materials Middle School classrooms. Teachers and students use the new materials for a few years. And, while the student reading scores continue to be above average, they are far from being among the best in the state. Why?

Principal Mackin did the right thing in providing his teachers and students with resources. But he did not provide the teachers with the training needed to use the materials effectively.

These three scenarios illustrate five of the seven building blocks required to initiate a comprehensive middle school reading program. All seven are needed to implement and sustain an effective reading program.

1. Moral Purpose Fullan (1999) defines moral purpose as ". . . making a positive difference in the lives of all citizens"—in this case, students. However, he also notes that achieving this positive difference is enormously complex, but not impossible. When good things happen in schools, it always starts with someone or a group of educators approaching an issue with a moral purpose.

2. Planning the Change The person or group who plans the middle school reading initiative should consider Fullan's (1991) recommendations in planning the change. As they relate to planning a middle school reading initiative, planners should recognize several things:

- Initial ideas of what the change should be will transform and continue to develop.
- Teachers, the implementers, need to work out their own meaning of what the reading initiative will look like.
- Conflict and disagreement are fundamental to successful change.
- Relearning is at the heart of a change in a middle school reading program.
- Effective change takes time.
- Slow implementation does not mean outright rejection of the values inherent in the reading initiative.
- Not everyone will embrace the reading initiative.
- No amount of technical support and expertise will make it totally clear what action needs to take place to implement the reading initiative.
- The real agenda is changing the culture of the school.

3. Collaboration and "Buy In" Michael Fullan eloquently describes the meaning of a collaborative culture:
"Collaborative organizations fan the passion and emotions of its members because they so value commitment and the energy required to pursue complex goals. But instead of leaving passionate teachers to sink or swim, the true value of collaborative cultures is that they simultaneously encourage passion and provide emotional support as people work through the roller coaster of change" (Fullan, 1999, p. 38).

So what are the characteristics of a collaborative culture? According to Fullan, such cultures foster diversity while building trust, accept the presence of anxiety, create knowledge, combine connectedness with openhandedness, and fuse the spiritual, political, and intellectual.

It is in this kind of a culture that teachers will ultimately "buy in" to something like a middle school reading initiative. This will happen when the vast majority of the staff:

- believes the reading initiative addresses a need.
- is clear about what its role is in implementing the initiative.
- knows how the initiative affects their time, energy, and need for professional development.
- recognizes that the reading initiative will be rewarding in terms of interaction with peers and others (Fullan, 1991).

4. Resources In order for any reading initiative to be successful, the necessary resources must support it. Among the key resources for a successful secondary reading program are materials and time.

• **Materials** Simply stated, a classroom cannot have too many reading materials. To grow as readers and to learn the content of a discipline, students need the opportunity to explore and read a wide range of texts. These can include novels and nonfiction books, magazines and newspapers, and short stories, poetry, and essays. Make sure that the materials are in as good shape as possible. The subtle message that we give students when we offer them materials that are not well cared for is that we have little respect for the materials (or the students) and that they, in turn, need not show any respect for the materials (or us) (Burke, 2000).

Many schools and districts also provide students with locally developed language arts "guidebooks" that provide students with the tools they need to become stronger readers and more efficient learners. These guidebooks not only define basic standards for the types of activities in which students will engage, but also provide them with guidelines and strategies to help them solve learning and reading challenges they may encounter. They also provide content teachers with a tool for explaining and discussing the learning strategies of their discipline.

• **Time** The resource of time needs to be considered within the context of both implementing a reading initiative and supporting students as they become more successful readers and learners. Little can be accomplished without the necessary time. In the classroom, students must have the opportunity to both read and discuss their reading—its content and the processes they used to help themselves learn and understand. And initiatives aimed at supporting students' growth as readers and learners need time to develop and grow. In this era of quick fixes, the time to create, implement, reflect upon, and revise an initiative is becoming too rare while, at the same time, increasingly necessary (Braunger and Lewis, 1998).

5. Professional Development (PD) Lyons and Pinnell (2001) provide us with some characteristics to keep in mind when planning and developing PD for a middle school reading initiative. They suggest gathering information about the school; planning a wide variety of learning experiences; establishing clear goals and a common vision; assessing and focusing resources such as time, people, and materials; teaching specific instructional procedures; establishing a culture that encourages reflection, feedback, support, and problem solving; coaching and providing in-class demonstrations; using student data to inform the PD; monitoring the impact of PD; and designing ongoing opportunities.

While the typical PD involves a consultant or university presenter who works with teachers, Robb (2000a) suggests, among a number of PD alternatives, teacher study groups led by a facilitator. For a middle school initiative, for example, math teachers might form a group to discover ways of helping students read word problems and symbols, social studies teachers might focus on maps, charts, and graphs, and language arts teachers might study the reading-writing connection.

6. Key Components of a Comprehensive Reading Program The key components of a comprehensive reading program can be distilled into three simple elements: opportunity, choice, and instruction. Each of these elements applies to all students: our best readers, average readers, and students in need of special intervention.

• **Opportunity** Students (and all members of the school community) need the chance to read often and widely. Initiatives that support this opportunity are independent reading, reading aloud, and programs that provide students with the time to read, such as Sustained Silent Reading (Robb, 2000b).

• **Choice** Allowing students to have a voice in selecting the materials they read ensures that they will be engaged in their reading and that they will read texts that are comprehensible. It is easy to see how choice links directly with the resource of "materials" identified above, since a range of materials provides students with options and relieves teachers of the burden of assigning texts that may be too simple or too challenging for students (Burke, 1999).

• **Instruction** Good teaching supports the role of schools in helping students grow to become literate adults. It is through instruction that we "show them how to do it better." Instruction is the opportunity for schools and teachers to share with students the processes for getting meaning from text as well as the understanding that reading is a problem-solving activity—one that constantly poses challenges to the reader and requires a variety of strategies (Langer, 2000).

7. Sustaining the Effort In these days of high-stakes testing, one of the greatest challenges facing teachers and schools that recognize the importance of establishing a school-wide reading initiative is to support and maintain the effort long enough for it to have an effect on the school and its culture. Too often, we find ourselves forced to take on the short-range focus of a discipline's content rather than the long-range view of developing the processes that make students independent learners of a discipline. One simple strategy for ensuring that any initiative is sustained and supported over time is the use of long- and short-term planning processes.

In the processes, the faculty establishes a year-long goal. It then identifies a step that all staff members can take over the next 30 days. Members work individually or in teams to accomplish the step agreed upon. One month later the staff meets to discuss the outcome of the small step it took: what worked and what did not. Informed by this discussion, the faculty then identifies a second step toward the long-term goal that it will take for the next 30 days. The process of action, reflection, and planning continues throughout the school year, culminating in an evaluation of how well the long-term goal was achieved and the establishment of a new long-term goal for the next school year.

An Example

Let's take a look at how this model might play out using the *Reader's Handbook*. Westside Middle School has declared that improving student learning and reading abilities are its focuses for the school year, and it is committed to using the *Reader's Handbook* as a key tool. At the initial staff meetings for the school year, the staff works to turn this declaration into a plan of action by identifying two long-term goals that it will work to achieve during the school year:

1. to establish a school-wide common language for students and staff to use when talking about how to learn from and understand text.
2. to provide students with the tools to be successful learners in each of their courses.

These two goals are fairly comprehensive, and experience has shown us that working to achieve goals that are too broad can often doom them to failure. So, the staff of Westside, while keeping its long-term goals in mind, establishes a more achievable objective that will move it toward accomplishing the broader goal. After discussion, the Westside faculty determined that during the first half of the school year it would focus only on the first goal: establishing a school-wide common language.

At its initial meeting of the year, the staff worked to achieve the first short-term goal for the year: introduce the *Reader's Handbook* to all students by presenting the opening section, "How to Use This Book." Grade-level teams of math, science, social studies, and language arts teachers planned the specifics of how, over the next 30 days, they would accomplish this short-term goal and shared their plans with the entire staff. During the next month, the teams worked to implement their plan.

At the October staff meeting, each team reported its progress. Successes were shared, and problems were presented. The full group discussed the successes and shared potential solutions to the problems. Then, within the context of both the previous month's accomplishments and the long-term goal of establishing a common language, a new short- term goal for the entire school was established: to introduce the reading process to all students using Chapter 2 of the *Reader's Handbook*.

Again, teams met to devise their plans. Those plans were shared with the full staff and, over the next 30 days, implemented. At the next staff meeting, successes and problems were discussed, and within the context of the long-term goal, a short-term goal for the next 30 days was established.

This process of short-term planning within the context of progress toward long-term goals continued throughout the school year and provided the entire school with the focus and direction that resulted in the successful achievement of its goals. This process has several benefits:

- It provides an opportunity for all members of the school community to contribute to establishing both long- and short-term goals.
- It allows for both successes and issues to be raised and discussed in the process of reflecting and planning. (Too often we only hear about the positives when, in fact, helping to solve the negatives can be the key to a successful initiative.)
- It keeps the initiative up front, as a critical part of the community's discussion and fabric at each monthly meeting.

It is through the use of this or other "stay the course" efforts that the success of any initiative can be assured.

REFERENCES

Braunger, J. & Lewis, J. (1998). *Building a knowledge base in reading.* Portland: Northwest Regional Education Laboratory.

Burke, J. (1999). *The English teacher's companion.* Portsmouth: Boynton/Cook Heinemann.

Burke, J. (2000). *Reading reminders: tools, tips, and techniques.* Portsmouth: Boynton/Cook Heinemann.

Fullan, M. (1991). *The new meaning of education change.* New York: Teachers College Press.

Fullan, M. (1999). *Change forces: the sequel.* New York: Routledge/Falmer Press.

Langer, J. (2000). *Guidelines for teaching middle and high school students to read and write well.* Albany: Center on English Learning & Achievement.

Lyons, C. A & Pinnell, G.S. (2001). *Systems for change in literacy education: a guide to professional development.* Portsmouth: Heinemann.

Robb, L. (2000a). *Redefining staff development.* Portsmouth: Heinemann.

Robb, L. (2000b). *Teaching reading in middle school.* New York: Scholastic.

Introduction

For use with *Reader's Handbook* pages 13–29

Daily Lessons	**Summary***
Lesson 1 **What Is the *Reader's Handbook*?**	Build an understanding of what the *Reader's Handbook* is and how students can use it.
Lesson 2 **Getting to Know the Handbook**	Work with students to explore the organization of the *Reader's Handbook*. Invite students to get to know the handbook by previewing it.
Lesson 3 **Using the Handbook**	Help students use what they know about the handbook to set a purpose for reading.
Lesson 4 **Reflect on Reading**	Build background about the reading process by asking students to reflect on their own reading experiences and practices.

*Use these notes to help you teach a mini-lesson or to teach a briefer, shorter version of the lessons for more proficient students.

Lesson Resources

See *Student Applications Book* 7 pages 6–7.

See *Lesson Plan Book* pages 30–32

See Website www.greatsource.com/rehand/

For more practice, see also *Daybook* Grade 7, page 10.

The Reading Process

For use with *Reader's Handbook* pages 32–37

Daily Lessons	**Summary***
Lesson 1 **The Reading Process**	Build background about the reading process by exploring the Before, During, and After Reading stages.
Lesson 2 **Before Reading**	Discuss why it is important to set a purpose, preview, and plan before reading.
Lesson 3 **During Reading**	Explore methods active readers use during reading.
Lesson 4 **After Reading**	Help students understand why it is important to take the time after reading to reflect, reread, and remember.

*Use these notes to help you teach a mini-lesson or to teach a briefer, shorter version of the lessons for more proficient students.

Lesson Resources

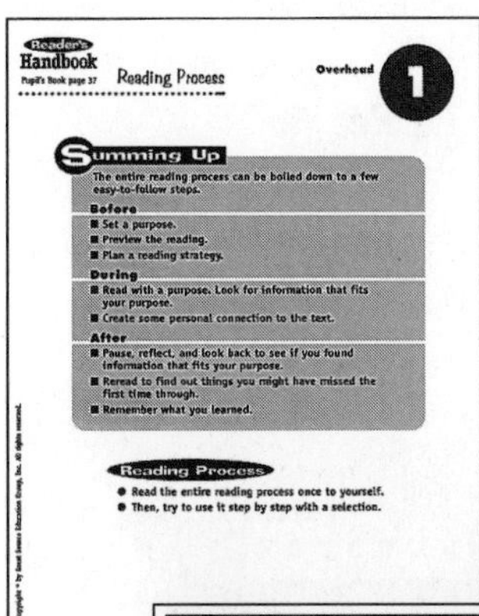
Reader's Handbook
Pupil's Book page 37
Reading Process
Overhead 1

Summing Up
The entire reading process can be boiled down to a few easy-to-follow steps.

Before
- Set a purpose.
- Preview the reading.
- Plan a reading strategy.

During
- Read with a purpose. Look for information that fits your purpose.
- Create some personal connection to the text.

After
- Pause, reflect, and look back to see if you found information that fits your purpose.
- Reread to find out things you might have missed the first time through.
- Remember what you learned.

Reading Process
- Read the entire reading process once to yourself.
- Then, try to use it step by step with a selection.

Overheads

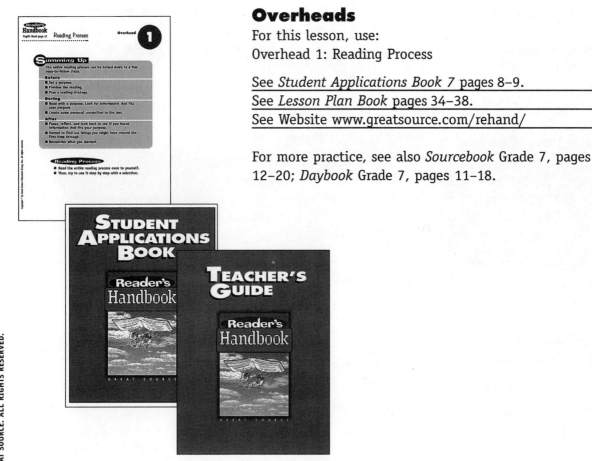

For this lesson, use:
Overhead 1: Reading Process

See *Student Applications Book 7* pages 8–9.
See *Lesson Plan Book* pages 34–38.
See Website www.greatsource.com/rehand/

For more practice, see also *Sourcebook* Grade 7, pages 12–20; *Daybook* Grade 7, pages 11–18.

WEEK 1 Lesson 1

What Is the *Reader's Handbook?*

For use with *Reader's Handbook* pages 13–15

Goals

In this lesson, students learn what the *Reader's Handbook* is and connect the goals of the handbook to their own reading experiences.

Teaching Focus

Background

The *Reader's Handbook* teaches, models, and reinforces a variety of skills and strategies that enhance comprehension and promote reading fluency across a variety of learning situations. The handbook teaches reading as an *active* process. In it, students will find the tools and strategies that they need to become more active, confident, and capable readers.

Instruction

Invite student volunteers to reflect on what the term *handbook* means. Guide students to come up with a definition similar to the following: *a guide or manual that can be used as a reference on a particular subject.* Then ask students to brainstorm the kinds of information they would expect or want to find in a *Reader's Handbook*. Tell students that in this unit they will learn more about the *Reader's Handbook* and how to use it.

Teaching Approach

Use of the Handbook

Read and discuss pages 13–15 of the *Reader's Handbook* as a class. Help students connect the goals of the handbook to their own experiences by asking questions such as the following: Have you ever learned how to do something from watching a model? How can a good model help you become a better reader? Explore with students the kinds of reading they find easy or difficult.

Extend the Handbook

Have students use their journals to jot down ideas about what they would like to learn from the *Reader's Handbook*. Encourage students to use this opportunity to reflect on both their strengths and weaknesses as readers.

Assessment

Ask students:

- What are the goals of the *Reader's Handbook*?
- What reading strategies do you use now?
  What strategies would you like to learn more about?

WEEK 1
Lesson 2

Getting to Know the Handbook

For use with *Reader's Handbook* pages 17–21

Goals

In this lesson, students learn more about the *Reader's Handbook* and how it is organized.

Teaching Focus

Background

The goal of this lesson is to familiarize students with the organization and components of the *Reader's Handbook*. Understanding how the book is put together—its layout, features, and structure—will create interest, promote ease of use, and help students generate questions prior to reading.

Instruction

Ask students to describe what they do before starting a book. Do they scan the table of contents? Read the boldface headings? Check out graphics or illustrations? Point out that these are all *previewing* techniques, or methods that help the reader get to know the material before reading. Lead students to see that readers preview a book in order to 1) see how it is organized and 2) get a sense of its contents.

Teaching Approach

Use of the Handbook

Have students work in small groups to preview the handbook. Encourage groups to make notes or jot down questions about the book's organization and contents. Guide students to identify both recurring and special features, such as the Reader's Almanac. Then, come together as a class to review pages 17–21. Invite students to share their questions and thoughts on the handbook's structure and contents.

Extend the Handbook

Invite students working in small groups to take part in a scavenger hunt. Explain that the purpose of the scavenger hunt will be to identify and find different parts of the *Reader's Handbook*. See pages 24–25 of the *Teacher's Guide* for a scavenger hunt activity.

Assessment

Ask students:

- What did you learn about the handbook by previewing it?
- What part(s) of the handbook do you find the most interesting?
- What questions do you still have about the handbook? How might you find answers?

WEEK 1
Lesson 3

Using the Handbook

For use with *Reader's Handbook* page 16

Goals

In this lesson, students learn and discuss different ways to use the *Reader's Handbook.*

Teaching Focus

Background

Previewing the handbook not only familiarizes students with its structure and content; it also helps them set purposes for reading. Developing their own purposes and reasons for using the *Reader's Handbook* will help students get the most out of this resource.

Instruction

After students have previewed the handbook, they will probably have some ideas about how they might use it. Engage the class in a discussion about what they hope to learn from the handbook and which parts of it they are interested in exploring further. Explain to students that in this lesson they will find out more about how and why to use the handbook.

Teaching Approach

Use of the Handbook

Ask student volunteers to read through the four uses of the handbook on page 16. Build understanding of any uses students have questions about. For example, you may want to walk students through a sample mini-lesson, or use the table of contents to discuss the different kinds of reading material the handbook covers.

Extend the Handbook

Have students choose one section or lesson in the handbook that interests them. Ask them to set a purpose for reading this section of the handbook. As they read the pages they've selected, encourage students to explore the organization, content, and features of the section. For an additional challenge, have students pair up and "teach" a partner all about the section they've explored and what they learned from it.

Assessment

Ask students:

- How will this lesson help you use the handbook?
- What is at least one purpose you have for using the *Reader's Handbook*?

WEEK 1
Lesson 4

Reflect on Reading

For use with *Reader's Handbook* pages 24–27

Goals

In this lesson, students reflect on their own reading experiences and practices in preparation for using the handbook.

Teaching Focus

Background

Successful readers are self-monitoring readers. They know what confuses them, what they understand, and how to apply strategies flexibly to different types of texts and different reading challenges. In order to become self-monitoring readers, students must first become aware of how they read. The introduction to the *Reader's Handbook* will help students begin to build this awareness.

Instruction

Invite students to reflect on what reading is like for them by writing the following questions on the board: *What is reading? Why do you read? What happens when you read?* Ask students to work in small groups to respond to these questions. Come together as a class to discuss the groups' thoughts and responses.

Teaching Approach

Use of the Handbook

Ask students to read pages 24–26 of the handbook. Encourage them to compare their own responses to the questions, What is reading? Why do you read? What happens when you read? to those provided in the handbook. To help students visualize what the reading process is like for them, have them create sketches as described on page 27.

Extend the Handbook

To help students further explore who they are as readers, ask them to create personal reading autobiographies. In their autobiographies, encourage students to respond to questions such as the following: What is my attitude toward reading? In what ways am I an effective reader? What kinds of reading do I find difficult? What were my most positive/negative reading experiences? Why?

Assessment

Ask students:

- After reading this section of the handbook, how would you define the word *reading*?
- What have you discovered about yourself as a reader?
- What questions do you still have about reading? How might you get answers?

WEEK 2
Lesson 1

The Reading Process

For use with *Reader's Handbook* pages 28–29

Goals

In this lesson, students explore how using a process can help them become better readers.

Teaching Focus

Background

One of the goals of the handbook is to enable students to develop an in-depth understanding of Before, During, and After Reading stages. As students learn, practice, and integrate the steps in the reading process, they will also become more active, critical readers.

Instruction

Invite students to reflect on the steps involved in an everyday activity, such as eating dinner. Write *Before, During,* and *After* on the board and have students list the steps involved in each stage of the dinner process. For example, the "before dinner" steps might include planning the meal, purchasing food, preparing the meal, and setting the table.

Point out that reading is also a process. Introduce the three main stages in the reading process: Before Reading, During Reading, and After Reading. Explain that, as in the example above, there are steps involved in each stage of the reading process.

Teaching Approach

Use of the Handbook

Continue to build understanding of the reading process by helping students link it to another familiar process—the writing process. Have students read pages 28–29 of the *Reader's Handbook*. Use the "Questions for Writers" on page 28 and the "Questions for Readers" on page 29. Ask students why it is helpful to break down complex activities, such as reading and writing, into smaller steps. How does having a process make reading and writing easier?

Extend the Handbook

Either in their journals or orally in small groups, have students reflect on the reading process. Ask them to describe what they usually do before, during, and after reading. Encourage them to note which aspects of the reading process they are comfortable with and which parts they would like to learn more about.

Assessment

Ask students:

- What is the reading process and why is it important?
- What steps in the reading process do you use now?
  What steps could you add to help you get the most out of your reading?

WEEK 2 Lesson 2 Before Reading

For use with *Reader's Handbook* pages 32–33

Goals

In this lesson, students learn about the first step in the reading process and why it is important to prepare for reading by setting purposes, previewing, and planning.

Teaching Focus

Background

Many students dive right into their reading without putting much thought into what they are about to read or why they are reading it. When students prepare for reading by setting a purpose, previewing, and planning, they get more out of the material. Prereading steps provide students with a reason to read before diving in and also help stimulate students' curiosity about the text or topic.

Instruction

Ask students to reflect on what they do before they go on a trip. Do they pack, plan an itinerary, look at a map? Point out that just as these activities help them make the most of their vacation time, so can preparing and planning before reading help them get the most out of their reading time. Have students brainstorm different kinds of prereading steps they currently take or could take to prepare before reading.

Teaching Approach

Use of the Handbook

Have students read pages 32–33 of the handbook to learn more about the first step of the reading process. Based on their reading in this section and their own experiences, have students generate a list of prereading steps as a class. On chart paper, write the heads *Setting a Purpose*, *Previewing*, and *Planning*. Help students cluster their ideas under these three headings. Save the chart so that it can be posted as a classroom reference.

Extend the Handbook

Have on hand a variety of reading material, such as a chapter from an informational book, a passage from a textbook, picture books, magazine articles, and short stories. Invite students to choose one of the texts and use it to practice the prereading steps of setting a purpose, previewing, and planning. Encourage students to pair up with another student to share and compare what the prereading process was like for them: Did the process differ for different types of reading material?

Assessment

Ask students:

- What are three steps you can use before reading?
- How can these steps help you become a stronger reader?

WEEK 2 Lesson 3 During Reading

For use with *Reader's Handbook* pages 34–35

Goals

In this lesson, students learn how to read with a purpose and make connections to their reading.

Teaching Focus

Background

Proficient readers read with a purpose, and they know how to change or adjust their purposes during reading, if necessary. They also engage in an ongoing "dialogue" with the text; they ask questions and note reactions that help them make connections to what they read. Finding texts to which students can make connections is particularly important in order to get struggling or reluctant readers involved with reading.

Instruction

Encourage students to reflect on what they think about during reading. Do they slow down to make sense of important information? Do they compare the characters and situations in books to their own lives? On chart paper, write the headings *Read with a Purpose* and *Connect*. Help students cluster their ideas for During Reading into these categories. If necessary, add additional categories. Students can use this chart as a reference.

Teaching Approach

Use of the Handbook

Have students read pages 34–35 of the handbook. Come together as a class to discuss why it is important to read with a purpose and connect to the text. To help students see these processes "in action," read aloud one of the passages, modeling for students how you set purposes or make connections to the text.

Extend the Handbook

Have students return to the reading material they selected in Lesson 2. In their journals, have them write down one purpose for reading the material they've selected. Then invite them to read a page or two of the text, jotting down any connections they make to what they read. If students find it difficult to connect to their reading, refer them to the checklist on page 35 of the handbook.

For more practice, see pages 8–9 of the *Student Applications Book 7*.

Assessment

Ask students:

- Why is it helpful to read with a purpose in mind?
- Why is it important to connect with what you read?
  What are some different ways you make connections during reading?

WEEK 2
Lesson 4

After Reading

For use with *Reader's Handbook* pages 35–37

Goals

In this lesson, students learn about the final stage in the reading process and why it is important to pause and reflect, reread, and remember.

Teaching Focus

Background

When students take the time to reflect after reading, they recall more of what they've read and gain a deeper appreciation of the text's meaning. Unfortunately, many students are already going on to the next activity almost as soon as they turn the last page. Helping students build in time after reading for reflecting, rereading, and remembering will help them make the material their own.

Instruction

Remind students that the reading process does not end when they finish the last page of a book. Ask students to brainstorm steps they use after reading to help them retain and reflect on what they've read. Write the headings *Pause and Reflect, Reread,* and *Remember* on chart paper and help students group common ideas together under each heading. Save the chart so it can be used as a classroom reference.

Teaching Approach

Use of the Handbook

Organize the class into three groups. Have one group read the section on pausing and reflecting (page 35). Ask another group to read the section on rereading (page 36) and the third group to read about remembering (page 36). Have each group provide a brief oral summary of the section they read for the rest of the class. As a whole class, use the summary on page 37 to discuss and review the reading process.

Extend the Handbook

To help students synthesize what they've learned about the Before, During, and After Reading stages, have them create a "road map" of the reading process for the book or article they've been working on throughout this unit. Invite students to be creative as they demonstrate how the reading process works with the particular text they've selected.

Assessment

Ask students:

- Why is it important to pause and reflect after reading?
- What steps of the reading process are easy for you? Why?
- What steps of the reading process are hard for you? Why?

Reading Know-how

For use with *Reader's Handbook* pages 40–46

Daily Lessons	**Summary***
Lesson 1 **Make Inferences**	Discuss as a class how students can use what they already know to make inferences.
Lesson 2 **Compare, Contrast, and Evaluate**	Help students make links between everyday activities and the reading skills of comparing, contrasting, and evaluating.
Lesson 3 **Question and React**	Review why marking the text is an important aspect of active reading. Have students practice this technique as they question and react to what they read.
Lesson 4 **Predict, Visualize, and Clarify**	Examine how active readers mark up the text in order to predict, visualize, and clarify.

*Use these notes to help you teach a mini-lesson or to teach a briefer, shorter version of the lessons for more proficient students.

Lesson Resources

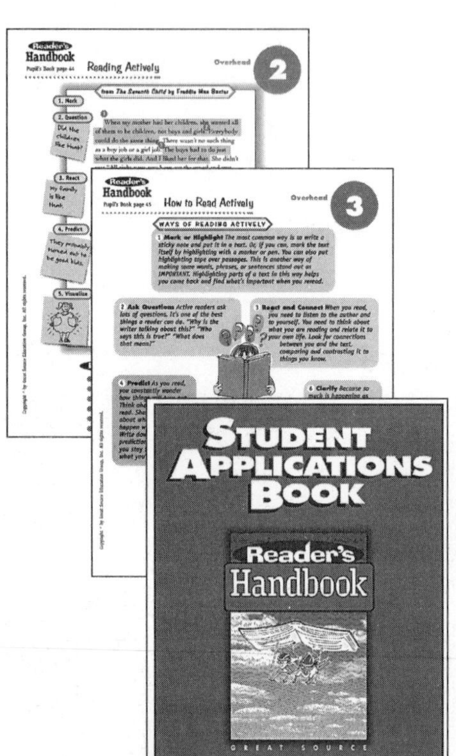

Overheads

For this lesson, use:
Overhead 2: Reading Actively
Overhead 3: How to Read Actively

See *Student Applications Book 7* pages 10–12.

See *Teacher's Guide* pages 40–49.

See Website www.greatsource.com/rehand/

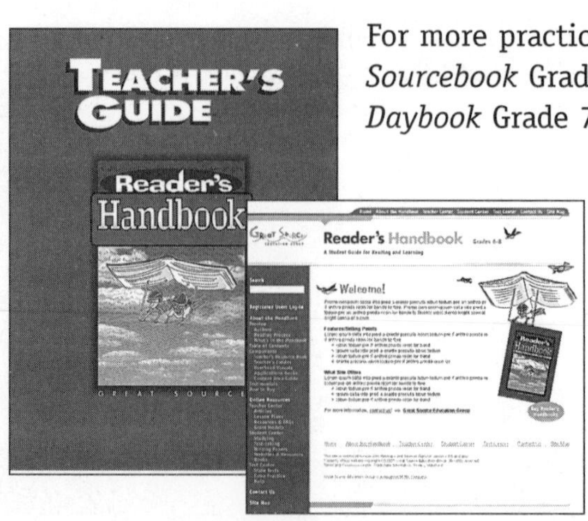

For more practice, see also *Sourcebook* Grade 7, pages 21–30; *Daybook* Grade 7, pages 142–143.

Reading Paragraphs

For use with *Reader's Handbook* pages 47–63

Daily Lessons	**Summary***
Lesson 1 **Identifying the Main Idea**	Review with the class how to identify the main idea of a paragraph.
Lesson 2 **Kinds of Paragraphs**	Discuss the four kinds of paragraphs students are likely to encounter: narrative, persuasive, descriptive, and expository.
Lesson 3 **Paragraph Organization**	Review different ways of organizing paragraphs. Discuss as a class the importance of being able to identify paragraph organization.
Lesson 4 **Order of Importance**	Build understanding of paragraphs organized in order of importance.

*Use these notes to help you teach a mini-lesson or to teach a briefer, shorter version of the lessons for more proficient students.

Lesson Resources

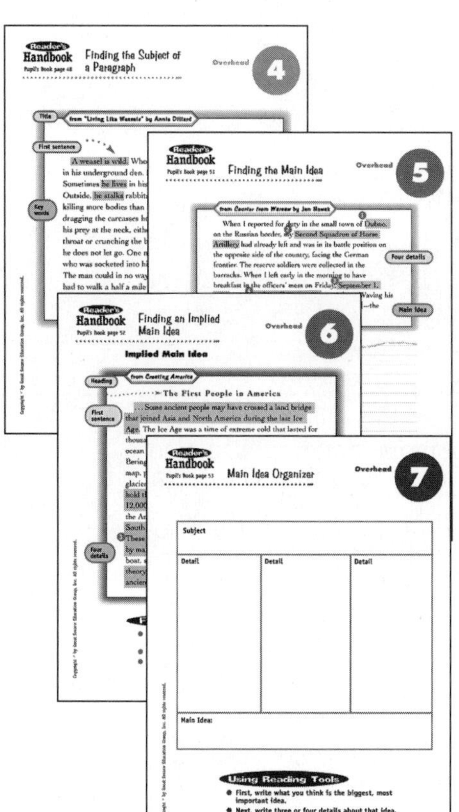

Overheads

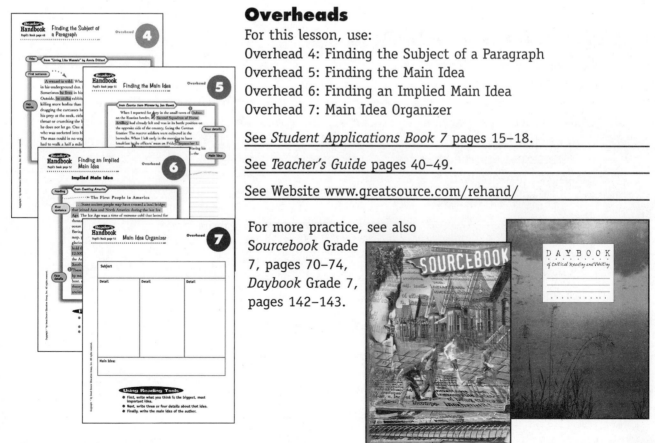

For this lesson, use:

Overhead 4: Finding the Subject of a Paragraph

Overhead 5: Finding the Main Idea

Overhead 6: Finding an Implied Main Idea

Overhead 7: Main Idea Organizer

See *Student Applications Book 7* pages 15–18.

See *Teacher's Guide* pages 40–49.

See Website www.greatsource.com/rehand/

For more practice, see also *Sourcebook* Grade 7, pages 70–74, *Daybook* Grade 7, pages 142–143.

WEEK 3 Lesson 1 Make Inferences

For use with *Reader's Handbook* page 40

Goals

In this lesson, students expand their understanding of the importance of making inferences.

Teaching Focus

Background

Making inferences enables readers to go beyond the literal level of a text to fully understand and appreciate its meaning. To make this essential reading skill more accessible to students, emphasize that making inferences involves using what students *already know,* along with information provided by the author.

Instruction

Ask the class to imagine that in the middle of a summer day, it suddenly grows dark, the wind begins to blow, and thunder rumbles in the distance. What do students think is happening? Point out that students' own knowledge and experiences, along with the information provided, enables them to make the inference that a storm is brewing. Remind them that readers, too, use what they already know, along with information provided by the author, to make inferences.

Teaching Approach

Use of the Handbook

Invite students to read page 40 of the handbook, focusing on the example at the bottom of the page. Copy the "inference equation" onto the board and fill it in as a class. What information do students *learn* about the character? (He is glaring and has clenched fists.) What do students *already know* that helps them to make an inference about the character? (They know how people look and act when they are angry.) What *conclusion* can be drawn? (The character is angry.)

Extend the Handbook

Ask students to select a character from a book they are currently reading or from a movie or TV show they've viewed recently. Have them fill in an inference equation for the character they've chosen. Remind them to use the information provided (the character's words, appearance, or actions) and what they already know to make an inference about the character's underlying thoughts or feelings.

For additional practice, see pages 15–18 of the *Student Applications Book 7*.

Assessment

Ask students:

- What does "making an inference" mean?
- Why is it important to make inferences when you read?

WEEK 3
Lesson 2

Compare, Contrast, and Evaluate

For use with *Reader's Handbook* page 42

Goals

In this lesson, students practice the reading skills of comparing, contrasting, and evaluating.

Teaching Focus

Background

Comparing, contrasting, and evaluating are key skills for critical reading. Because these are also skills that students use in a variety of circumstances, it is helpful to link comparing, contrasting, and evaluating to everyday experiences.

Instruction

Invite students to compare and contrast two or more items, such as sneaker brands or CDs. Ask how the items are alike and how they are different, and have a volunteer record the responses on the board. Then ask students to rate the items on a scale of one to ten. Explain that rating items is one way of evaluating them.

Teaching Approach

Use of the Handbook

Have students read the section on comparing and contrasting on page 42 of the handbook. Use the examples provided to help students explore the idea that there are many different ways to examine how things are alike and different. Invite students to generate additional ideas about how they might use the skills of comparing and contrasting during or after reading.

Have students continue reading page 42 to learn about the skill of evaluating. Point out that any time students make judgments—for example, about books, clothes, or music—they are evaluating. Lead students to understand that being able to explain *why* they like or dislike something is an important part of making an evaluation.

Extend the Handbook

Have students work in small groups to compare two authors or books they have read in class. Ask them to first compare and contrast the books or authors. Then invite students to evaluate the two books or authors, reminding them that it is important to back up their evaluations with reasons.

Assessment

Ask students:

- Why is it helpful to compare and contrast when reading?
- How does evaluating what you read make you a stronger reader?

WEEK 3 Lesson 3 Question and React

For use with *Reader's Handbook* pages 43–45

Goals

In this lesson, students learn how to become more active readers by marking up the text, questioning, and reacting to what they read.

Teaching Focus

Background

Active readers monitor their own reading. They check comprehension by raising questions, connect the text to their own experiences, and reflect on meaning by noting their reactions. To help students get into the habit of actively monitoring their own reading, encourage them to mark up the text, highlight, and/or take notes as they read.

Instruction

Discuss with the class the concept of "active reading." If necessary, review the concept by having a volunteer read aloud the first paragraph on page 45 of the handbook. Ask students what methods they use to get involved with what they read: What methods help them remember what they've read? What do they do when something they read is confusing or unclear? Make a list of students' ideas. (Save this list for use in Lesson 4.)

Teaching Approach

Use of the Handbook

Point out that there are many different ways of reading actively. Compare the list generated by students (above) with the ideas listed under *Ways of Reading Actively* on page 45 of the handbook. If student suggestions did not include marking and highlighting, reacting and connecting, or asking questions, add these to the class list. Use the handbook to review these active reading methods with the class.

Extend the Handbook

Ask students to use a content-area textbook from one of their classes to practice active reading skills. As they read one or two pages of the textbook, have them use a separate piece of paper to note important ideas or information, react and connect to the text, and jot down questions about their reading.

Assessment

Ask students:

- What active reading methods do you use most often?
- Are there active reading methods that you could try to use more?
- How can reading actively help you become a better reader?

WEEK 3
Lesson 4

Predict, Visualize, and Clarify

For use with *Reader's Handbook* pages 43–46

Goals

In this lesson, students learn how to become more active readers by predicting, visualizing, and clarifying what they read.

Teaching Focus

Background

Active readers are more likely to comprehend and remember what they read. This lesson continues the instruction in Lesson 3 by introducing three additional ways of reading actively. Opportunities for guided and independent practice in this lesson will help students add predicting, visualizing, and clarifying to their arsenal of active reading skills.

Instruction

Review with students the techniques for active reading they employed in the previous lesson. Have students revisit the list of active reading methods they generated as a class. If student suggestions did not include the techniques of predicting, visualizing, and clarifying, add these to the students' list.

Teaching Approach

Use of the Handbook

Divide the class into three groups. Assign one group the skill of predicting, another group the skill of visualizing, and the third group the skill of clarifying. Have each group read the relevant section on pages 43–45 of the handbook and then summarize the information for the rest of the class. Use the excerpt from *The Seventh Child* on page 44 of the handbook to clarify and model active reading skills learned in Lessons 3 and 4 of this unit.

Extend the Handbook

Have students return to the textbook passages they read in the previous lesson. Ask students to add to their notes, this time applying the active reading skills of predicting, visualizing, and clarifying.

Assessment

Ask students:

- Which active reading skills do you find easy to use?
- Which active reading skills are more difficult? Why?
- How will you use this unit to become a stronger reader?

WEEK 4

Lesson 1 Identifying the Main Idea

For use with *Reader's Handbook* pages 47–54

Goals

In this lesson, students learn how to identify the main idea of a paragraph.

Teaching Focus

Background

Identifying the main idea is essential to understanding the meaning of nonfiction. For some students, the skill of finding the main idea requires a little practice. Although every paragraph is different, there are basic methods that can help students locate and recognize main ideas.

Instruction

Ask students why it is important to be able to identify the main idea of a piece of nonfiction. Lead students to understand that the main idea contains the central meaning of a paragraph, a passage, or an entire piece. Point out that the main idea is the most important point the author wants to make about the subject. Write the following equation on the board, and explain that the main idea of a paragraph or passage can often be found by using the following rule of thumb:

Subject + What the Author Says About the Subject = Main Idea

Teaching Approach

Use of the Handbook

Tell students that sometimes authors will state the main idea in one of the sentences—often the first or last—in a paragraph. Point out that more often, however, the main idea is not stated. In this case, the main idea is implied, and the reader must pull together information from different sentences to find it. Have students read through pages 52–53 of the handbook to learn more about how to find the main idea. Then come together as a class to review and discuss the steps for identifying main ideas on page 54.

Extend the Handbook

Have students find the main idea in a nonfiction passage. Provide students with a short nonfiction essay or have them use a paragraph or passage from one of their textbooks. Encourage students to use a Main Idea Organizer (see model provided on page 53 of the handbook) to help them identify the main idea.

Assessment

Ask students:

- What is a "main idea"?
- Why is it important to look for the main idea when you are reading nonfiction?
- What are some methods you can use to identify the main idea of a piece?

WEEK 4
Lesson 2

Kinds of Paragraphs

For use with *Reader's Handbook* page 55

Goals

In this lesson, students explore the four basic types of paragraphs and their purposes.

Teaching Focus

Background

Experienced readers understand that the features of paragraphs vary depending on the type of text and the author's purposes for writing. In this lesson, students will learn to recognize four basic types of paragraphs—narrative, persuasive, descriptive, and expository. Building understanding of these paragraph types will help students read and evaluate paragraphs more effectively.

Instruction

Introduce the four types of paragraphs by writing the following heads on the board: *Narrative*, *Persuasive*, *Descriptive*, and *Expository*. Explain that these are the most common types of paragraphs students will encounter in their reading. To activate prior knowledge, discuss with students what they know about each type of writing.

Teaching Approach

Use of the Handbook

Have volunteers read aloud page 55 of the handbook. As a class, brainstorm to expand on the definitions provided for each type of paragraph. For example, students might note that descriptive paragraphs use words that help readers see, hear, smell, taste, or feel what is being described while expository paragraphs address questions such as *who, what, when, why,* and *how?*

Extend the Handbook

Invite students to choose one of the paragraph types described in this lesson. Ask them to explore the format by writing a brief paragraph. Then have students exchange paragraphs with a friend who chose a different paragraph type. Encourage pairs to compare and contrast the characteristics of the two paragraphs.

For more practice, see pages 15–18 of the *Student Applications Book 7*.

Assessment

Ask students:

- What are the four basic kinds of paragraphs?
- Why is it important to identify the kind of paragraph you are reading?

WEEK 4 Lesson 3 Paragraph Organization

For use with *Reader's Handbook* pages 56–63

Goals

In this lesson, students examine the different ways writers organize paragraphs.

Teaching Focus

Background

In this lesson, students will take a closer look at how the organization of a paragraph both reflects the author's purpose and shapes meaning. Being able to identify the structure of paragraphs will help students make sense of them and determine what information is important.

Instruction

Point out to students that authors structure their paragraphs in different ways depending on their purposes for writing. To draw a comparison, point out that buildings can be structured in different ways, depending on their purposes. For example, warehouses are built to provide large open spaces low to the ground. On the other hand, apartment buildings are structured to provide living space for many people on multiple levels. Different paragraphs are also put together differently, depending on the authors' purposes.

Teaching Approach

Use of the Handbook

As a class, read page 56 of the handbook. On the board, identify the six different ways paragraphs can be organized: time order, location order, order of importance, cause-effect order, comparison-contrast order, and classification order. Then assign small groups to each read one of the sections and summarize it for the rest of the class.

Extend the Handbook

Have students divide a piece of paper into six sections, labeling each section with one of the six types of paragraph structures. Then ask them to reflect on when and why an author might use each type of structure. Have them record their ideas on the chart. As students work, they may want to review the sample paragraph structures in the handbook to help them determine what purpose the different types serve.

Assessment

Ask students:

- What are the six main ways in which paragraphs can be structured?
- What purpose does each type of paragraph serve?

WEEK 4 Lesson 4 Order of Importance

For use with *Reader's Handbook* pages 60–61

Goals

In this lesson, students will examine in greater depth paragraphs structured according to order of importance.

Teaching Focus

Background

Paragraphs organized by order of importance can be either inductive or deductive in nature. Good examples of inductive paragraphs can typically be found in newspaper articles. Deductive paragraphs can be found in a variety of expository and persuasive writing. Because many types of writing utilize order of importance, it is important for students to develop a basic understanding of this paragraph structure.

Instruction

Explain to students that when paragraphs are organized by order of importance, the most important idea may come either first *or* last. Read aloud the sample paragraph from *Creating America* on page 60 of the *Reader's Handbook*. Discuss the excerpt as a class, leading students to understand that the writer of this paragraph begins with the most important idea, followed by several supporting details. Then read aloud the second excerpt from *Creating America* on page 61. Work with students to identify that this paragraph uses details to build up to the main idea in the last sentence.

Teaching Approach

Use of the Handbook

Ask students to review pages 60–61 of the handbook independently. Come together as a class to discuss the Main Idea Organizer provided for each of the sample paragraphs. Use the charts to emphasize the difference between paragraphs organized inductively and paragraphs organized deductively.

Extend the Handbook

Have students write brief paragraphs that utilize order of importance. After they choose a topic, encourage students to create a graphic to organize their main idea and details before writing (see sample organizers on pages 60–61). If time permits, read aloud student examples of both inductive and deductive paragraphs so that students can compare them.

Assessment

Ask students:

- What are the characteristics of paragraphs organized in order of importance?
- Of the six paragraph types, which do you find easiest to read and understand? Which type do you usually use in your own writing?

Reading History

For use with *Reader's Handbook* pages 66–76

Daily Lessons	**Summary***
Lesson 1 **Reading History: An Overview**	Work with the class to activate prior knowledge and build background about reading history.
Lesson 2 **Asking *Who, What, Where, When,* and *Why***	Help students set a purpose for reading history texts by asking the 5 W's questions: *who, what, where, when,* and *why.*
Lesson 3 **Previewing and Planning**	Continue utilizing Before Reading steps as students preview a history text and plan for reading.
Lesson 4 **Reading Strategy: Note-taking**	Build understanding of how to take notes to keep track of information in a history textbook. Help students make connections between the notes they take and their purposes for reading.

*Use these notes to help you teach a mini-lesson or to teach a briefer, shorter version of the lessons for more proficient students.

Lesson Resources

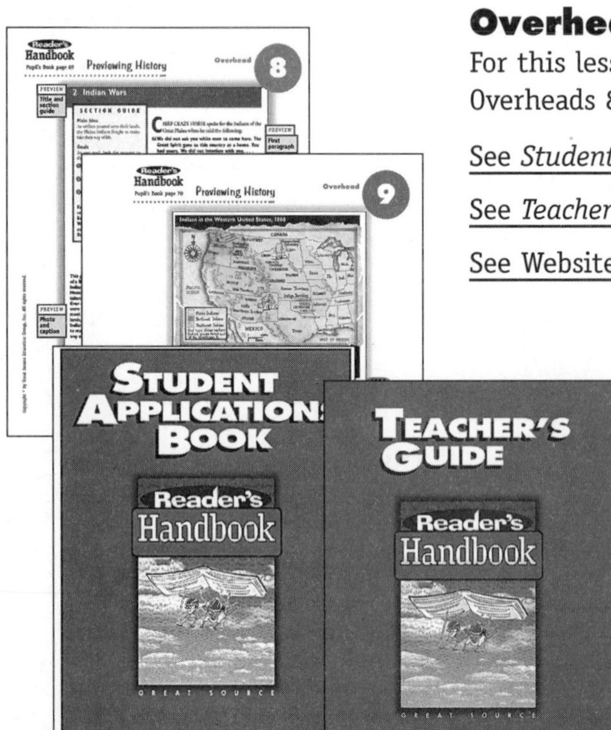

Overheads

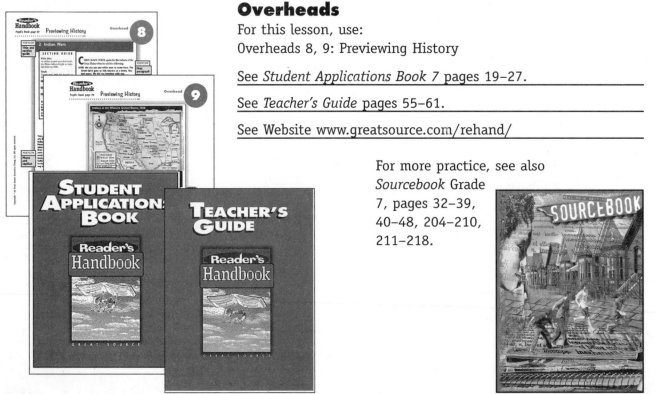

For this lesson, use:
Overheads 8, 9: Previewing History

See *Student Applications Book 7* pages 19–27.

See *Teacher's Guide* pages 55–61.

See Website www.greatsource.com/rehand/

For more practice, see also *Sourcebook* Grade 7, pages 32–39, 40–48, 204–210, 211–218.

Reading History (continued) For use with *Reader's Handbook* pages 77–83

Daily Lessons	**Summary***
Lesson 5 **How History Textbooks Are Organized**	Build understanding of how history texts are organized. Help students use the structure of a history text to locate, understand, and keep track of information.
Lesson 6 **Connecting to History Texts**	Explore with students how to make connections to history texts.
Lesson 7 **Rereading Strategy: Outlining**	Ask students to outline as they reread history in order to track ideas and information.
Lesson 8 **Remembering**	Help students practice After Reading steps to reinforce recall and retention of history material.

*Use these notes to help you teach a mini-lesson or to teach a briefer, shorter version of the lessons for more proficient students.

Lesson Resources

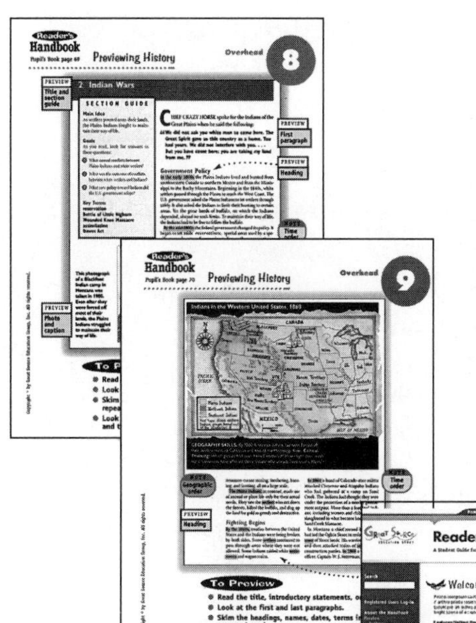

Overheads

For this lesson, use:
Overheads 8, 9: Previewing History

See *Student Applications Book 7* pages 19–27.

See *Teacher's Guide* pages 51–61.

See Website www.greatsource.com/rehand/

For more practice, see also *Sourcebook* Grade 7, pages 32–39, 40–48, 204–210, 211–218.

WEEK 5
Lesson 1

Reading History: An Overview

For use with *Reader's Handbook* pages 66–83

Goals

In this introductory lesson, students activate prior knowledge and build background about reading history texts.

Teaching Focus

Background

In this unit, students will use the reading process to walk through a chapter in a prototypical history textbook. Students will examine the features and organization of the sample chapter, as well as how to apply Before, During, and After Reading steps to a history text.

Instruction

Invite volunteers to describe what they do when they read their history textbooks. Do they preview the questions or study guide before reading? Do they reread to master parts of the text that are important or difficult? Lead students to understand that they probably already use some key methods before, during, and after reading history texts. Explain that in this unit they will learn more about how to use the reading process to understand and remember information in a history textbook.

Teaching Approach

Use of the Handbook

Activate prior knowledge by asking students to reflect on their experiences with history texts. What do they like about reading history? What aspects of reading history do they find challenging? Then read aloud page 66 of the handbook. Help students see that history is not just about names and dates, but also about real people and actual events. Discuss the goals listed on of page 66 to familiarize students with what they will learn in this unit.

Extend the Handbook

Ask students to reflect on their own goals for reading this section of the handbook. Have students jot down their thoughts about what they hope to learn as they read. Encourage them to turn their thoughts into personal goals. Have students review their goals as they work through this unit.

Assessment

Ask students:

- What aspects of reading history do you find easy or enjoyable?
- What about reading a history textbook is difficult or challenging for you?
- What do you hope to learn about reading history textbooks from this unit?

WEEK 5
Lesson 2

Asking *Who, What, When, Where,* and *Why*

For use with *Reader's Handbook* page 67

Goals

In this lesson, students learn how to set a purpose for reading history by asking the 5 W's—*who, what, where, when,* and *why.*

Teaching Focus

Background

Because history textbooks can contain a wealth of new information, it is important to help students set clear purposes for reading. Setting a purpose for reading history provides students with a focus for learning and a motivation for reading on. Because it enables them to monitor their own reading goals and progress, setting a purpose helps students become more independent learners.

Instruction

Help students link the skill of setting a purpose to their own lives. For example, ask students whether they've ever gone to the store without having a clear purpose in mind. If so, chances are that they forgot items that were important or that they returned home with some things they didn't really need. Point out that setting a purpose for the shopping trip beforehand would have made them more effective shoppers. Similarly, setting a purpose before reading will help make students more effective readers. Explain that in this lesson, students will learn how to set a purpose for reading history textbooks.

Teaching Approach

Use of the Handbook

As a whole class, read page 67 of the handbook. Discuss why asking the questions *who, what, where, when,* and *why* can be helpful when setting a purpose for reading history texts. Have a volunteer read the five questions at the bottom of the page. Can students think of any other questions or purposes for reading "Indian Wars"?

Extend the Handbook

Ask students to flip through their history textbooks and find a chapter that interests them. Have them use the 5 W's to set a purpose for reading the chapter. Is there anything students hope to learn from the chapter that can't be answered by asking the 5 W's questions? If so, what question would students need to ask instead?

Assessment

Ask students:

- Why is it important to set a purpose before reading?
- What are the 5 W's, and how do they help you set a purpose for reading history?

WEEK 5 Lesson 3 Previewing and Planning

For use with *Reader's Handbook* pages 68–73

Goals

In this lesson, students learn how to preview a history text and plan for reading.

Teaching Focus

Background

When reading in history, or in any other content area, previewing and planning are key steps in the Before Reading process. Previewing gives students a sense of the text's topic, length, structure, and difficulty. It also enables students to activate prior knowledge about the topic and begin to plan for reading.

Instruction

Remind students of the purposes they set for reading "Indian Wars" in Lesson 2. Ask students what other steps they might take before reading this chapter from an American history textbook. Then have students recall what they know about previewing and planning. Discuss how setting a purpose, previewing, and planning help readers get a sense of what the text will be about. (If students need to review any steps in the Before Reading stage of the reading process, refer them to pages 32–33 of the handbook.)

Teaching Approach

Use of the Handbook

Have a student volunteer read aloud page 68 in the *Reader's Handbook*. Then invite students to preview "Indian Wars" on pages 69–72. Encourage students to use the preview checklist on page 68 as a guide. Come together as a class to discuss what students learned from previewing the history selection. Conclude the discussion by working with the class to plan for reading (p. 73). Remind students that their plan for reading should be related to, and shaped by, their purpose for reading.

Extend the Handbook

Have students return to the chapter in their history textbooks they used in the previous lesson. Ask them to review their purposes for reading. Then have students preview the chapter and determine a plan for reading. Given their purpose and plan, what strategy might they use to read the chapter? Have students record their ideas in their journals.

Assessment

Ask students:

- What are important text elements to note when you preview a history text?
- Why are previewing and planning important steps before reading history?

WEEK 5 Lesson 4 Reading Strategy: Note-taking

For use with *Reader's Handbook* pages 73–76

Goals

In this lesson, students learn how to take notes to keep track of information in history textbooks.

Teaching Focus

Background

Note-taking is an important tool for reading and learning. The process of taking notes requires students to read actively, summarizing information and separating key ideas from nonessential details. It also helps students organize and remember what they read.

Instruction

Ask students how they keep track of important ideas and information when reading history textbooks. Student responses are likely to include ideas such as highlighting, taking notes, or using sticky notes. Point out to students that there are several ways of taking notes and organizing information from reading. Explain that in this lesson they will learn a variety of methods for taking history notes.

Teaching Approach

Use of the Handbook

Have a student volunteer read page 74 in the *Reader's Handbook*. Then divide the class into four groups. Ask the first group to read about Summary Notes, the second group to read about Webs, the third to read the section on Timelines, and the fourth to read about Thinking Trees. Have each group summarize what they learned from their reading for the rest of the class. Engage students in a discussion about the benefits of each method of note-taking. Lead students to see that the method readers choose depends on the text and their purposes for reading it.

Extend the Handbook

Have students use one of the note-taking tools they learned in this lesson as they read a passage or chapter from their history textbooks. Remind students that in order to choose a note-taking method that will be effective, they first should preview and set a purpose for reading. After they've finished, invite students to share and compare their notes in small groups.

For more practice, see pages 19–27 of the *Student Applications Book 7*.

Assessment

Ask students:

- How can you decide which note-taking method to use when reading different texts?
- How can taking notes help you read and understand history texts?

WEEK 6
Lesson 5

How History Textbooks Are Organized

For use with *Reader's Handbook* page 77

Goals

In this lesson, students explore how history textbooks are organized.

Teaching Focus

Background

The organization and structure of history textbooks provide built-in scaffolding to support students' learning. Unfortunately, many students don't know how to recognize and use the structure of their textbooks to support comprehension. The goal of this lesson is to familiarize students with some of the structural clues embedded in their history texts.

Instruction

Use an analogy to introduce the idea of organization and structure. For example, ask students to reflect on the organization of a supermarket: Grocery carts are located at the entrance, similar foods and products are grouped together, frozen foods are usually in the last aisle, and checkout lines are near the exits. Lead students to see that grocery stores are organized to make it easy for shoppers. Explain that history textbooks are also user-friendly. They are organized to make it easy for readers to locate, understand, and keep track of information.

Teaching Approach

Use of the Handbook

Have students read page 77 in small groups. Then find and discuss examples of time order and location order in "Indian Wars." You may want to have students use a timeline to track time order in the selection. Alternatively, have students use the map on page 70 of "Indian Wars" to keep track of location order.

Extend the Handbook

Have students work in pairs to examine the organization of a chapter in their history textbooks. Encourage pairs to use a Timeline, Web, or other organizer to keep track of how the passage is organized.

For more practice, see pages 19–27 of the *Student Applications Book 7*.

Assessment

Ask students:

- What are some common ways in which history textbooks are organized?
- What are some methods to keep track of the information in history texts?
- Why is it important to understand how a history textbook is organized?

WEEK 6
Lesson 6

Connecting to History Texts

For use with *Reader's Handbook* page 78

Goals

In this lesson, students discover ways to connect history to their own lives.

Teaching Focus

Background

Most seventh graders have little trouble making connections between their own lives and their favorite works of fiction. What they may not realize is that it is equally important to make connections to other types of texts, including their history textbooks. When students are able to link their own lives and knowledge to a text, students become involved with what they read and learning becomes personal.

Instruction

Review with students the importance of connecting to the text. Explore students' ideas about how they might make connections to their history textbooks. If students have trouble seeing how the text relates to their own experiences, guide them to see that they can make many different kinds of links to their reading. For example, students can make connections between the information in the text and current events, figures, or issues. Students can also connect what they learn in history to learning or reading in other subject areas.

Teaching Approach

Use of the Handbook

Read aloud or have a student volunteer read aloud the top of page 78 of the *Reader's Handbook*. Use the class discussion (see above) and the examples in the text to list ways students can connect to history reading. Invite students to brainstorm other examples to add to the list.

Extend the Handbook

Have students return to the history text they used in previous lessons. Ask them to read a chapter or passage of the textbook, and then use sticky notes to flag and jot down any connections they make to their reading. Was it easy or difficult for students to make connections? Why?

Assessment

Ask students:

- Why is it important to connect to history textbooks?
- What are two ways you can connect to your history reading?

WEEK 6
Lesson 7

Rereading Strategy: Outlining

For use with *Reader's Handbook* pages 79–81

Goals

In this lesson, students practice outlining to review the key information in a history chapter.

Teaching Focus

Background

Because history textbooks are rich sources of information, it is important for students to pause and reflect on their learning after reading. Questions such as the following are useful for assessing learning: Have I met my purposes for reading? Were there parts of the text that were confusing or difficult? Are there any gaps in the information in my notes? After students have answered these questions, they can return to the text and reread with specific purposes in mind.

Instruction

Ask students what they do after they finish a chapter in their history textbook. If necessary, remind them that it is important to pause after reading to reflect on the material and check comprehension. Walk through the questions from the Looking Back section (p. 79) with students. Explain to students that if the answer to any of these questions is "no," then it is probably a good idea to go back and reread.

Teaching Approach

Use of the Handbook

Once students have used the Rereading Checklist to set a purpose for rereading, they can choose a rereading strategy. Have students read page 80 in the handbook. Explain that outlining is a useful rereading strategy because it helps students organize and focus their thinking. Use the sample outline of "Indian Wars"on page 81 of the handbook to familiarize students with outlining.

Extend the Handbook

Explain that outlines are also helpful to use when preparing for discussions, presentations, or writing. Invite students to build on the outline on page 81, adding other important ideas and key details. Then ask students to use the outline to write a summary of the history chapter.

Assessment

Ask students:

- Why is it important to reread after finishing a history text?
- What questions can you ask yourself to set a purpose for rereading?
- Why is outlining a useful tool when rereading history texts?

WEEK 6
Lesson 8

Remembering

For use with *Reader's Handbook* page 82

Goals

In this lesson, students learn techniques to help them review and remember information in history texts.

Teaching Focus

Background

For many students, the most difficult part of history is not reading the information, but retaining it. One good way to process and remember information is by talking about it—as a whole class, in small groups, or one to one. Graphic organizers can also help students review and recall learning. Organizers such as Cause-Effect Organizers, Webs, and Venn Diagrams visually support both learning and memory. (For more information on graphic organizers, see pages 662–684 of the handbook.)

Instruction

Ask students to share techniques they use to review and recall information after reading. Use students' ideas as a springboard for exploring two methods in more depth. First explain to students that *sharing ideas*—engaging in a conversation with others to explore questions and thoughts about reading—is one good way to get involved with a text and remember it. Add that *creating a chart or graphic* is a second method that can help students recall and organize information from reading.

Teaching Approach

Use of the Handbook

Have students work in pairs to read page 82 of the handbook. As a class, review and discuss the Cause-Effect Organizer at the bottom of the page. Then invite students to compare the two methods for remembering described in this lesson (sharing ideas and using an organizer). Which method do students prefer? Which technique do they think would be more effective for them? Why?

Extend the Handbook

Ask half the class to break into small groups to share ideas about "Indian Wars." Ask the other half of the class to work in small groups also, but to use a Cause-Effect Organizer to keep track of information in "Indian Wars." After they've completed the exercise, have groups come together to discuss and compare what they learned.

Assessment

Ask students:

- Is remembering what you read in history easy or difficult? Why?
- What methods can you use to help you better remember what you read?
- What is the most important thing you learned about reading history in this unit? Explain.

Reading Mathematics

For use with *Reader's Handbook* pages 117–131

Daily Lessons	**Summary***
Lesson 1 **Mathematics: Before Reading**	Discuss why students should apply Before Reading steps to mathematics material. Help students set a purpose, preview, and plan for reading a math text.
Lesson 2 **Mathematics: During Reading**	Build understanding of the reading strategy of visualizing and thinking aloud to help students read and solve math problems.
Lesson 3 **How Math Textbooks Are Organized**	Explore the structure and features of math texts with students.
Lesson 4 **Mathematics: After Reading**	Discuss After Reading steps students can take to help them learn and remember math material.

*Use these notes to help you teach a mini-lesson or to teach a briefer, shorter version of the lessons for more proficient students.

Lesson Resources

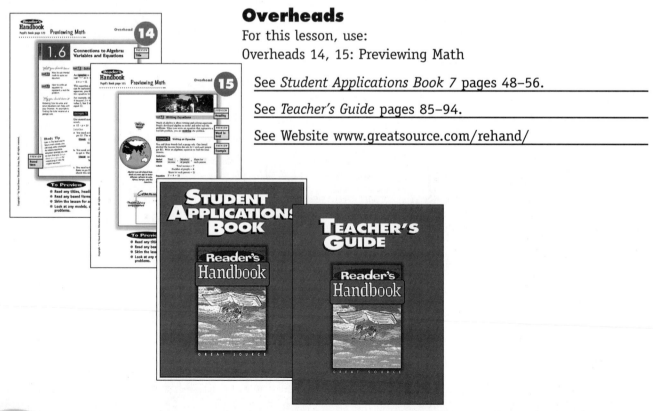

Overheads

For this lesson, use:

Overheads 14, 15: Previewing Math

See *Student Applications Book 7* pages 48–56.

See *Teacher's Guide* pages 85–94.

See Website www.greatsource.com/rehand/

Focus on Word Problems

For use with *Reader's Handbook* pages 143–154

Daily Lessons	**Summary***
Lesson 1 **Planning for Word Problems**	Introduce students to a four-step plan they can use to read and break down word problems.
Lesson 2 **Reading Strategies for Word Problems**	Support students as they use the strategy of visualizing and thinking aloud to work through and solve word problems.
Lesson 3 **Making Sense of Word Problems**	Examine the structure of word problems with students. Compare word problems to other types of math problems.
Lesson 4 **Problem-solving Tips**	Teach students techniques they can use when they have difficulty solving word problems.

*Use these notes to help you teach a mini-lesson or to teach a briefer, shorter version of the lessons for more proficient students.

Lesson Resources

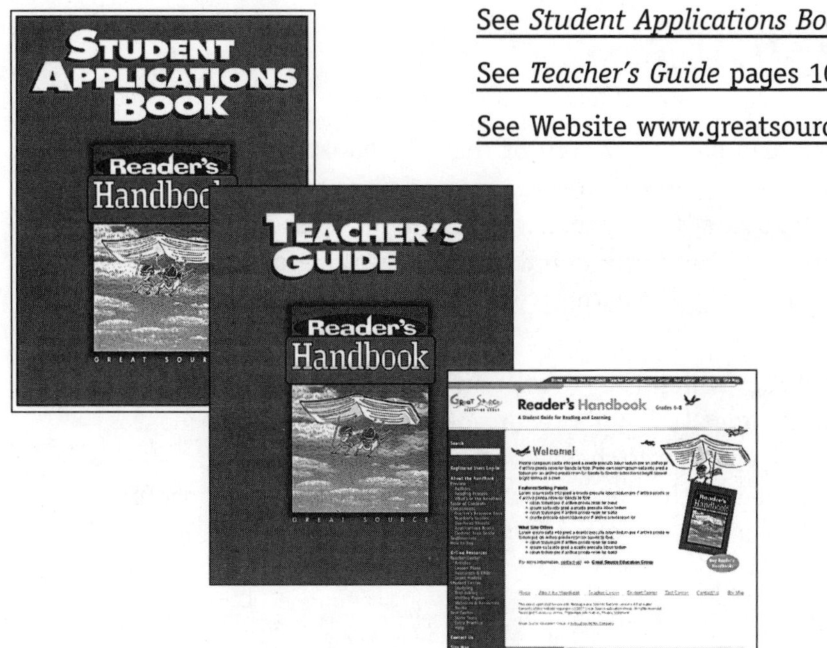

See *Student Applications Book 7* pages 59–60.

See *Teacher's Guide* pages 100–104.

See Website www.greatsource.com/rehand/

WEEK 7
Lesson 1

Mathematics: Before Reading

For use with *Reader's Handbook* pages 117–122

Goals

In this lesson, students review the Before Reading stage of the reading process and learn how to set a purpose, preview, and plan before reading math texts.

Teaching Focus

Background

Students may not be in the habit of applying the stages of the reading process to their mathematics textbooks. However, the best way to learn content in math—as in other content areas—is by reading actively to construct meaning from the text. In this lesson, students will learn how to apply the Before Reading stage of the reading process to math texts.

Instruction

The idea of "reading math" may be new to many students. If so, explain that making sense of math involves more than just reading numbers. The same skills and methods students use to read a book or to make sense of an article can also help them learn the material in their math books. Review with students what they know about the Before Reading stage of the reading process. Conclude by explaining that in this lesson students will take Before Reading steps for reading a math text.

Teaching Approach

Use of the Handbook

Have students work in pairs to read pages 117–119 of the handbook. Then ask partners to preview the math text on pages 120–121. Invite students to share what they learned about the math text from their preview. Finish by discussing why it is useful to work with a partner to read and talk about math material. Have students continue to work in pairs as they make a reading plan.

Extend the Handbook

Have students begin a learning log, which they'll use throughout the unit. Explain to students that they will use the logs to keep a record of their learning and ideas about reading math. For the first entry in their logs, ask students to reflect on the Before Reading steps they practiced in this lesson. Ask them: Were the steps useful when applied to the math text? Explain. Was it helpful to work with a partner? Why or why not?

Assessment

Ask students:

- What are important text elements to note when you preview a math text?
- Why should you apply Before Reading steps to mathematics material?

WEEK 7 Lesson 2 Mathematics: During Reading

For use with *Reader's Handbook* pages 123–126, 128

Goals

In this lesson, students learn how to visualize, think aloud, and make connections to real life in order to solve math problems.

Teaching Focus

Background

The language of math is unique in that it combines numbers, words, signs, and letter symbols. To make the language of math less abstract, many students find it useful to "translate" math problems into more familiar terms. This can be done visually with a sketch or graphic or verbally by talking through and rephrasing problems. Students may also find it helpful to link the content of math problems to their own lives.

Instruction

Ask students how they approach the problems in their math textbooks. Many students probably follow a series of steps similar to the following: 1) read the problem, 2) plan how to solve it, 3) solve the problem, 4) check work. Discuss with students what they do if they get stuck on one of these steps. Explain that in this lesson students will learn three strategies they can use when they have difficulty solving math problems.

Teaching Approach

Use of the Handbook

Have students work with partners to read and discuss pages 123–124 of the handbook. As a class, walk through the three techniques: visualizing (page 125), thinking aloud (top of page 126), and connecting to real life (page 128). Then discuss the different techniques. When and why would students use each?

Extend the Handbook

Invite students to choose a problem from their math textbooks. Ask them to solve the problem first using visualization, then doing a think-aloud, and finally connecting the problem to real life. After they've completed the exercise, have students reflect on the process in their learning logs: Which strategy was easiest for them to use? Why? Which strategy was the most difficult to apply? Why?

Assessment

Ask students:

- What rereading strategy can you use to help you solve math problems?
- How will this lesson help you next time you "read math"?

WEEK 7
Lesson 3

How Math Textbooks Are Organized

For use with *Reader's Handbook* pages 126–127

Goals

In this lesson, students explore the organizational features of math textbooks.

Teaching Focus

Background

Chapters in math textbooks are often organized in similar ways. Most chapters begin with an explanation of key concepts, which may include graphics and diagrams. After concepts are introduced, guided practice is provided in the form of examples or sample problems. Finally, most math chapters end with exercises for independent practice. This structure serves to both guide learning and support students' comprehension.

Instruction

Ask students to recall what they remember about the key features of a math textbook from their preview in Lesson 1. List responses, such as headings, explanations, examples, and boxed items, on the board. Explain that math books contain features like these to help organize the material and support students' learning. Point out that the structure of math textbooks can serve as a guide map, helping students to navigate through the text and exercises.

Teaching Approach

Use of the Handbook

Read aloud the bottom half of page 126. On the board, write the four parts of a math chapter (explanation, sample problems, graphs/diagrams, exercises). Discuss the purpose and importance of each of these four elements. Then have students locate these elements on the sample on page 127 of the handbook.

Extend the Handbook

Ask students to examine the organization of their math textbook. In their learning logs, have them jot down notes about the book's organization and features. Then have students reflect on the organization of the text: In what ways does its structure act as a guide map?

Assessment

Ask students:

- What are some common features of math textbooks?
- How can understanding how your textbook is organized help you "read math" more effectively?

WEEK 7
Lesson 4

Mathematics: After Reading

For use with *Reader's Handbook* pages 129–131

Goals

In this lesson, students learn how to apply the After Reading stage of the reading process to mathematics texts.

Teaching Focus

Background

Because math texts are dense and contain technical vocabulary, it is especially important for students to pause and reflect on their understanding after reading. In this lesson, students will learn how to assess their comprehension of math texts. They'll also learn activities that will help them reread and remember math material more effectively.

Instruction

Review with students the After Reading stage of the reading process. (Have students reread pages 35–37 of the *Reader's Handbook* if they need more information on this stage of the reading process.) Discuss the three After Reading steps: pause and reflect, reread, and remember. Explain that in this lesson students will learn how to apply the steps to their mathematics textbooks.

Teaching Approach

Use of the Handbook

Have a volunteer read aloud the pause and reflect step on page 129. Invite students to add additional assessment questions to the list in the handbook. Ask another volunteer to read aloud the section on note-taking. Then have students examine the Key Word Notes on page 130. To conclude, read and discuss the two steps for remembering math material. Point out that a math journal is similar to the learning log students have been keeping in this unit.

Extend the Handbook

Have students use a chapter in their math books to practice one of the After Reading activities they learned in this lesson. Invite students to either take notes on key words or create a sample test for the chapter. Then have students reflect on their learning in their logs: How did applying the After Reading strategy affect students' understanding of the chapter? Which steps in the reading process do students feel confident about using with math texts? Which steps do they feel unsure about?

For more practice, see pages 48–56 of the *Student Applications Book 7*.

Assessment

Ask students:

- How can you apply After Reading steps to mathematics textbooks?
- What is the most important thing you learned in this unit? Explain.

WEEK 8 Lesson 1

Planning for Word Problems

For use with *Reader's Handbook* pages 143–145

Goals

In this lesson, students learn a four-step plan for solving word problems.

Teaching Focus

Background

When asked what aspect of math they find most challenging, many students answer word problems. Although students may find them intimidating, the majority of word problems can be solved in essentially the same way. This lesson provides students with a basic plan of attack for word problems. Once students understand how to read and break down a word problem, they'll be able to focus more of their attention on solving it.

Instruction

Talk with students about their experiences solving word problems: Do they find this type of problem easy or difficult? What do they like or dislike about word problems? Build an understanding of why it is a good idea to approach word problems with a plan in mind. It may be helpful to draw an analogy by asking students how planning can be helpful when solving other kinds of problems. Then explain to students that in this lesson they will learn a four-step plan that will help them read, understand, and solve word problems.

Teaching Approach

Use of the Handbook

Have students read page 143 of the handbook. Then read aloud page 144, focusing students' attention on the four-step plan. Ask students whether they follow these four steps when they solve word problems. If not, find out which steps they skip and why. Lead students to see that all four steps are important.

Extend the Handbook

Ask students to apply the four-step plan to some of the word problems in their math textbooks. Then have them reflect on the process with a partner or in their learning logs: Was using the four-step plan helpful? Why or why not? Did they have trouble with any of the steps? If so, which ones?

Assessment

Ask students:

- What four steps should you follow when solving word problems?
- Why is it helpful to approach word problems with a plan in mind?

WEEK 8
Lesson 2

Reading Strategy for Word Problems

For use with *Reader's Handbook* pages 145–146

Goals

In this lesson, students learn how to visualize and think aloud to solve word problems.

Teaching Focus

Background

In order to solve word problems, students need to use both reading *and* mathematical skills. First, students need to use a reading strategy in order to identify the main idea (what is being asked) and how it relates to the rest of the word problem. Then students need to use math knowledge to identify and apply the appropriate mathematical concept(s) to the problem.

Instruction

Discuss with students the strategy they use to solve word problems. Do they jot down key information? Draw pictures or diagrams? Rewrite the problem in their own words? Point out that these are all forms of note-taking. Then ask students to compare the notes they take when solving word problems to the notes they take when they read an essay or an article. Lead students to see that in both cases the notes serve to identify and organize important information.

Teaching Approach

Use of the Handbook

Explain to students that this lesson focuses on the reading strategy they can use to keep track and make sense of the information in word problems. Have students read pages 145–146 in the handbook. Either as a whole class or in small groups, work through the sample problem to see how the strategy of visualizing and thinking aloud work.

For more practice, see pages 59–60 of the *Student Applications Book 7*.

Extend the Handbook

Ask students to practice the strategy of visualizing and thinking aloud as they work through two or three word problems in their math textbooks. Then have students reflect on this lesson in their learning logs.

Assessment

Ask students:

- What reading strategy can you use to solve word problems?
- What is the purpose of taking notes to solve word problems?

WEEK 8
Lesson 3

Making Sense of Word Problems

For use with *Reader's Handbook* pages 147–149

Goals

In this lesson, students analyze the structure of word problems and then use appropriate techniques to solve them.

Teaching Focus

Background

One of the most difficult aspects of word problems is that they require students to move back and forth between everyday language and the mathematical language of numbers, symbols, and equations. In this lesson, students learn how to read word problems in order to determine what information is given, what they need to find out, and how to "translate" the problem into mathematical terms.

Instruction

Ask students how solving word problems is different from solving other math problems. Help students break down the process of solving word problems into the following steps: 1) Reading the problem to see what information is given, 2) asking, "What do I need to find out?" 3) changing words into numbers and equations, and 4) solving the equation. Lead students to see that other math problems typically only involve one step—step 4.

Teaching Approach

Use of the Handbook

Read aloud or have a student volunteer read aloud page 147 of the *Reader's Handbook*. Discuss and clarify how to use sequence and word clues when solving word problems. Then have students work in pairs to read and work through the examples on pages 148–149.

Extend the Handbook

To make the learning methods in this lesson more concrete, ask students to divide a page in their learning logs into three sections. Have them label the sections with the following questions: 1) "What information is given?" 2) "What do I need to find out?" and 3) "How can I solve the problem?" Have them answer these questions in their logs as they work through two or three word problems in their math textbooks.

Assessment

Ask students:

- What questions can you ask yourself to help make sense of word problems?
- How are word problems different from other math problems?

WEEK 8 Lesson 4 Problem-solving Tips

For use with *Reader's Handbook* pages 150–154

Goals

In this lesson, students review techniques they can use when they have difficulty solving word problems.

Teaching Focus

Background

When proficient readers encounter text that is difficult for them, they know how to use techniques to get back on track. Students can use problem solving techniques in math as well. In this lesson, students learn four tips for getting back on track when they get stumped trying to solve word problems.

Instruction

Open by asking students what they do when they encounter a new word or a difficult passage during reading. Possible responses include *reread, read on, use context clues,* and *ask for help.* Point out that there are also techniques students can use when they run into difficulty in math. Explain that in this lesson, students will learn four tips that will help them if they get stuck trying to solve word problems.

Teaching Approach

Use of the Handbook

To introduce the material in this lesson, ask a student volunteer to read page 150 aloud. Divide the class into four groups, and assign each group one of the four problem-solving tips: guess, check, and revise (p. 151); work backward (p. 152); use simpler numbers (p. 153); and work with a partner (p. 154). Have each group give a short presentation on the tip they read about to the rest of the class.

Extend the Handbook

Have students work in small groups to apply the methods they learned to the sample problems in this unit or to word problems in their math textbooks. Then have them use their logs to reflect on their learning in this unit: What reading tool(s) for solving word problems did students find most useful? Has this unit changed the way students think about or approach word problems? Explain.

Assessment

Ask students:

- What are two techniques you can use if you get stuck trying to solve a word problem?
- What is the most important thing you learned in this unit? Explain your answer.

Elements of Textbooks

For use with *Reader's Handbook* pages 155–169

Daily Lessons	**Summary***
Lesson 1 **Textbooks: An Overview**	Introduce this unit by reviewing what students know about the elements of textbooks.
Lesson 2 **Features of Textbook Chapters**	Discuss with the class how to utilize the following features of textbook chapters: previews, boldface terms, and headings.
Lesson 3 **Textbook Graphics**	Work with students to explore the purposes of charts, graphs, and maps in textbooks.
Lesson 4 **Glossary, Index, and Table of Contents**	Discuss with the class how to use the glossary, table of contents, and index. Help students recognize the purposes of each.

*Use these notes to help you teach a mini-lesson or to teach a briefer, shorter version of the lessons for more proficient students.

Lesson Resources

See *Teacher's Guide* pages 105–113.

See Website www.greatsource.com/rehand/

Elements of Nonfiction

For use with *Reader's Handbook* pages 273–291

Daily Lessons	**Summary***
Lesson 1 **Fact or Opinion?**	Discuss as a class the importance of distinguishing facts from opinions when reading nonfiction.
Lesson 2 **Connotation and Denotation**	Build understanding of the terms *connotation* and *denotation*. Examine how connotation can affect how readers feel about a topic.
Lesson 3 **Is It Persuasive?**	Teach students how to identify and evaluate the author's viewpoint when reading persuasive writing.
Lesson 4 **Editorials**	Build background about editorials. Have students apply what they've learned about elements of nonfiction as they evaluate an editorial piece.

*Use these notes to help you teach a mini-lesson or to teach a briefer, shorter version of the lessons for more proficient students.

Lesson Resources

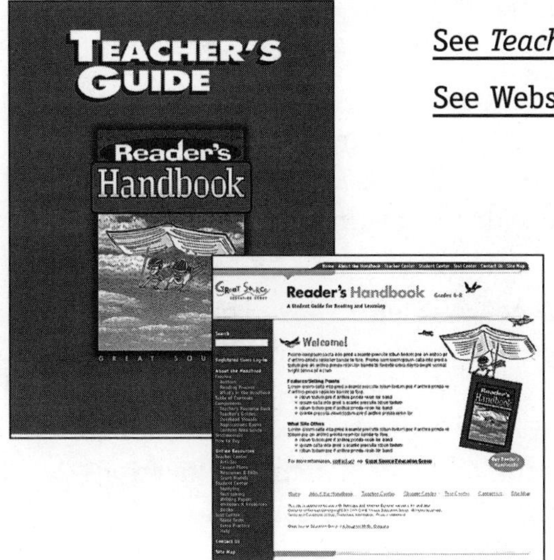

See *Teacher's Guide* pages 182–193.

See Website www.greatsource.com/rehand/

WEEK 9
Lesson 1

Textbooks: An Overview

For use with *Reader's Handbook* pages 155–169

Goals

In this introductory lesson, students learn about the features and organization of textbooks.

Teaching Focus

Background

Textbooks use common features such as headings, graphics, glossaries, and indexes, in predictable ways. Familiarizing students with these elements and building background about their purposes will enable students to utilize them more effectively. This lesson will provide students with a frame of reference for reading textbooks across the curriculum.

Instruction

Ask students to recall or to page through one of their textbooks. Have volunteers identify common features of most textbooks. Record students' ideas on the board. Then engage students in a discussion about features such as glossaries and indexes: When and how do students use these features? Which features of textbooks do they find most useful? Are there any features that students don't use or don't know how to use?

Teaching Approach

Use of the Handbook

Have a volunteer read aloud page 155 of the handbook. Invite students to compare the ten basic parts of a textbook to the list of textbook features generated by the class. Then encourage students to preview this section of the *Reader's Handbook*, noting its contents and flagging any pages they want to return to later.

Extend the Handbook

Now that students have identified common textbook elements, have them work in small groups to identify and discuss the purpose of each element. Encourage students to create a chart to organize their thinking. On one axis, they might list features such as headings, index, and glossary. On the other axis students can chart purposes such as "Can be used to preview the text" or "Useful for locating information." Lead students to see that many textbook features serve more than one purpose.

Assessment

Ask students:

- What are some key features of textbooks?
- How do these features help you read textbooks?
- What would you like to learn about textbooks from reading this unit?

WEEK 9
Lesson 2

Features of Textbook Chapters

For use with *Reader's Handbook* pages 156, 160–161, 166–167

Goals

In this lesson, students take a closer look at textbook chapters, examining features such as previews, headings, and boldface terms.

Teaching Focus

Background

Chapters in textbooks contain cues—such as previews, headings, and boldface terms—that call students' attention to key topics, information, and ideas. Proficient readers know how to recognize and use these features to find and get the information they need from the text.

Instruction

Have students thumb through a chapter in one of their textbooks to locate the following features: previews, headings, and boldface terms. Engage students in a discussion about these three features: In what ways are they similar? How are they different? Lead students to see that these features call attention to key words, topics, and ideas. They help readers focus on important information in the text.

Teaching Approach

Use of the Handbook

Divide the class into three groups. Assign each of the groups one of the following textbook elements: boldface terms (page 156), headings (pages 160–161), and previews (pages 166–167). After they've read through the assigned section, ask each group to "teach" their textbook feature to the class. Then discuss as a whole class how these features can help students read and understand the chapters in their textbooks.

Extend the Handbook

To build understanding of the function of previews, headings, and boldface terms, provide students with a variety of brief, simple texts. Informational picture books and magazine articles work well. Invite students to work on a text in small groups, using sticky notes to add headings and to flag key terms. Then ask students to create a preview for the text. Encourage students to make their previews clear and concise. Display them or have students share their previews with the class.

Assessment

Ask students:

- What are some common features of textbook chapters?
- Why do you think authors of textbooks include these features?
- How can you use these features to help you read textbooks?

WEEK 9 Lesson 3 Textbook Graphics

For use with *Reader's Handbook* pages 157, 159, 163–164

Goals

In this lesson, students explore various non-text features of textbooks, including charts, graphs, and maps.

Teaching Focus

Background

Graphics are used in textbooks to present key information in an alternative format. Often, graphics clarify or synthesize ideas more effectively than text alone can. Not all students, however, are comfortable with reading and interpreting information presented graphically. Reading graphics such as maps, charts, and graphs requires a specialized type of reading that can take some practice.

Instruction

Have students skim though class textbooks to explore the types of graphics used. Ask them to compare the information presented in the graphics to the information in the accompanying text. Which is easier for them to read and understand? What do the graphics add to the text? How do the text and graphics work together? Lead students to see that textbooks use graphic aids to emphasize and make clear important ideas or concepts.

Teaching Approach

Use of the Handbook

Explain that in this lesson students will learn more about three types of graphics: charts, graphs, and maps. As in the previous lesson, divide the class into three groups and have the first group read page 157; the second, 159; and the third, pages 163–164. Ask each group to share what they learned with the rest of the class. Then have students compare and contrast the different graphics. How are charts, graphs, and maps alike? How are they different?

Extend the Handbook

Ask groups to return to the text they worked with in Lesson 2. Have them reread the text, this time noting key information or concepts that could be represented graphically. Have groups create a chart or any other form of graphic to represent the information in the text.

Assessment

Ask students:

- What are three kinds of graphics commonly found in textbooks?
- Why do textbooks use graphics in addition to text?
- Do you find it easy or difficult to read and understand textbook graphics? Explain.

WEEK 9
Lesson 4

Glossary, Index, and Table of Contents

For use with *Reader's Handbook* pages 158, 162, 168–169

Goals

In this lesson, students examine how and when to use glossaries, indexes, and tables of contents.

Teaching Focus

Background

The glossary, index, and table of contents are standard features of many textbooks. Although most seventh-graders are familiar with these elements, they may not understand their importance or know how to utilize them as learning tools. In this lesson, students will learn how and when to use these parts of a textbook.

Instruction

Gauge students' prior knowledge about tables of contents, indexes, and glossaries by asking them to compare and contrast the three elements. Use a Venn Diagram with three overlapping circles to record students' ideas. Many students think that an index and a table of contents can be used interchangeably. If this is the case, lead students to understand that a table of contents presents a broad outline of the topics in a textbook, while the index lists specific terms, names, and ideas.

Teaching Approach

Use of the Handbook

Have student volunteers read aloud page 158 (Glossary), page 162 (Index), and pages 168–169 (Table of Contents). As students read and discuss each section, continue to add new information to the Venn Diagram. Then use a think-aloud to summarize the information in the Venn Diagram. For example: "The items in indexes and glossaries are in alphabetical order, while the order of a table of contents follows the organization of the book. Glossaries and indexes contain key terms, but indexes are used to locate page numbers, and glossaries provide a definition for each term."

Extend the Handbook

Ask students once again to return to their small groups. Have groups revisit the text they used in the previous two lessons. This time have students generate either a table of contents, an index, or a glossary for the text.

Assessment

Ask students:

- Why do textbooks include a table of contents? An index? A glossary?
- What information in this unit will be most helpful to you next time you read a textbook?

For use with *Reader's Handbook* page 281

Goals

In this lesson, students learn why it is important to distinguish facts from opinions when reading nonfiction.

Teaching Focus

Background

In their day-to-day lives, students are inundated with written information from multiple sources, including books, advertisements, newspapers, magazines, and the Internet. To make their way through this jungle of information, students need a variety of "survival skills." One of these skills is the ability to distinguish facts from opinions.

Instruction

Point out to students that it is their job to distinguish facts from opinions when reading nonfiction. Write the following statements on the board:

In 2001, Tiger Woods earned more money than any other player in the PGA.
Tiger Woods is the best player in the history of golf.
The computer was the most important invention of the 20th century.
Computers can perform certain tasks more quickly than humans.

Ask students to evaluate the above statements to determine which are facts and which are opinions. How can they tell?

Teaching Approach

Use of the Handbook

Have students read the description and definition of *fact* and *opinion* on page 281 of the handbook. Then ask a volunteer to read aloud the excerpt from *The Boys' War* on the same page. Discuss as a class what makes the first highlighted statement a fact and the second an opinion.

Extend the Handbook

Provide students with movie reviews from magazines or newspapers. Ask students to read the reviews, noting which statements are facts and which are opinions. Then ask students to evaluate the reviews: Do the reviews consist mostly of facts or opinions? Do the writers of the reviews use facts to support their opinions?

Assessment

Ask students:

- What is a fact? What is an opinion?
- Why is it important to distinguish facts from opinions when reading nonfiction?

WEEK 10 Lesson 2 Connotation and Denotation

For use with *Reader's Handbook* page 279

Goals

In this lesson, students examine how the connotation and denotation of words can affect how readers feel about a topic.

Teaching Focus

Background

While students are probably aware that all words have a dictionary meaning, or *denotation,* they may not be aware that many words also have an emotional meaning, or *connotation.* It is important for students to be aware of the difference between a word's denotation and its connotation because in nonfiction writing, the choice of words often reflects the author's opinion. Word choice can also slant the reader's opinion or feelings about the topic.

Instruction

Introduce the topic by asking students, "Would you rather have your best friend describe you as talkative or big-mouthed? Confident or conceited?" Point out that sometimes the words we choose can have a positive or negative emotional impact, called a *connotation.* Explain that these words are also sometimes called *loaded* or *slanted* words. Discuss with students how the connotation of a word is different from its dictionary definition, or *denotation.*

Teaching Approach

Use of the Handbook

Read aloud the sample paragraph on page 279 of the handbook, calling attention to the use of words that have an emotional appeal. Think aloud to illustrate how the author's word choice affects your feelings about the topic. Then have students read and discuss the description and definition of *connotation* and *denotation* at the bottom of the page.

Extend the Handbook

Invite students to create mini-glossaries of words that have positive or negative connotations in addition to their dictionary meanings. Have available thesauruses and dictionaries to help students find words and meanings. After they complete the glossaries, ask volunteers to share entries from their glossaries with the class.

Assessment

Ask students:

- What is the difference between a word's connotation and its denotation?
- Why do authors use words with connotations in their writing?

Is It Persuasive?

For use with *Reader's Handbook* page 274

Goals

In this lesson, students learn how to evaluate the author's viewpoint when reading persuasive writing.

Teaching Focus

Background

To get middle-schoolers involved with the genre of argument and persuasion, ask them to think about what they do when they want to convince someone else to agree with their opinion. Conversations about students' own viewpoints and opinions can be used as a springboard for identifying and evaluating the viewpoints they encounter in reading.

Instruction

Write the following definition on the board: *Persuade (verb): to win a person over to a desired belief or action by strong urging or arguing that appeals both to reason and feeling.* Ask students to think of a time they tried to persuade someone to agree with their opinion. Did they urge and argue? Did they use both logical and emotional appeals? Point out that these same methods are used by persuasive writers to convince readers to adopt a particular viewpoint.

Teaching Approach

Use of the Handbook

Have students work in pairs to read page 274 of the handbook. Call attention to the opinion statement, or viewpoint, at the top of the page. Make sure students understand that good persuasive writers support their opinion statements with facts and details.

For additional information on persuasive writing, see pages 247–255 of the handbook.

Extend the Handbook

Do students agree that public-school students should be required to wear uniforms? Assign groups of students to each side of the issue. Encourage groups to use an Argument Chart (such as the one on page 274) to organize details and facts in support of the position they were assigned. If time permits, invite groups to debate the school uniform issue.

Assessment

Ask students:

- What is persuasive writing?
- What are some techniques persuasive writers use?

WEEK 10 Lesson 4 Editorials

For use with *Reader's Handbook* page 280

Goals

In this lesson, students use what they've learned about the elements of nonfiction to analyze newspaper editorials.

Teaching Focus

Background

Because they are concise, timely, and can be marked and annotated, newspaper editorials provide an excellent medium for students to practice the skills they have learned in this unit. In this lesson, students will use editorials to apply and synthesize what they know about fact and opinion, connotation and denotation, and persuasive writing.

Instruction

Ask students to share what they know about editorials. Explain that while the intention of most newspaper articles is to report objective facts, editorials express the opinion, or viewpoint, of the writer. Make available to students a variety of opinion and editorial pages from local papers. Encourage students to preview the those pages, noting headlines, length, style, and other features of editorials.

Teaching Approach

Use of the Handbook

Have a volunteer read aloud the example from a student newspaper on page 280 of the *Reader's Handbook*. Call students' attention to the techniques the writer uses to persuade readers that Rosa Parks Middle School is overcrowded. After reading the description and definition of an editorial, discuss with the class whether the editorial was persuasive: Did it convince them to "vote 'yes' for a new school"?

Extend the Handbook

Invite students to choose an editorial from those they previewed earlier. Have them read the editorials critically, marking facts with an *F* and opinions with an *O*, and putting a plus (+) next to words with a positive connotation and a minus (–) next to words with a negative connotation. Then ask students to evaluate the editorials: How well did the writers support their opinions? Did they rely on logic, emotional appeals, or both? Were students persuaded by the editorials? Why or why not?

Assessment

Ask students:

- What is an editorial?
- What kinds of techniques do editorial writers use to persuade readers?
- How has this unit helped you become a more critical reader of nonfiction?

Reading an Essay

For use with *Reader's Handbook* pages 172–180

Daily Lessons	**Summary***
Lesson 1 **Reading an Essay: An Overview**	Help students build background and activate prior knowledge by previewing this section of the handbook. Have students reflect on the previewing process in their journals.
Lesson 2 **Before Reading an Essay**	Work with students to use Before Reading methods when reading an essay. Discuss the importance of identifying author's purpose.
Lesson 3 **Reading Strategy: Outlining**	Build students' understanding of the use of outlining when reading essays and other nonfiction texts.
Lesson 4 **Reading an Essay**	Discuss with students strategies for reading an essay, including identifying its main idea and supporting details.

*Use these notes to help you teach a mini-lesson or to teach a briefer, shorter version of the lessons for more proficient students.

Lesson Resources

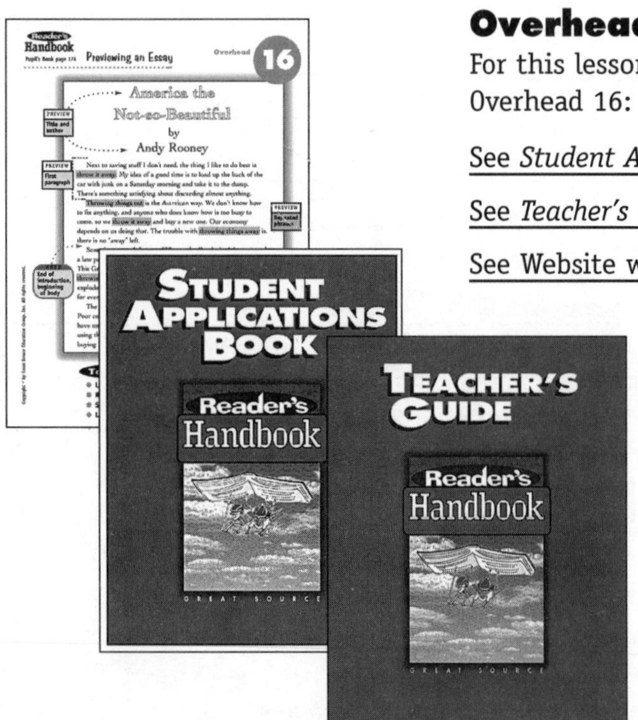

Overhead

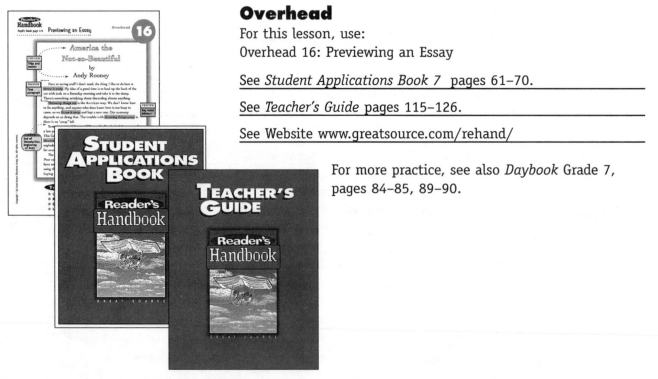

For this lesson, use:
Overhead 16: Previewing an Essay

See *Student Applications Book 7* pages 61–70.

See *Teacher's Guide* pages 115–126.

See Website www.greatsource.com/rehand/

For more practice, see also *Daybook* Grade 7, pages 84–85, 89–90.

Reading an Essay (continued)

For use with *Reader's Handbook* pages 181–187

Daily Lessons	**Summary***
Lesson 5 **How Essays Are Organized**	Work with students to identify the typical organization of narrative and expository essays. Students analyze the organization of an essay.
Lesson 6 **After Reading an Essay**	Build an understanding of the techniques students can use after reading an essay to help them understand and evaluate it.
Lesson 7 **Rereading Strategy: Questioning the Author**	Help students understand how and why to use the questioning the author strategy after reading an essay.
Lesson 8 **Essays and Graphic Organizers**	Reinforce students' understanding of graphic organizers they can use to help them read and evaluate essays.

*Use these notes to help you teach a mini-lesson or to teach a briefer, shorter version of the lessons for more proficient students.

Lesson Resources

Overheads

For this lesson, use:
Overhead 16: Previewing an Essay

See *Student Applications Book 7* pages 61–70.

See *Teacher's Guide* pages 115–126.

See Website www.greatsource.com/rehand/

For more practice, see also *Daybook* Grade 7, pages 84–85, 89–90.

WEEK 11

Lesson 1

Reading an Essay: An Overview

For use with *Reader's Handbook* pages 172–187

Goals

In this lesson, students build background and activate their prior knowledge of essays by previewing this section of the *Reader's Handbook*.

Teaching Focus

Background

While many students have experience writing essays by now, they most likely haven't read many. Previewing this section of the *Reader's Handbook* will enable students to activate their prior knowledge of nonfiction writing in general and to begin building background on essays.

Instruction

Ask students what they know about writing essays. What distinguishes essay writing from other forms of writing? Lead students to see that essays are short pieces of nonfiction that center on a single subject. Explain that methods for reading essays are similar to those used when reading other forms of nonfiction. Work with students to set purposes for reading this section.

Teaching Approach

Use of the Handbook

Have students preview pages 172–187 of the *Reader's Handbook*. Ask them to begin by reading the unit opener and goals on page 172. Then have them skim the section, concentrating on headings, boldface terms, graphics, and anything else that piques their curiosity. Come together as a class and discuss the preview. What stood out to students about this section? Did they notice that the unit is organized around the reading process?

Extend the Handbook

Have students reflect on the preview in their journals. Since previewing is such a critical component of the reading process and one used throughout the handbook, encourage students to focus on the act of previewing itself as well as what they discovered about essays by previewing. Questions they might consider: Was the preview helpful to me? What did I gain from doing it? What do I need to work on the next time I preview?

Assessment

Ask students:

- What do you know about essays? What questions do you have about them?
- What do you hope to learn about reading essays from this unit?

WEEK 11
Lesson 2

Before Reading an Essay

For use with *Reader's Handbook* pages 172–177

Goals

In this lesson, students take Before Reading steps to prepare for reading an essay.

Teaching Focus

Background

Repeated exposure to the steps in the reading process will help students begin to integrate it into their own reading practice. Different genres call for different emphases; The *Reader's Handbook* guides students to adapt the process to fit the needs of particular genres. In this unit, students will focus on determining the author's purpose, finding the main idea and supporting details, and evaluating the information presented in an essay.

Instruction

Review the Before Reading stage of the reading process. Discuss with students what readers' purposes might be for reading an essay. Then talk about the author's purpose for writing an essay. Explain that essay writers can have a number of purposes: to inform, to persuade, or to tell about a personal experience. Discuss the relationship between the reader's and writer's purposes. How might the author's purpose influence students' purposes? Lead students to see that identifying the author's purpose before reading an essay will help them set their own purpose and provide a focus for reading.

Teaching Approach

Use of the Handbook

Have student volunteers read aloud the bottom of page 172 and the information under "Set a Purpose" on page 173 of the handbook. Then have students preview and plan for reading by working through pages 174–176 independently. Remind students to use the preview to help them determine Rooney's purpose for writing.

Extend the Handbook

Gather examples of essays for students to preview. (John F. Kennedy's *Profiles in Courage* and James Herriott's *All Creatures Great and Small* include a number of essays from which to choose.) After previewing, have students reflect on both the author's purpose and their own reading purposes in their journals.

Assessment

Ask students:

- Why is it important to identify the author's purpose before reading an essay?
- What did you learn about this selection by previewing it?

WEEK 11
Lesson 3

Reading Strategy: Outlining

For use with *Reader's Handbook* pages 177–178

Goals

In this lesson, students learn how to use the reading strategy of outlining to help them organize and evaluate information in an essay.

Teaching Focus

Background

When used appropriately, outlining promotes active reading and facilitates readers' understanding of text. It also promotes effective evaluation of arguments and helps readers see the way information is organized. In order for outlining to be a success, allow students to explore various outlining structures (e.g., bullets versus numerical or alphabetical formats).

Instruction

Discuss what students know about outlining. Point out that outlining can help students keep track of ideas and information in an essay. Talk about why it is important to evaluate the ideas and information in an essay or any kind of nonfiction material. Explain that even writing that appears objective can include false statements of facts as well as biased or missing information.

Teaching Approach

Use of the Handbook

Have students read the information on outlining on page 177 of the *Reader's Handbook* independently. Then walk students through the sample outline on page 178. Point out that not all outlines will look like the sample. The organization of the outline depends on the organization of the essay, but most likely the largest part of the outline will focus on the body of the essay.

Extend the Handbook

Outlines are useful tools for tracking and organizing the information in almost any type of nonfiction text. Have students practice the skill by outlining a chapter from a content-area textbook or other nonfiction text.

For more practice, see pages 61–70 of the *Student Applications Book 7*.

Assessment

Ask students:

- What is the purpose of outlining an essay?
- How can outlining help you read an essay?

WEEK 11
Lesson 4

Reading an Essay

For use with *Reader's Handbook* pages 178–183

Goals

In this lesson, students learn techniques for reading an essay, including identifying its main idea and supporting details.

Teaching Focus

Background

Armed with a purpose and plan for reading, as well as a reading strategy (outlining), students are now ready to begin reading the essay. A discussion of the importance of identifying main ideas and details will help students stay focused on the "big picture" as they read.

Instruction

Review During Reading steps with students. Explain that since expository essays are organized around a single point, identifying that point—the main idea—will help students understand the essay as a whole. Review with students the concepts of *main idea* and *supporting details*. (See pages 284–285 for more information on main idea.) Discuss how outlining can help students identify the main idea and supporting details.

Teaching Approach

Use of the Handbook

Read aloud the bottom of page 178 of the *Reader's Handbook*. Have students read "America the Not-so-Beautiful" independently. Encourage them to keep their purpose in mind as they read. Then have students work in pairs to read and discuss page 179 of the handbook. Come together as a class and work through the sample outline on page 180. Help students identify the various parts of the outline, using the outline framework on page 178 as a guide. Ask students to read about ways to connect to essays on page 183.

Extend the Handbook

Have students revisit the essay that they previewed in Lesson 2. As they read the essay, ask students to focus on identifying the main idea and supporting details. Then have them create an outline for the essay.

For additional practice, see pages 61–70 of the *Student Applications Book 7*.

Assessment

Ask students:

- Why is it important to determine the main idea and supporting details in an essay?
- What is the connection between an outline and the main idea and supporting details?

WEEK 12
Lesson 5

How Essays Are Organized

For use with *Reader's Handbook* pages 181–182

Goals

In this lesson, students examine the organization of narrative and expository essays.

Teaching Focus

Background

Understanding the organization of an essay can help readers stay focused on the material and, in the case of expository essays, identify the main idea and details. This lesson concentrates on three common structures used to organize essays.

Instruction

Discuss with students how they organize essays when they write. Talk about the differences in organizing a narrative essay and an expository one. Ask student volunteers to create diagrams illustrating ways they might organize narrative and expository essays. Discuss the similarities among the diagrams. Then explain that authors also rely on some common frameworks for organizing their essays.

Teaching Approach

Use of the Handbook

Have students work in small groups to examine the three organizational structures for essays on pages 181–182 of the *Reader's Handbook*. Ask groups to compare the two models of expository organization. What are the benefits of each? Remind students that writers, including themselves, are not restricted to these three structures. Work with groups to diagram the organizational structure of "America the Not-so-Beautiful."

Extend the Handbook

Have students return to the essay they have been working with throughout the unit to examine its organization. Ask students to diagram its organization and then compare it to the diagrams in the handbook. Did the author follow one of the typical frameworks? Discuss how identifying the organization affected students' understanding of the essay.

For more practice, see pages 61–70 of the *Student Applications Book 7*.

Assessment

Ask students:

- What can readers learn by examining an essay's organization?
- What are some of the differences between the organization of a narrative essay and an expository essay?

WEEK 12 Lesson 6 After Reading an Essay

For use with *Reader's Handbook* pages 184, 186–187

Goals

In this lesson, students develop an understanding of the techniques they can use after reading an essay to help them understand and evaluate it.

Teaching Focus

Background

While the main purpose of an expository essay may be to inform, essays often include persuasive elements as well. Proficient readers rely on After Reading steps to ensure that they understand and can evaluate the information in an essay effectively.

Instruction

Review with students the After Reading stage of the reading process. Reinforce their understanding of the importance of taking time after reading to reflect on what they have read. Explain that after reading an essay it is important to think not only about what the essay was all about but also how they feel about the author's message.

Teaching Approach

Use of the Handbook

Ask students to think back to "America the Not-so-Beautiful" as they work through the After Reading strategies on pages 184 and 186 of the *Reader's Handbook*. (Questioning the author on page 185 will be discussed in detail in the next lesson.) Have them jot down answers to the Looking Back section questions to ensure that they have met their purpose for reading. Encourage students to reread as necessary in order to restate the main idea and supporting details in their own words. Discuss how students can take After Reading steps to help them evaluate the author's message.

Extend the Handbook

Have students apply the After Reading techniques discussed in this section of the handbook to the essay they have been reading throughout the unit. Remind them to check to see if they have met their purpose for reading and can restate the main idea. Encourage them to write their thoughts about the author's message in their journals. Do they agree with the author's message? Why or why not?

Assessment

Ask students:

- How can After Reading steps help you understand and evaluate an essay?
- Why is it important to evaluate essays?

WEEK 12 Lesson 7 Rereading Strategy: Questioning the Author

For use with *Reader's Handbook* pages 185

Goals

In this lesson, students learn how and why to use the Questioning the Author strategy after reading an essay.

Teaching Focus

Background

Questioning the author is a powerful strategy to employ after reading, particularly when working with difficult text or passages. Questioning the author requires the reader to play an active role in the reading (or rereading) process. It helps engage the reader in the text and provides a framework for understanding it.

Instruction

Ask student volunteers to share what they would do if after reading an essay, they discovered that they didn't quite understand what the essay was all about. List their ideas on the board. Explain that there is a particularly effective rereading strategy they might use called questioning the author. Have students predict what the strategy is, based on its title.

Teaching Approach

Use of the Handbook

Since questioning the author might be an unfamiliar rereading strategy for students, walk them through the information on page 185 of the *Reader's Handbook*. Then choose a short excerpt from the essay and think aloud as you reread, concentrating on questions you would ask the author and textual clues that help you answer them. Scaffold the lesson by asking students to work in small groups to continue the questioning process.

Extend the Handbook

Have students apply the questioning the author strategy to the essay they have been using throughout this unit. Encourage students to reread any difficult or confusing parts of the essay and jot down questions they might ask the author. Encourage students to look for clues in the text to help find answers.

Assessment

Ask students:

- Describe the questioning the author strategy. What is its purpose?
- How did applying this strategy to an essay affect your understanding of the material?

WEEK 12
Lesson 8

Essays and Graphic Organizers

For use with *Reader's Handbook* pages 178–187

Goals

In this lesson, students reinforce their understanding of graphic organizers they can use to help them read and evaluate an essay.

Teaching Focus

Background

In order for the strategies discussed in this section of the *Reader's Handbook* to be effective, students must be able to integrate them into their own reading practices. A review of graphic organizers used for reading essays will promote students' continued use of the strategies.

Instruction

Review with students what they learned about reading essays in this unit. Discuss how well they think they can remember the methods presented. Explain that revisiting the graphic organizers used before, during, and after reading an essay and reflecting on their purposes will provide "hooks" for students to hang the strategies on.

Teaching Approach

Use of the Handbook

Divide the class into five groups. Assign each group one of the following: Outline (pages 178 and 180), essay organization diagrams (pages 181–182), Main Idea Organizer (p. 182), Double-entry Journal (p. 185), Summary Notes (p. 186). Have each group revisit one of the graphics then explain the graphic to the rest of the class. Ask groups to include a description of the graphic, what reading technique it reinforces, and its benefits.

Extend the Handbook

Have students choose one of the graphic organizers that they have not already used and apply it to the essay they worked on throughout the unit. Encourage students to reflect on how the organizer helps them use the corresponding reading technique more effectively.

Assessment

Ask students:

- How can graphic organizers help you read an essay? Choose one organizer from the unit and explain its purpose.
- What is the most important thing you learned about essays from this unit?

Reading a Magazine Article

For use with *Reader's Handbook* pages 234–246

Daily Lessons	**Summary***
Lesson 1 **Previewing a Magazine Article**	Build an understanding of the importance of previewing a magazine article before reading it. Ask students to work in small groups to preview an article.
Lesson 2 **Reading with a Purpose**	Work with students to examine how the questioning the author strategy can help them read with a purpose.
Lesson 3 **How Magazine Articles Are Organized**	Help students understand two ways magazine articles can be organized. Discuss how identifying the structure of an article can help readers keep track of the information in it.
Lesson 4 **Rereading Strategy: Reading Critically**	Discuss with students how reading a magazine article critically can help them evaluate it. Have students create a Critical Reading Chart to help them evaluate an article.

*Use these notes to help you teach a mini-lesson or to teach a briefer, shorter version of the lessons for more proficient students.

Lesson Resources

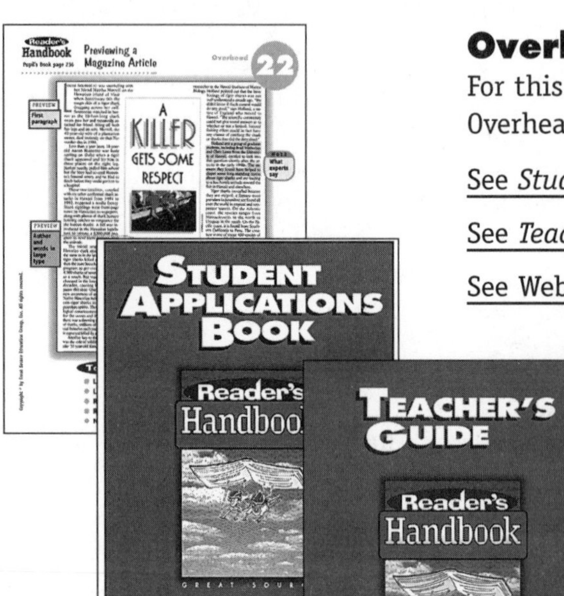

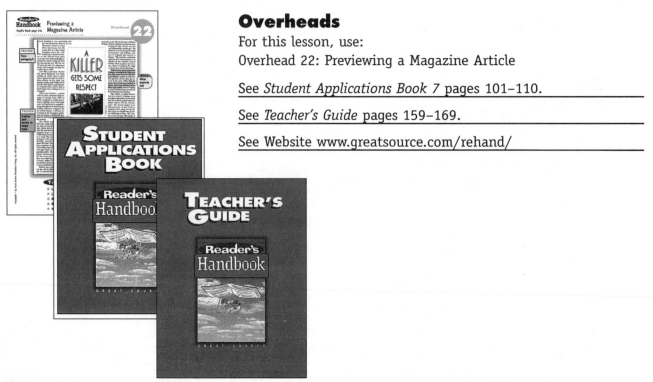

Overheads

For this lesson, use:
Overhead 22: Previewing a Magazine Article

See *Student Applications Book 7* pages 101–110.

See *Teacher's Guide* pages 159–169.

See Website www.greatsource.com/rehand/

Focus on Speeches

For use with *Reader's Handbook* pages 256–264

Daily Lessons	**Summary***
Lesson 1 **Understanding the Purpose of a Speech**	Help students understand why determining the purpose of a speech is critical for understanding and evaluating it successfully. Have students preview a speech.
Lesson 2 **Reading Strategy: Reading Critically**	Expand students' understanding of the benefits of reading nonfiction texts critically.
Lesson 3 **How Speeches Are Organized**	Work with students to identify how speeches are typically organized. Students create a graphic organizer to illustrate the structure of a speech.
Lesson 4 **Evaluating a Speech**	Build students' understanding of methods for evaluating speeches effectively, including recognizing propaganda techniques and loaded words.

*Use these notes to help you teach a mini-lesson or to teach a briefer, shorter version of the lessons for more proficient students.

Lesson Resources

See *Student Applications Book 7* pages 113–115.

See *Teacher's Guide* pages 174–177.

See Website www.greatsource.com/rehand/

For more practice, see also Sourcebook Grade 7, pages 93–102; Daybook Grade 7, pages 92–93.

WEEK 13

Lesson 1

Previewing a Magazine Article

For use with *Reader's Handbook* pages 234–240

Goals

In this lesson, students preview a magazine article to get ready for reading.

Teaching Focus

Background

Before reading a magazine, most experienced readers preview it. They might first skim the articles to determine which ones interest them. Then, after choosing an article, they continue the preview to build background and activate prior knowledge of the article's topic. Students will benefit from a review of the previewing process and a discussion of how it can be used before reading magazine articles.

Instruction

Ask student volunteers to share what they do before reading a magazine article. Do they skim the article? Look over the photographs? Read the captions? Point out that these are all ways of previewing an article. Review the process and purpose of previewing. Help students recognize that previewing an article helps them get a sense of what the article is all about.

Teaching Approach

Use of the Handbook

Read aloud or have a student volunteer read aloud the unit opener on page 234 of the *Reader's Handbook*. Discuss the goals of the unit. Ask students to think about their own goals for reading the unit. What do they hope to learn? Have students read the rest of page 234 and the top of page 235 independently. Then have students work in pairs to preview "A Killer Gets Some Respect" on pages 236–239. After previewing, ask partners to discuss what they learned. Have them plan for reading, using the information on page 240 as a guide.

Extend the Handbook

Bring in a variety of magazine articles for students to work with throughout the unit. Divide the class into small groups and assign each group an article to preview. Ask students to preview the articles on their own and then gather in groups to discuss what they learned. Have groups discuss the effectiveness of previewing.

Assessment

Ask students:

- Why should readers preview a magazine article before reading it?
- Describe strategies for previewing a magazine article.
  Which do you think is the most effective? Explain.

WEEK 13
Lesson 2

Reading with a Purpose

For use with *Reader's Handbook* pages 240–241

Goals

In this lesson, students build an understanding of the questioning the author strategy to help them read with a purpose.

Teaching Focus

Background

Questioning the author was introduced in Week 12, Lesson 7. Questioning the author is a strategy that helps readers of differing ability levels get actively involved with a variety of texts. In this lesson, the strategy is used to help make students aware of how the author of a magazine article writes and thinks about his or her topic.

Instruction

Review the strategy of questioning the author. Remind students that this strategy involves thinking about the decisions the author made when writing the article. Explain that students can use the strategy to help them read with a purpose and to get more involved in the article.

Teaching Approach

Use of the Handbook

Walk students though the information on questioning the author on pages 240–241 of the *Reader's Handbook*. Help students work though the sample questions and answers on page 241. Then have students read the article independently. Encourage them to question the author as they read. They might jot down questions on sticky notes next to the specific passages or else list them in their journals, as shown on page 241. Ask student volunteers to share their questions. Have the class work together to search for textual clues that help answer them.

Extend the Handbook

Have students use the strategy of questioning the author as they read the magazine article they previewed in the last lesson. Ask students to gather in groups to share their questions and discuss possible answers. Encourage students to talk about how they used the strategy. What did they gain from it? What did they find difficult about it?

For more practice, see pages 102–110 of the *Student Applications Book 7*.

Assessment

Ask students:

- How does questioning the author as you read affect your understanding of a magazine article?
- Do you think this is an effective strategy for reading a magazine article? Why or why not?

WEEK 13
Lesson 3

How Magazine Articles Are Organized

For use with *Reader's Handbook* pages 242–243

Goals

In this lesson, students learn two ways magazine articles can be organized.

Teaching Focus

Background

As with other genres, understanding how a magazine article is organized provides a framework for reading. This lesson concentrates on two common structures—chronological order and viewpoint-supporting details order. Using graphic organizers can both help students visualize the structure and reinforce comprehension.

Instruction

Explain that in this lesson, students will examine two ways magazine articles are commonly organized. Discuss the purpose of analyzing an article's organization. Point out that if students know how an article is organized, they can use the structure of the article to organize and track the information contained within it.

Teaching Approach

Use of the Handbook

Walk students through the information on pages 242–243 of the *Reader's Handbook*. Discuss the differences between chronological, or time-order organization, and viewpoint-supporting details organization. (For more information on chronological order, see page 276 of the handbook.) Talk about clue words in the text that students can use to determine an article's organization (such as *then*, *next*, and *later* for chronological order).

Extend the Handbook

Have students analyze the organization of the article they have been using throughout the unit. Remind them that not all articles will be organized in chronological or viewpoint-supporting details order. Challenge students to create a diagram to show the article's structure if it is different from those diagrammed in the handbook. As a class, discuss the various methods of organization used in the articles. Does one type of structure dominate?

For more practice, see pages 102–110 of the *Student Applications Book 7*.

Assessment

Ask students:

- What are two common ways of organizing a magazine article?
- What is the purpose of analyzing an article's structure?

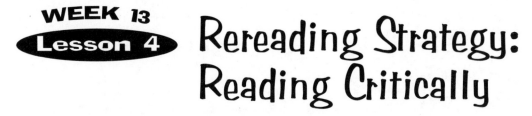

WEEK 13
Lesson 4

Rereading Strategy: Reading Critically

For use with *Reader's Handbook* pages 244–246

Goals

In this lesson, students learn how to read critically in order to evaluate a magazine article.

Teaching Focus

Background

Perhaps the most important strategy proficient readers rely on when reading any type of nonfiction material is evaluating the text. Even a seemingly objective article can contain biased information. Building students' understanding of critical reading will help them evaluate magazine articles and other forms of nonfiction.

Instruction

Ask students if they expect magazine articles to be objective or subjective; that is, do magazine writers just report the facts, or do they include their opinions? Ask students to reflect on the information in "A Killer Gets Some Respect." Is this an objective or subjective piece? Explain that in order to effectively answer this question, students need to evaluate the information presented (and not presented) in the article.

Teaching Approach

Use of the Handbook

Ask students to read page 244 of the *Reader's Handbook* and answer the questions in the Looking Back section. Explain that if students do not feel they can answer the questions, they might need to reread all or part of the article. Work with students to read and discuss the strategy of reading critically on page 245. Walk the class through the Critical Reading Chart. Do students think the author has supported his viewpoint with enough evidence? Have students finish the section by reading page 246 on their own.

Extend the Handbook

Ask students to apply the After Reading strategies explored in this section to the article they have been using. Encourage them to reread critically and then create a Critical Reading Chart to help them evaluate the article. Have students discuss their evaluations with other students who have read the same piece.

Assessment

Ask students:

- Describe the reading strategy of reading critically. What is its purpose?
- Why should readers evaluate the information in a magazine article?

WEEK 14
Lesson 1

Understanding the Purpose of a Speech

For use with *Reader's Handbook* pages 256–259

Goals

In this lesson, students learn why determining the purpose of a speech is critical for understanding and evaluating it successfully.

Teaching Focus

Background

In order to understand and evaluate a speech, readers must first identify its purpose. Knowing the purpose helps readers stay focused during reading. Help students identify the purpose of a speech by previewing to look for clues about its purpose, reflecting on its title, and reading the opening and closing paragraphs.

Instruction

Ask whether students have ever heard or read any speeches. Explain that reading a speech requires many of the same methods as reading other forms of nonfiction. Talk about the purpose of speeches. In what situations do people make speeches? Lead students to see that speeches are used to persuade people of an opinion or to provide information about a subject (even then, chances are the underlying purpose is to persuade).

Teaching Approach

Use of the Handbook

Have students work in small groups to read and discuss the Before Reading strategies for reading a speech on pages 256–259 of the *Reader's Handbook*. Build understanding of how previewing the speech can help readers determine the speaker's purpose. Talk about the relationship between a speaker's viewpoint and his or her purpose.

Extend the Handbook

There are a limited number of published speeches that are accessible to seventh graders. One of the best known is Dr. Martin Luther King, Jr.'s "I Have a Dream." Provide copies of Dr. King's speech for students to preview or see if copies of student-government candidates' speeches are available. Have students preview the speech to identify the speaker's purpose.

Assessment

Ask students:

- Why is it important to determine the purpose of a speech?
- What technique can you use to determine the writer's or speaker's purpose?

WEEK 14
Lesson 2

Reading Strategy: Reading Critically

For use with *Reader's Handbook* page 260

Goals

In this lesson, students build on their understanding of the benefits of reading nonfiction texts critically.

Teaching Focus

Background

Once students have identified the purpose of a speech, they can take the related step of identifying the speaker's viewpoint. As students read or listen to speeches, they need to critically evaluate how well the speaker supports that viewpoint. Critical reading was introduced as a rereading strategy in Week 13, Lesson 4. In this lesson, students will turn a critical eye (and ear) to evaluating speeches.

Instruction

Review with students the strategy of critical reading. If they utilized critical reading as a strategy in the unit on magazine articles, ask students to revisit what the process was like for them. Point out that reading critically is a powerful strategy for nonfiction material in general, particularly when pieces include persuasive elements. Talk about the benefits of reading a speech critically.

Teaching Approach

Use of the Handbook

Read aloud the information on reading critically on page 260 of the *Reader's Handbook*. Model the strategy by thinking aloud as you read the first paragraph of President Reagan's speech on page 258. Work with students in small groups as they continue reading the speech critically.

Extend the Handbook

Ask students to critically read the speech that they previewed in the last lesson, using your think-aloud and the tips in the handbook as guides. Come together as a class and talk about the critical reading process. Did students find it helpful for reading the speech? Why or why not?

For additional practice, see pages 113–115 of the *Student Applications Book 7*.

Assessment

Ask students:

- What should readers concentrate on when reading a speech critically?
- What is the purpose of reading critically?

WEEK 14
Lesson 3

How Speeches Are Organized

For use with *Reader's Handbook* pages 261–262

Goals

In this lesson, students examine the structure and organization of speeches.

Teaching Focus

Background

Determining the structure of speeches and other nonfiction material enables readers to construct meaning from the text more effectively. One of the benefits of analyzing the structure of a speech is that while students might be unfamiliar with reading this genre, they should be familiar with its underlying organization (typically, viewpoint-supporting details order).

Instruction

Review what students know about nonfiction text structures. Point out that speeches are often organized in ways similar to other forms of nonfiction. Reinforce students' understanding of the purpose of identifying text structure. Explain that readers can use the organization of a speech to keep track of the author's viewpoint and the evidence used to support it.

Teaching Approach

Use of the Handbook

Have students read pages 261–262 of the *Reader's Handbook* on their own. Then discuss common ways of organizing information in a speech. Work through the two graphic organizers with students, and discuss the purpose of each.

Extend the Handbook

Have students work in small groups to analyze the structure of the speech they have been working with throughout the unit. Ask groups to create a graphic organizer for the speech that reflects its organization. Have groups discuss how identifying the text structure affected their understanding of the speech.

For more practice, see pages 113–115 of the *Student Applications Book 7*.

Assessment

Ask students:

- Describe two ways in which speeches can be organized.
- How can identifying its organization help you read a speech?

WEEK 14
Lesson 4

Evaluating a Speech

For use with *Reader's Handbook* pages 263–264

Goals

In this lesson, students learn strategies for evaluating speeches, including recognizing propaganda techniques and identifying loaded words.

Teaching Focus

Background

In order to effectively evaluate a speech, readers need to be aware of propaganda techniques speakers often rely on to sway their audience. Students will benefit from an overview of common propaganda techniques as well as a closer investigation of the use of loaded words in speeches.

Instruction

Ask student volunteers to describe their favorite television commercial. Work with the class to analyze the ad. What makes it effective? How do the ad-makers try to get the viewer to buy the product? Explain that there are a variety of propaganda techniques that writers of persuasive pieces use to persuade their audience. Point out that identifying these techniques will help students evaluate speeches and other forms of persuasive writing.

Teaching Approach

Use of the Handbook

Have student volunteers read aloud the first three paragraphs on page 263 of the *Reader's Handbook*. Walk students through the seven common propaganda techniques. Work with students to brainstorm examples of each technique. Then have students work in pairs to read about loaded words on the bottom of page 263 and page 264. Ask pairs to reread Reagan's speech to look for additional examples of loaded words. Discuss the effects of his word choices.

Extend the Handbook

Have students skim magazine ads to find examples of the various propaganda techniques discussed in this section. Ask students to share their ads in small groups and talk about the effectiveness of the ads and the techniques they employed.

Assessment

Ask students:

- What is the purpose of propaganda techniques? Why do speakers rely on them?
- What are "loaded words" and why do speakers use them?
- How can you use your understanding of propaganda techniques to effectively evaluate a speech?

Reading a Short Story

For use with *Reader's Handbook* pages 294–314

Daily Lessons	**Summary***
Lesson 1 **Getting Ready to Read**	Work with students to explore techniques for previewing and planning to read a short story.
Lesson 2 **Reading a Short Story**	Review active reading methods that can help students get involved with reading fiction. Have students form reading groups to discuss the short story "Charles."
Lesson 3 **Using Graphic Organizers**	Build an understanding of the various graphic organizers students can use as they read short stories.
Lesson 4 **Rereading Strategy: Close Reading**	Introduce students to the rereading strategy of close reading. Have students reread to deepen their appreciation and understanding of a short story.

*Use these notes to help you teach a mini-lesson or to teach a briefer, shorter version of the lessons for more proficient students.

Lesson Resources

Overheads

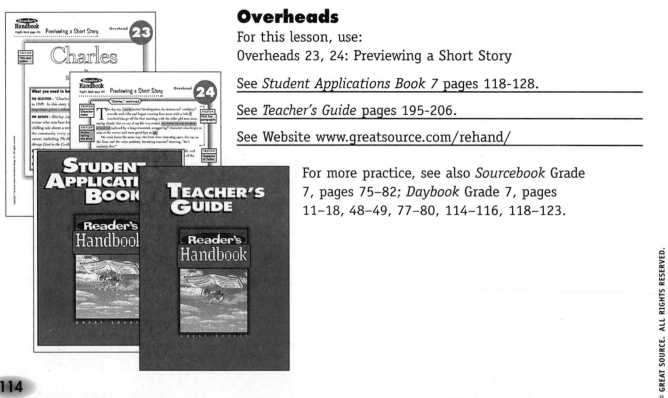

For this lesson, use:
Overheads 23, 24: Previewing a Short Story

See *Student Applications Book 7* pages 118-128.

See *Teacher's Guide* pages 195-206.

See Website www.greatsource.com/rehand/

For more practice, see also *Sourcebook* Grade 7, pages 75–82; *Daybook* Grade 7, pages 11–18, 48–49, 77–80, 114–116, 118–123.

Reading a Novel

For use with *Reader's Handbook* pages 315–339

Daily Lessons	**Summary***
Lesson 1 **Before Reading a Novel**	Have students use what they know about story elements to set a purpose and plan for reading a novel.
Lesson 2 **Reading with a Purpose**	Work with students to explore point of view, character, and setting in a novel.
Lesson 3 **Reading with a Purpose (continued)**	Continue examining story elements with students. Discuss graphic organizers students can use to keep track of plot, theme, and author's style in a novel.
Lesson 4 **Rereading Strategy: Close Reading**	Review rereading strategies with the class. Have students use the strategies to help them synthesize learning and respond to reading.

*Use these notes to help you teach a mini-lesson or to teach a briefer, shorter version of the lessons for more proficient students.

Lesson Resources

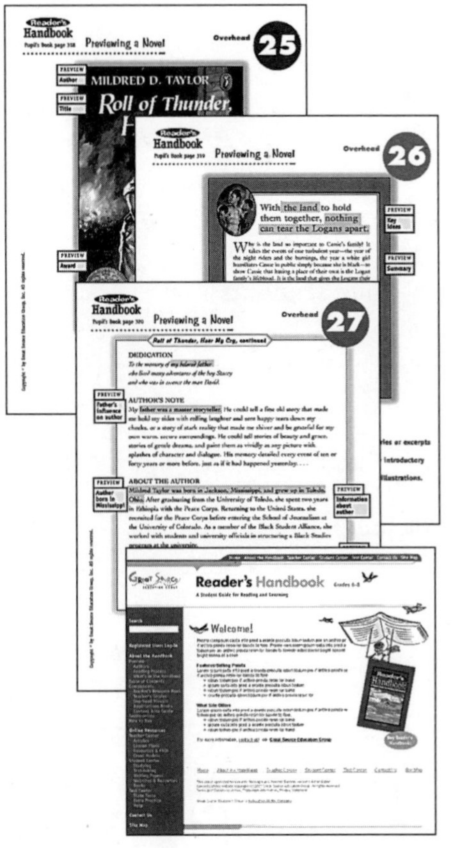

Overheads

For this lesson, use:

Overheads 25, 26, 27: Previewing a Novel

See *Student Applications Book 7* pages 129–140.

See *Teacher's Guide* pages 207-219.

See Website www.greatsource.com/rehand/

For more practice, see also *Sourcebook* Grade 7, pages 50–58, 59–66; *Daybook* Grade 7, pages 40-44, 162–163.

WEEK 15 Lesson 1 Getting Ready to Read

For use with *Reader's Handbook* pages 294–305

Goals

In this lesson, students learn how to set a purpose, preview, and plan for reading a short story.

Teaching Focus

Background

Because a short story can be read in one class period, it is an ideal genre for modeling and reviewing the steps in the reading process. In this lesson, students will take Before Reading steps to get ready to read the short story "Charles." As for other genres, previewing, setting a purpose, and planning will help students focus their reading and engage with the text.

Instruction

Invite students to preview the story "Charles." Begin by reading and talking about the background and biographical information on page 296. Have students continue the preview by reading the first paragraph of the story on page 297. Then ask students to jot down predictions about what the story might be about and what they think will happen. Remind them to support their predictions with information they learned from the preview.

Teaching Approach

Use of the Handbook

Read the information on page 295 of the handbook to help students set a purpose for reading. Students can use the purpose on page 295 or come up with their own purposes for reading "Charles." Encourage students to pay attention to the preview callouts as they continue previewing the story on their own. Have students use what they learned from their preview and the information on pages 304–305 to plan for reading.

Extend the Handbook

Ask students to return to the predictions they made about "Charles." Have students meet in small groups to share their predictions and discuss how they arrived at them. Engage students in a discussion about how the skill of predicting relates to the steps in the Before Reading process—setting a purpose, previewing, and planning.

Assessment

Ask students:

- What did you learn about this short story by previewing it?
- What is one purpose you have for reading "Charles"? What is your plan for reading this story?

WEEK 15
Lesson 2

Reading a Short Story

For use with *Reader's Handbook* pages 296–303, 310

Goals

In this lesson, students practice using active reading methods to get involved with a short story.

Teaching Focus

Background

Throughout the handbook, students learn and practice methods that help them become more active readers. The compelling characters and dramatic plot turns in "Charles" make this story a "natural" for getting readers actively involved. As students read "Charles," encourage them to enter into the world of the story by noting reactions, making connections, and continuing to jot down predictions about what will happen next.

Instruction

Ask students to reflect on the methods they use to get involved with the action and characters in stories. Do students relate events in stories to their own experiences? Do they identify with characters who remind them of themselves or someone they know? Do they try to guess what will happen next or how the story will end? Record students' ideas on chart paper so they can refer to them as they read "Charles."

Teaching Approach

Use of the Handbook

Have students read the short story "Charles" (pages 296–303). As students read, encourage them to confirm or adjust the predictions they generated during the preview in Lesson 1. If students need help getting involved with the story, refer them to the ideas they generated as a class (see above) and to page 310 of the handbook.

Extend the Handbook

Have students break into small groups to discuss "Charles." You many want to provide the following prompts as starting points for discussion: 1) Were you surprised by the ending of "Charles"? Why or why not? 2) What point do you think the author, Shirley Jackson, was trying to make? and 3) If you could ask the author one question, what would it be?

Assessment

Ask students:

- Why is it important to get involved with what you read?
- What do you do to get involved with the action and characters in stories you read?

WEEK 15
Lesson 3

Using Graphic Organizers

For use with *Reader's Handbook* pages 306–308

Goals

In this lesson, students explore various graphic organizers they can use to build understanding of short story elements.

Teaching Focus

Background

Short stories such as "Charles" provide readers with the opportunity to "zoom in" and take a closer look at story elements. In this lesson, students will focus on characterization and plot in the short story "Charles." Students will review a variety of graphic organizers they can use to deepen their understanding of how writers of short stories develop these story elements.

Instruction

Invite students to preview pages 306–308 in the *Reader's Handbook*. Ask them to note the many different types of graphic organizers in this section. When they finish previewing, come together as a class to discuss the graphics: Which graphic organizers have they used before? Which ones are new to students? What do the different graphic organizers on these pages have in common? Lead students to see that these organizers can help them focus on and organize important information about plot and characters.

Teaching Approach

Use of the Handbook

Ask student volunteers to read aloud the description of the five main parts of a plot on page 309 of the handbook. Ask students to identify the climax of the story "Charles." Then, discuss how the diagram on this page "fits" the plot of "Charles" and how it does not. Next, divide the class into five groups. Assign each group to read about one of the graphic organizers on pages 306–308. Ask groups to "teach" the rest of the class how to use the graphic organizer.

Extend the Handbook

Invite students to use one of the graphic organizers they learned about in this lesson to help them keep track of character or plot development in a familiar fairy tale such as "Cinderella" or "Jack and the Beanstalk."

Assessment

Ask students:

- Why is it helpful to use graphic organizers when reading a short story?
- What graphic organizers do you use during reading? What new graphic organizers did you learn about in this unit?

WEEK 15
Lesson 4

Rereading Strategy: Close Reading

For use with *Reader's Handbook* page 312

Goals

In this lesson, students explore close reading, an After Reading strategy designed to help readers reflect on and remember what they've read.

Teaching Focus

Background

In order for readers to fully understand and appreciate a short story, they may need to read it more than once. In this lesson, students revisit the short story "Charles" to gain additional insights into its meaning, point of view, and characters.

Instruction

Ask students to reflect on when and why they reread texts. Do they reread their favorite parts of stories or poems? Do they return to passages in books that are difficult or complex? Explain that good readers go back into texts all the time—to gather more information, to clarify something that is confusing, or just for the enjoyment of it.

Teaching Approach

Use of the Handbook

Explain that in this lesson, students will the use rereading strategy of close reading to help them get more out of the short story "Charles." Have students read pages 312–314 of the *Reader's Handbook* on their own. Then have them come together as a class to discuss the information on close reading, point of view, and comparing characters. Ask students why these might be good methods to use when rereading. What purpose does each method serve?

Extend the Handbook

Have students return to "Charles." As they reread, ask them to explore the parts of a story by choosing one of the following options: 1) create a close reading organizer for part of the story, 2) rewrite a portion of the story from a different character's point of view, or 3) use a Venn Diagram to compare two of the story's characters.

For more practice, see pages 118–128 of the *Student Applications Book 7*.

Assessment

Ask students:

- What is close reading?
- How did using this rereading strategy help you better understand the short story "Charles"?

WEEK 16 Lesson 1 Before Reading a Novel

For use with *Reader's Handbook* page 315–321

Goals

In this lesson, students use what they know about story elements to set a purpose and plan for reading a novel.

Teaching Focus

Background

In this unit, students will examine six key ingredients of novels—point of view, characters, setting, plot, theme, and style. Begin by reviewing what students know about these basic story elements. Then help students use what they know as a springboard to set purposes and plan for reading a novel.

Instruction

On the chalkboard, create a Fiction Organizer like the one on page 321 of the handbook. Point out that the organizer lists the six basic elements of a novel: point of view, characters, setting, plot, theme, and style. Explain that students will return to the organizer throughout this unit as they read parts of Mildred Taylor's *Roll of Thunder, Hear My Cry.*

Teaching Approach

Use of the Handbook

Have students work in pairs to read pages 315–317 of the *Reader's Handbook*. Then ask partners to preview *Roll of Thunder, Hear My Cry* by examining its front and back covers (pages 318–319) and its dedication, author's note, and author's biography (page 320). Come together as a class to read page 321 and plan for reading. Use information from previewing to begin to fill in the Fiction Organizer for *Roll of Thunder, Hear My Cry.*

Extend the Handbook

For additional practice in previewing, setting a purpose, and planning before reading a novel, have students complete pages 129–140 in the *Student Applications Book 7*.

Assessment

Ask students:

- What are the six basic parts of a novel?
- How can you use your understanding of these elements of a novel to set a purpose and plan for reading?

WEEK 16 Lesson 2 Reading with a Purpose

For use with *Reader's Handbook* page 322–330

Goals

In this lesson, students examine point of view, characters, and setting in a novel.

Teaching Focus

Background

Novels offer rich opportunities for students to examine how one writer develops fundamental story elements. In this lesson, students deepen their understanding of three of those elements—point of view, characters, and setting—as they take a closer look at *Roll of Thunder, Hear My Cry*.

Instruction

Circle the story elements point of view, character, and setting on the Fiction Organizer for *Roll of Thunder, Hear My Cry* (see Lesson 1). Ask students what they know about each of these elements. Build background by introducing into the discussion terms such as *narrator* and *first person*. Tell students that they will explore these three elements in more depth as they read excerpts from Mildred Taylor's novel.

Teaching Approach

Use of the Handbook

Review with the class the purposes they set for reading (see page 322). Ask a student volunteer to read aloud the excerpt from *Roll of Thunder, Hear My Cry* on page 323. Use the excerpt and the information on this page to engage students in a discussion of point of view in the story. Repeat this process as students examine characters (pages 323–326) and setting (pages 327–330). Then work with the class to add what they learned about point of view, characters, and setting to the Fiction Organizer begun in the previous lesson.

Extend the Handbook

Have students work in pairs to extend their understanding of story elements in *Roll of Thunder, Hear My Cry*. Invite pairs to choose one of the following options:

- Explore character and point of view by rewriting the scene on pages 323–324 from Little Man's point of view.
- Visualize the setting by drawing one of the scenes from pages 327–330.

Assessment

Ask students:

- How does the Mildred Taylor reveal the characters' personalities in *Roll of Thunder, Hear My Cry*? Why is the setting an important part of this novel?
- What questions do you still have about character, point of view, and setting?

WEEK 16 Lesson 3: Reading with a Purpose (continued)

For use with *Reader's Handbook* pages 331–334

Goals

In this lesson, students examine plot, theme, and author's style in a novel.

Teaching Focus

Background

Students continue learning about story elements in this lesson as they focus on plot, theme, and style in *Roll of Thunder, Hear My Cry.* As they explore these elements, students will learn about the important role conflict plays in novels, how to develop a theme statement, and how to analyze an author's style.

Instruction

Return to the Fiction Organizer (see previous lessons) and circle the three remaining story elements: plot, theme, and author's style. Ask student volunteers to share what they know about each of these elements. If necessary, build background by bringing into the discussion relevant terms, such as *climax* and *resolution*.

Teaching Approach

Use of the Handbook

Have students read pages 331–334 in the handbook on their own. Encourage students to compare the three graphic organizers that can be used to explore the plot of a novel (Summary Notes, Timelines, and Plot Diagrams). Review with students how to use a Topic and Theme Organizer to develop a theme statement (page 333). Finally, discuss how a Double-entry Journal can help students analyze an author's style (page 334). Continue filling in the Fiction Organizer as students discuss plot, theme, and style in *Roll of Thunder, Hear My Cry.*

Extend the Handbook

Organize students into small discussion groups. Ask groups to reflect on either plot, theme, or author's style in a novel they have recently read for class. Encourage groups to use one of the graphics they learned about in this lesson to organize their thinking about this story element.

Assessment

Ask students:

- How can you keep track of the plot in a novel?
- How would you define *theme*? How can you determine the theme(s) of a novel?
- How would you describe Taylor's writing style? How would your describe your own writing style?

WEEK 16
Lesson 4

Rereading Strategy: Close Reading

For use with *Reader's Handbook* pages 336–339

Goals

In this lesson, students use After Reading steps to check understanding, synthesize learning, and formulate personal responses to a novel.

Teaching Focus

Background

Because novels are longer than other forms of fiction and can be more complex, it is particularly important for students to take the time afterward to think about what they've read. As students look back at *Roll of Thunder, Hear My Cry,* they will reflect on their understanding of the story, synthesize what they've learned about story elements, and formulate their own responses and reactions to the novel.

Instruction

Return to the Fiction Organizer students have been working on throughout this unit. If it has any remaining gaps, have students fill them in now. Then read aloud the paragraph under "Looking at the Whole Novel" on page 337 of the handbook. Invite students to compare their Fiction Organizer for *Roll of Thunder, Hear My Cry* with the sample organizer in the handbook. Encourage students to discuss any differences in the two organizers.

Teaching Approach

Use of the Handbook

Remind students of the importance of taking the time after reading to pause, reflect, and reread. Have students review these steps in the reading process by reading pages 336–338 in the handbook. Help students differentiate between graphics that capture the "big picture" of a novel (such as a Fiction Organizers) and graphics used to gather specific information (for example, Character Maps). Then have students read about how to recommend and review novels on pages 338–339 of the handbook.

Extend the Handbook

Have students practice formulating their own responses and reactions to reading by 1) sending a letter or an email recommending a novel they've read to a friend or 2) writing a book review of a novel that utilizes a rating chart (see the example on page 339 of the handbook).

Assessment

Ask students:

- Why is it important to use After Reading steps when you finish a novel?
- How will you use what you learned in this unit the next time you read a novel?

Focus on Dialogue

For use with *Reader's Handbook* pages 360–367

Daily Lessons	**Summary***
Lesson 1 **The Form of Dialogue**	Review with students the form of dialogue, including how it is punctuated and the purpose of speech tags.
Lesson 2 **Dialogue and Character**	Analyze a story's dialogue for character clues. Use a Double-entry Journal to examine the connection between dialogue and characterization.
Lesson 3 **Dialogue, Plot, and Mood**	Develop an understanding of how authors use dialogue to advance the plot and contribute to the mood of a story.
Lesson 4 **Pulling It All Together**	Explore how to use a Thinking Tree to reflect on the relationship between a story's dialogue and its characters, plot, and mood.

*Use these notes to help you teach a mini-lesson or to teach a briefer, shorter version of the lessons for more proficient students.

Lesson Resources

See *Student Applications Book 7* pages 146-147.

See *Teacher's Guide* pages 232-236.

See Website www.greatsource.com/rehand/

Focus on Theme

For use with *Reader's Handbook* pages 376–382

Daily Lessons	**Summary***
Lesson 1 **Identifying the General Topic**	Work with students as they examine technique for identifying the general topic(s) of a fictional piece. Create a bibliography of common topics of young adult literature.
Lesson 2 **Connecting Story Details to the Theme**	Build understanding of how details in a story can provide clues to the story's theme. Have students create Summary Notes or a Double-entry Journal to examine theme.
Lesson 3 **Character and Theme**	Discuss how analyzing characters can help readers infer a story's theme. Students work in small groups to brainstorm a list of favorite stories and their themes.
Lesson 4 **Developing a Theme Statement**	Help students use the methods explored in this unit to create a theme statement.

*Use these notes to help you teach a mini-lesson or to teach a briefer, shorter version of the lessons for more proficient students.

Lesson Resources

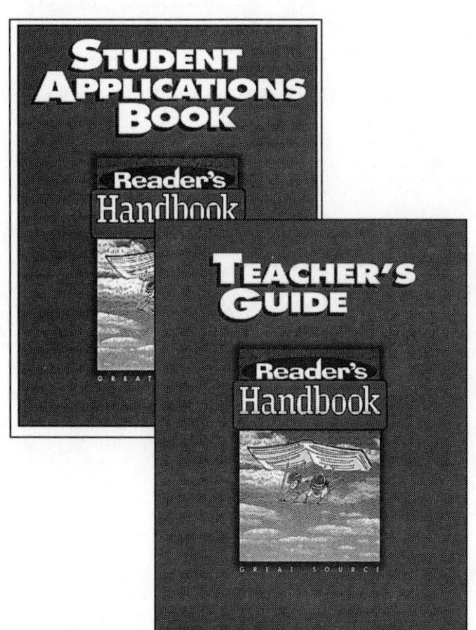

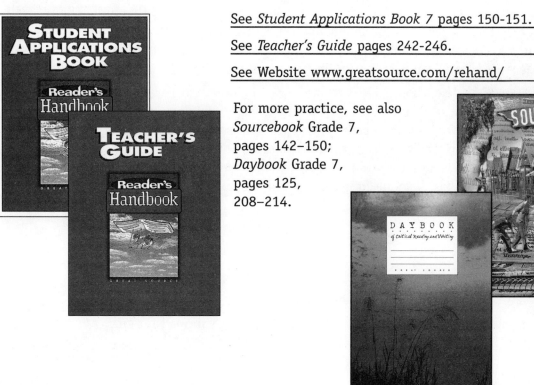

See *Student Applications Book 7* pages 150-151.

See *Teacher's Guide* pages 242-246.

See Website www.greatsource.com/rehand/

For more practice, see also *Sourcebook* Grade 7, pages 142–150; *Daybook* Grade 7, pages 125, 208–214.

WEEK 17 Lesson 1 The Form of Dialogue

For use with *Reader's Handbook* pages 360–362

Goals

In this lesson, students review the form of dialogue, including how it is punctuated and the use of speech tags.

Teaching Focus

Background

Before students can analyze the meaning of dialogue, they need to understand how to read it. In this lesson, students will review "dialogue rules," such as setting dialogue off with quotation marks and starting a new paragraph for each new speaker. An understanding of the basic mechanics of dialogue will benefit students in their roles both as readers and writers.

Instruction

Discuss with students what rules they follow when they write dialogue. List their ideas on the board. Talk about the purpose of these rules. How do they help the reader understand what is going on in the story?

Teaching Approach

Use of the Handbook

Read aloud the unit opener on page 360 of the *Reader's Handbook*. Discuss the goals of the unit. Encourage students to share their own goals for reading this unit. Then have students read pages 361–362 independently. Come together as a class and review the class list of rules for writing dialogue. Work with students to modify the rules as necessary based on information in this section of the handbook.

Extend the Handbook

To help students recognize how rules for writing dialogue help readers keep track of a story's action, ask them to choose a dialogue-rich excerpt from a novel or short story they are reading. Have them rewrite the passage without following any rules for writing dialogue. Then have students share their rewrites with a partner. How does the lack of familiar dialogue form affect students' understanding of the excerpt?

For additional practice, see pages 146–147 of the *Student Applications Book 7*.

Assessment

Ask students:

- What are three rules for writing dialogue?
- What is the purpose of these rules? How do they help you read fiction?

WEEK 17
Lesson 2

Dialogue and Character

For use with *Reader's Handbook* pages 363–364

Goals

In this lesson, students learn how to analyze dialogue to find clues about a story's characters.

Teaching Focus

Background

Writers often rely on dialogue to provide clues to characters' personalities and motivations. In this lesson, students will explore reading strategies and tools that will help them analyze dialogue and make inferences about story characters.

Instruction

Talk with students about what they can learn about people from listening to what they say and how they say it. Explain that readers can infer much about a character's personality and motivation by looking for similar clues in the story's dialogue. Remind students that making inferences involves reading "between the lines" to find the implied meaning of the text.

Teaching Approach

Use of the Handbook

Review the strategy of close reading as a class. Then have students work in pairs to read and discuss the information on pages 363–364 of the *Reader's Handbook.* Encourage partners to read aloud the excerpt from *Roll of Thunder, Hear My Cry* on page 364, with each student reading one character's dialogue.

Extend the Handbook

Ask students to look for clues about characters' personalities and motivations by focusing on the dialogue in a favorite novel or short story. Have students skim the text for examples of dialogue that offer clues about characters. Encourage students to use a Double-entry Journal to help them make inferences. Come together as a class and discuss the activity. Did using the Double-entry Journal help students? Why or why not? If students found the activity difficult, what could they do to make it easier?

Assessment

Ask students:

- What can dialogue tell you about a story's characters?
- How can a Double-entry Journal help you examine the relationship between dialogue and characterization?

WEEK 17 Lesson 3 Dialogue, Plot, and Mood

For use with *Reader's Handbook* page 365-366

Goals

In this lesson, students learn how authors use dialogue to advance the plot and contribute to the mood of a story.

Teaching Focus

Background

Proficient readers rely on dialogue not only to learn about characters but also to make inferences about a story's plot and mood. Examining the connection between these three story elements will deepen students' understanding of the text.

Instruction

Ask students to think about how authors use dialogue to advance a story's plot. What role can dialogue play in helping readers keep track of the action? Lead students to see that just as they can use dialogue to make inferences about characters, they can also use it to make inferences about the events in a story or its plot. Then discuss *mood*. Explain that the mood of a story is its general feeling or atmosphere. Point out that examining dialogue can provide clues about the mood of a piece.

Teaching Approach

Use of the Handbook

Have a student volunteer read aloud the top of page 365 of the *Reader's Handbook*. Then think aloud as you read the excerpt from *Roll of Thunder, Hear My Cry* to model how you make inferences about the plot based on the excerpt's dialogue. Discuss the reading tools students can use to help them make inferences about plot, including the Double-entry Journal discussed in the previous lesson.
To help students make connections between the story's dialogue and mood, perform another think-aloud as you read the next excerpt from *Roll of Thunder, Hear My Cry* on page 366.

Extend the Handbook

For additional practice using dialogue to find clues about a story's plot and mood, have students work though pages 146–147 of the *Student Applications Book 7*.

Assessment

Ask students:

- How can readers use dialogue to understand a story's plot? A story's mood?
- What reading tools can you use to make connections between a story's dialogue, plot, and mood?

WEEK 17 Lesson 4 Pulling It All Together

For use with *Reader's Handbook* page 367

Goals

In this lesson, students learn how to use a Thinking Tree to reflect on the relationship between a story's dialogue and its characters, plot, and mood.

Teaching Focus

Background

Reflecting on the clues dialogue can provide to a story's characters, plot, and mood helps readers construct meaning when they read fiction. Creating a Thinking Tree will help students broaden their understanding of the connection between dialogue and other literary elements.

Instruction

Discuss the role graphic organizers can play in helping students get more out of their reading. Point out that graphic organizers can be particularly helpful to students when they are trying to draw inferences by pulling together information and details from different parts of a text.

For more information on graphic organizers, see pages 666–684 of the *Reader's Handbook*.

Teaching Approach

Use of the Handbook

Walk students though the sample Thinking Tree for dialogue on page 367 of the *Reader's Handbook*. Discuss the purpose of the reading tool. Help students understand how they can use a Thinking Tree to pull together the various clues found in a story's dialogue.

Extend the Handbook

Have students create a Thinking Tree for one of the stories they used in this unit. Encourage them to reflect on how the graphic organizer affects their understanding of the relationship between the story's dialogue and its characters, plot, and mood.

For additional practice, see pages 146–147 of the *Student Applications Book 7*.

Assessment

Ask students:

- Which story element do you think dialogue can tell you the most about—character, plot, or mood? Explain your choice.
- What is difficult about using dialogue to make inferences about characters, plot, and mood? What can you do to make it easier to make these inferences?

WEEK 18 Lesson 1 Identifying the General Topic

For use with *Reader's Handbook* pages 376–377

Goals

In this lesson, students learn strategies for identifying the general topic(s) of a fictional piece.

Teaching Focus

Background

Quality fiction does more than tell stories; it provides fresh ways to reflect on familiar issues, or *themes*. Inferring the themes of a fictional piece is one of the reader's biggest responsibilities. This unit provides a three-step plan for inferring theme, beginning with identifying the general topics of fictional material.

Instruction

Brainstorm as a class a list of topics important to middle school student, such as friendship and growing up. List their suggestions on the board. Explain that writers of young adult literature often center their stories on topics such as these. Discuss what students know about theme. Explain that a story's theme revolves around a general topic such as those the class brainstormed. Identifying the general topic is the first step in determining theme.

Teaching Approach

Use of the Handbook

Have students read the unit opener on page 376 of the *Reader's Handbook* independently. Encourage them to reflect on both the goals of the unit and their own goals for reading. Then have students read the information on finding the general topic of a piece of fiction on page 377. Come together as a class and discuss the list of topics at the bottom of the page. Compare the topics with the list generated by the class above.

Extend the Handbook

Have students work in small groups to create a fiction bibliography for the topics listed on page 377 of the handbook. Ask groups to brainstorm familiar stories or novels that center on each of these general ideas. Have groups combine their lists into a master bibliography. Encourage students to add to the lists as they read throughout the year.

For more practice, see pages 150–151 of the *Student Applications Book 7*.

Assessment

Ask students:

- Why do you think various young adult authors focus on similar topics?
- Why should readers identify the general topic in a piece of fiction?

Connecting Story Details to the Theme

For use with *Reader's Handbook* pages 378–379

Goals

In this lesson, students develop an understanding of how details in a story can provide clues to the story's theme.

Teaching Focus

Background

Readers infer theme based on their prior knowledge and personal experiences with the topic. Different readers will infer different themes based on how they construct meaning from the text. There is no one correct theme; however, readers must use evidence from the text to provide support for their inferences.

Instruction

Discuss with students techniques they currently use to determine the theme of a story. Explain that determining theme is a subjective activity; there is no one right answer. Discuss how students' past experiences with a story's general topics affect their understanding of a story's themes. Point out that while readers might differ in what they consider to be the main theme(s) of a piece, every theme must be supported by evidence from the text.

Teaching Approach

Use of the Handbook

Ask students to read pages 378–379 of the *Reader's Handbook* on their own. Then discuss the two reading tools used in this section. Help students explore the similarities and differences between the two tools. Clarify how each tool can help students explore details related to theme.

Extend the Handbook

Have students explore the themes of a familiar short story or novel. Encourage them to begin by identifying its general topic, as discussed in the previous lesson. Then have them look for clues about theme by creating Summary Notes or a Double-entry Journal. Ask students to reflect on how the reading tool affected their understanding of the piece. Did it help them find clues to the story's theme? Why or why not?

Assessment

Ask students:

- How can you use reading tools to determine a story's theme?
- Why do readers need to support inferences about theme with evidence from the text?

WEEK 18
Lesson 3

Characters and Theme

For use with *Reader's Handbook* pages 347–348

Goals

In this lesson, students learn how analyzing characters can help them infer a story's theme.

Teaching Focus

Background

Experienced readers recognize that a character's words, thoughts, and actions can provide clues to the story's themes. This lesson focuses on two kinds of character clues: 1) what a character's statements or thoughts about life say about theme and 2) what a change in a character signifies about theme.

Instruction

Explain to students that one way to look for clues about theme is to examine the story's characters. Point out that often what characters say, think, or do can tell readers something about the big idea of the piece. For example, share Dorothy's classic line from *The Wonderful Wizard of Oz*: "There's no place like home." Point out how a theme of the story can be summed up in that one bit of dialogue.

Teaching Approach

Use of the Handbook

Have students work in pairs to read and discuss pages 347–348 of the *Reader's Handbook*. Encourage partners to take turns thinking aloud to point out clues about theme as they read the excerpts. After reading, have pairs discuss how the change in Phillip provides clues about a theme of the story.

Extend the Handbook

Classic tales such as *The Wonderful Wizard of Oz* are wonderful resources for examining the connection between characters and theme. Ask students to work in small groups to brainstorm a list of favorite classic stories or fairy tales and their themes. Have groups discuss how the tales' characters provide support for the themes of the pieces.

For more practice, see pages 150–151 of the *Student Applications Book 7*.

Assessment

Ask students:

- How can analyzing characters help readers identify a story's theme?
- What techniques can you use to help you make connections between the characters and a story's theme?

WEEK 18
Lesson 4

Developing a Theme Statement

For use with *Reader's Handbook* pages 380–382

Goals

In this lesson, students learn how to pull together the technique explored in this unit to develop a theme statement.

Teaching Focus

Background

Proficient readers not only recognize a story's themes; they can also articulate the themes effectively. Students will benefit from explicit instruction in techniques for developing a theme statement.

Instruction

Review with students the terms *topic* and *theme*. Help students understand the differences between the two. Explain that after reading, they can use the clues they found throughout the story to help them develop a theme statement. Point out that a theme statement is simply a sentence that states one of the story's themes. Remind students that different readers will develop different theme statements; every theme is appropriate as long as the reader can support it with evidence from the text.

Teaching Approach

Use of the Handbook

Work with students as they read the strategies for developing theme statements on pages 380–381 of the *Reader's Handbook*. Walk them through the Topic and Theme Organizer and discuss its purpose. Help them recognize that the Organizer follows the three steps for determining theme taught in this section of the handbook. Read through the tips for making theme statements. Work with students to create a class list of "do's" and "don'ts" for developing their statements of theme.

Extend the Handbook

Have students develop a theme statement for one of the stories discussed in the unit. Ask them to first create a Topic and Theme Organizer and then follow the tips on page 382 of the handbook for developing a theme statement. If more than one student is working with the same piece, ask students to compare their statements. Remind students to support their themes with evidence from the text.

Assessment

Ask students:

- What is the connection between a story's general topic and its theme?
- What methods can you use to determine a story's theme?

Elements of Fiction

For use with *Reader's Handbook* pages 389–405

Daily Lessons	**Summary***
Lesson 1 **Character**	Review and expand students' understanding of the use of characterization in fiction. Have students create a Character Map for a favorite character.
Lesson 2 **Point of View**	Build understanding of the effects different points of view have on a fictional piece.
Lesson 3 **Plot**	Examine the role conflict plays in the action of a story. Students create a Plot Diagram for a favorite piece of fiction.
Lesson 4 **Setting**	Discuss with students the role setting plays in fiction.

*Use these notes to help you teach a mini-lesson or to teach a briefer, shorter version of the lessons for more proficient students.

Lesson Resources

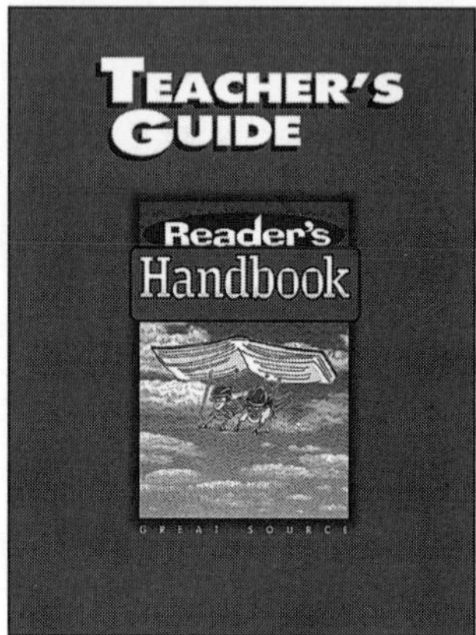

See *Teacher's Guide* pages 252–263.

See Website www.greatsource.com/rehand/

Elements of Poetry

For use with *Reader's Handbook* pages 446–469

Daily Lessons	**Summary***
Lesson 1 **Allusion**	Work with students as they examine the use of allusions in poetry. Have students look for examples of allusions in poems.
Lesson 2 **Free Verse**	Build an understanding of poetry written in free verse.
Lesson 3 **Symbol**	Help students understand the use of symbolism in poetry. Invite students to create poems that include symbolism.
Lesson 4 **Stanza**	Review what a stanza is and the purpose stanzas serve in poetry.

*Use these notes to help you teach a mini-lesson or to teach a briefer, shorter version of the lessons for more proficient students.

Lesson Resources

See *Teacher's Guide* pages 291– 307.

See Website www.greatsource.com/rehand/

Character

For use with *Reader's Handbook* pages 392–393

Goals

In this lesson, students expand their understanding of characterization.

Teaching Focus

Background

By seventh grade, students have undoubtedly read and been exposed to numerous novels. Have they ever thought about what sets novels apart from other forms of writing? In this lesson, students will identify these characteristics to better appreciate what makes a novel a novel.

Instruction

Explain to students that they are about to begin a two-week unit on reading a novel. Ask student volunteers to list what they know about novels. (Students might offer ideas such as *work of fiction, chapters,* and *characters.*) Use the list to compare and contrast novels with other forms of fiction.

Teaching Approach

Use of the Handbook

Have a student volunteer read aloud the excerpt from *To Kill a Mockingbird* on page 392 of the handbook. Ask students to describe Calpurnia based on the information provided in the excerpt. Discuss the textual clues students relied on for their description. Continue reading this page. Talk about characterization techniques. Revisit the excerpt and highlight Lee's use of these different techniques. Then have students read page 393 independently. Discuss the different character types. Build students' understanding by sharing examples of each type (i.e., the three stepsisters in *Cinderella* as examples of static characters).

For more information on characterization, see pages 340–350 of the *Reader's Handbook*.

Extend the Handbook

Have students focus on characterization techniques in a novel or short story they have read recently. Ask students to create a Character Map as shown on page 668. Encourage students to skim the text for specific examples of characterization techniques to include in their charts. Have students classify the character as either main or minor and static or dynamic, using evidence from the text to support their classification.

Assessment

Ask students:

- What are four techniques authors use to develop a character's personality?
- How do these techniques help you connect with the story?

WEEK 19
Lesson 2

Point of View

For use with *Reader's Handbook* pages 398–399

Goals

In this lesson, students build their understanding of point of view and the effects different points of view have on the text.

Teaching Focus

Background

Experienced readers understand that the point of view of a piece greatly affects both the amount and accuracy of information they receive. Identifying point of view (or who the narrator is) will deepen students' ability to understand and evaluate narratives in fiction.

Instruction

Review what students know about point of view. Work with students to identify the three main points of view used in literary works: first-person, third-person limited, and third-person omniscient. Explain that an author's choice of point of view determines not only who will tell the story but also what kind of information readers get about the characters and events in the piece.

Teaching Approach

Use of the Handbook

Read aloud the excerpt from *The Kid Comes Back* on page 398 of the *Reader's Handbook*. Work with students to identify the point of view of the excerpt. Discuss the textual clues that indicate point of view. Have students continue reading the rest of pages 398 and 399. Write the three points of view on the board. Work with students to list characteristics of each. Help students understand the advantages and disadvantages each point of view presents for readers.

Extend the Handbook

Ask students to reflect on a favorite novel or short story. Why might the author have chosen to tell the story from one point of view rather than another? How does it affect the story? How would the story have been different if told from another point of view? Have students share their ideas in small groups.

Assessment

Ask students:

- Why is identifying the point of view important when reading fiction?
- How can you use what you learned in this lesson the next time you read a short story or novel?

Plot

For use with *Reader's Handbook* pages 400–401

Goals

In this lesson, students expand their understanding of plot and examine the role conflict plays in the action of a story.

Teaching Focus

Background

Proficient readers use their understanding of the five parts of a plot to help them keep track of the story's action. Reviewing these components, as well as examining the role conflict plays in stories, will enhance students' understanding of the text.

Instruction

Create a Concept Web for *conflict*. Ask student what comes to mind when they think of conflict. List their ideas on the Web. Talk about the different kinds of conflicts students have experienced or have heard about. Add these to the Web. Explain that some kind of conflict is at the heart of every plot.

Teaching Approach

Use of the Handbook

Work with students to review the five parts of a plot on page 400 of the *Reader's Handbook*. Discuss the purpose of a Plot Diagram (p. 401). Then walk through the five main types of conflict. Compare the list to the ideas students included in the Concept Web. To build students' understanding of the various types of conflict and their role in fiction, discuss specific examples of each type of conflict (for example, *Hatchet* for person vs. nature, *The Diary of Anne Frank* for person vs. society).

For more information on plot, see pages 368–375 of the *Reader's Handbook*.

Extend the Handbook

Have students create a Plot Diagram for a favorite novel or short story. If the piece does not fit the traditional Plot Diagram format, challenge students to create their own diagram. Then ask students to reflect on the central conflict of the story. How would they categorize it? Have students jot down their thoughts about the conflict in their journals.

Assessment

Ask students:

- What is the relationship between conflict and the plot of a story?
- How does identifying the conflict in a story help you understand the story as a whole?

WEEK 19 Lesson 4 Setting

For use with *Reader's Handbook* pages 402

Goals

In this lesson, students expand their understanding of the role setting plays in a literary work.

Teaching Focus

Background

Setting, while often considered one of the more basic literary elements, can significantly impact the plot and characters in a story. In this lesson, students will expand their understanding and appreciation of the role that setting plays in fictional works.

Instruction

Review what students know about setting. Ask students what role they think setting plays in a story. How important is the story's setting? Explain that while in some pieces, setting seems inconsequential, in others it is central to the story's action. Engage students in a discussion of stories in which setting plays a central role, such as the Emerald City in *The Wonderful Wizard of Oz* or the chocolate factory in *Charlie and the Chocolate Factory*. Ask students how these stories would be different if the settings were changed.

Teaching Approach

Use of the Handbook

Read aloud or have student volunteers read aloud the excerpt from *Journey to Topaz* on page 402 of the *Reader's Handbook*. Discuss the setting described in the excerpt. Have students read the remainder of page 402 independently. Come together as a class and talk further about the relationship between a story's setting and its plot, using the excerpt as a focal point for discussion. (For students unfamiliar with *Journey to Topaz,* point out that it takes place in a Japanese-American internment camp in Utah during World War II.)

For more information on setting, see pages 351–359 of the *Reader's Handbook*.

Extend the Handbook

Have students gather in small groups to discuss favorite novels or short stories. Ask groups to reflect on the role of setting in these literary works. In which pieces is setting integral to the action of the plot? How would a different setting affect the story? Have each group summarize their discussion for the rest of the class.

Assessment

Ask students:

- Do you agree with the statement, "The setting in which a story takes place does not matter?" Explain your answer.

Allusions

For use with *Reader's Handbook* page 448

Goals

In this lesson, students learn about the use of allusions in poetry.

Teaching Focus

Background

Allusions enrich the reading experience, but only if readers can appreciate their meaning. Students will benefit from an examination of the use of allusions in poetry as well as strategies for understanding them.

Instruction

Write the following sentences on the board: *Rachel broke down the door with the strength of Hercules. Their fights seem like World War II all over again.* Ask students what these two sentences have in common. Lead them to see that each contains an *allusion*, or a reference to a familiar person or event. Explain that poets use allusions to express ideas in very few words.

Teaching Approach

Use of the Handbook

Have students work in pairs to read the information on allusions on page 448 of the *Reader's Handbook*. Build students' understanding of the purpose of allusions by discussing what they add to poetry. Think aloud as you reread the excerpt from "Alice," concentrating on how you make connections between the poem and *Alice's Adventures in Wonderland*. Discuss strategies students can use to help them figure out unfamiliar allusions, such as thinking about what the poet is trying to say or looking up the allusion in reference sources.

Extend the Handbook

Have students work in small groups to skim through a poetry anthology for examples of allusions. Ask groups to identify each allusion and explain its meaning. Remind students to use the strategies discussed above to unlock the meaning of unfamiliar allusions. Have groups discuss what the allusions add to the poems.

Assessment

Ask students:

- What is the purpose of an allusion?
- What strategies can you use to figure out an unfamiliar allusion?

Free Verse

For use with *Reader's Handbook* page 451

Goals

In this lesson, students build their understanding of the use of free verse in poetry.

Teaching Focus

Background

Students who read a lot of poetry are probably aware that poets rely on a variety of forms, including free verse, to express their ideas. Free verse can be difficult for students to grasp initially, since it doesn't follow a "traditional" format. Recognizing the characteristics of free verse will facilitate students' understanding of its use in poetry.

Instruction

Discuss with students what makes a poem a poem. Most likely, students will mention rhyme or rhyme scheme. Explain that poets do not have to use rhythm or a rhyme scheme to create a poem. Point out that free verse is a form of poetry written without a regular rhythm or rhyme scheme. Lead students to see that poetry can take many forms.

Teaching Approach

Use of the Handbook

Have a student volunteer read aloud "April Rain Song" on page 451 of the handbook. Then read the poem a second time, this time thinking aloud to call attention to the poem's informal use of stanzas, pauses, and line lengths. Ask students what else they notice about the structure of the poem. Lead them to see that while Hughes does not follow a regular system of rhythm or a rhyme scheme, he does rely on other poetic techniques, such as repetition, to get his ideas across.

Extend the Handbook

Have students work in pairs to skim poetry anthologies for examples of free verse. (Two possibilities: *Salting the Oceans, 100 Poems by Young People* edited by Naomi Shihab Nye and Langston Hughes's *The Dreamkeeper and Other Poems*.) Ask partners to examine the poems for poetic features, such as the use of repetition and figurative language.

Assessment

Ask students:

- What is free verse?
- Compare free verse to other forms of poetry. How is your reading and appreciation of the poem affected by the poet's use of free verse?

Symbol

For use with *Reader's Handbook* page 467

Goals

In this lesson, students expand their understanding of the use of symbols in poetry.

Teaching Focus

Background

Many students tend to read on a literal level. When reading poetry, however, readers need to go beyond what is stated on the page to get at implied or symbolic meanings. Helping students understand the use and importance of symbolism will prepare them to read poetry—and a variety of other texts—with greater depth and understanding.

Instruction

Display pictures of symbols such as a flag, a light bulb, and an olive branch. Ask students if they understand the significance of each of these symbols. Then have students reflect on what the word *symbol* means. Guide students to come up with a definition similar to the following: *A symbol is something that stands for or represents something else.* Point out that symbols are often used in poetry to represent larger concepts or ideas.

Teaching Approach

Use of the Handbook

Have a student volunteer read aloud "This Is My Rock" on page 467 of the *Reader's Handbook*. Reread the poem, this time thinking aloud as you use information in the poem to discover what the rock symbolizes. Then talk about the poem with students: Why do they think the poet chose the rock as a symbol? What other objects might represent safety and strength?

Extend the Handbook

Invite students to create short poems that include symbolism. Have students begin by linking an abstract idea—for example, freedom—to a concrete object—for example, a flag. Have students build their poems around this symbolic image, as McCord does in "This Is My Rock."

Assessment

Ask students:

- What is a symbol?
- Why do writers of poems often use symbols?

Stanza

For use with *Reader's Handbook* pages 465–466

Goals

In this lesson, students learn about stanzas and why they are used in poetry.

Teaching Focus

Background

Proficient readers recognize that poets use stanzas to group and hold ideas together. Understanding how stanzas are used will help students organize their reading and enhance their comprehension of meaning.

Instruction

Revisit "April Rain Song" on page 451 of the handbook. Ask students what they notice about how the words of the poem are organized on the page. Help students see that Hughes uses stanzas, or groups of lines separated by line spaces, to cluster and organize his ideas.

Teaching Approach

Use of the Handbook

Read aloud "Because I Could Not Stop for Death" on page 465 of the *Reader's Handbook*. Then work through the description and definition of *stanza* on page 466 with the class. Return to "Because I Could Not Stop for Death." Have student volunteers read aloud each stanza. Pause after each stanza and discuss why Dickinson might have grouped her ideas in this way. Explain that not all poems are divided into stanzas of equal lines and that some poems do not include stanzas at all; these poems are described as having *continuous form*.

Extend the Handbook

Provide students with xeroxed copies of sample poems. Invite students to cut apart the poems, keeping lines intact. Then ask students to work in small groups to reassemble the lines into new stanzas. How does altering the poem's form affect the way the poem looks and sounds? How does it affect the poem's meaning?

Assessment

Ask students:

- What is the purpose of stanzas in poetry?
- What is the most important thing you learned about poetry from this unit?

Reading Poetry

For use with *Reader's Handbook* pages 408–421

Daily Lessons	**Summary***
Lesson 1 **Read for Enjoyment**	Discuss with students the importance of reading a poem multiple times. Invite students to do an initial reading of "Winter Poem" for enjoyment.
Lesson 2 **Read for Meaning**	Have students do a second reading of "Winter Poem" to deepen their understanding of its language, images, and meaning.
Lesson 3 **Read for Structure**	Examine with students the role that structure plays in poetry. Have students note the characteristics of free verse.
Lesson 4 **Read for Feeling**	Discuss how the tone and mood of a poem affect the reader. Have students do a final reading of "Winter Poem" to note the responses and reactions it evokes.

*Use these notes to help you teach a mini-lesson or to teach a briefer, shorter version of the lessons for more proficient students.

Lesson Resources

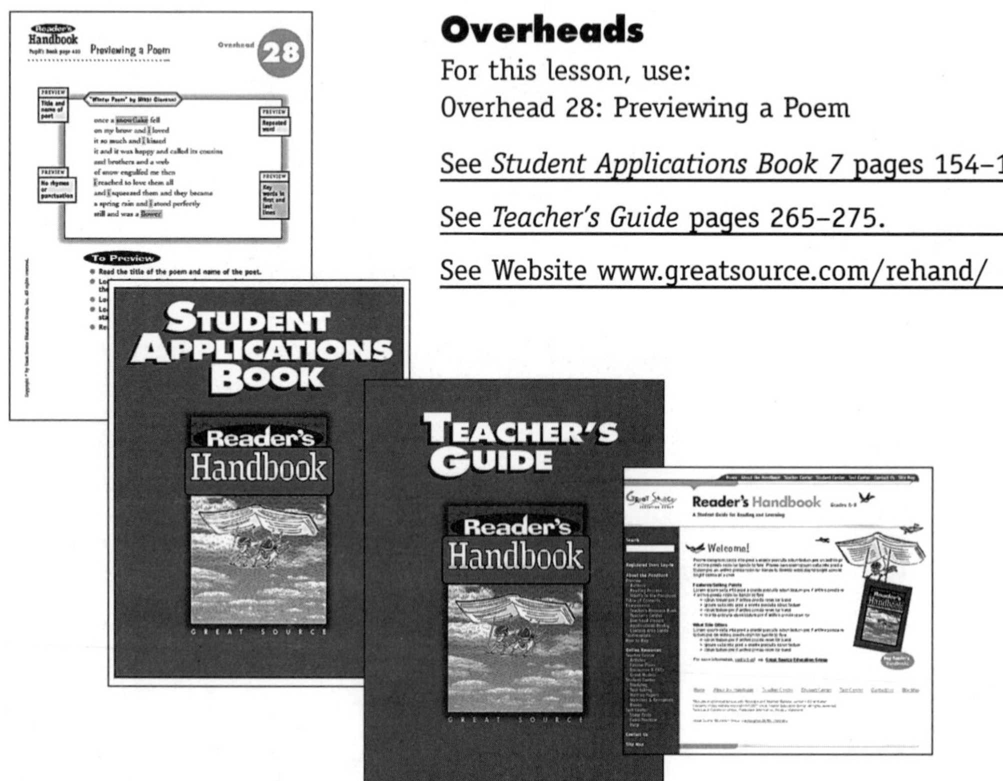

Overheads

For this lesson, use:

Overhead 28: Previewing a Poem

See *Student Applications Book 7* pages 154–163.

See *Teacher's Guide* pages 265–275.

See Website www.greatsource.com/rehand/

Focus on Language

For use with *Reader's Handbook* pages 422–429

Daily Lessons	**Summary***
Lesson 5 **Strategy: Close Reading**	Discuss the strategy of close reading and how it can be used to deepen students' understanding of poetry.
Lesson 6 **Key Words and Connotation**	Work with students to explore the denotations and connotations of key words in a poem.
Lesson 7 **Figurative Language**	Build students' understanding of figurative language. Have students identify examples of similes and metaphors in poems.
Lesson 8 **Imagery**	Discuss with students the use of imagery in poetry. Ask students to work in pairs to reflect on what they've learned in this unit.

*Use these notes to help you teach a mini-lesson or to teach a briefer, shorter version of the lessons for more proficient students.

Lesson Resources

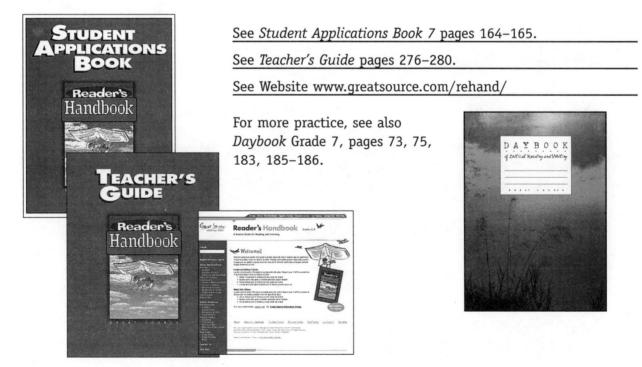

See *Student Applications Book 7* pages 164–165.

See *Teacher's Guide* pages 276–280.

See Website www.greatsource.com/rehand/

For more practice, see also *Daybook* Grade 7, pages 73, 75, 183, 185–186.

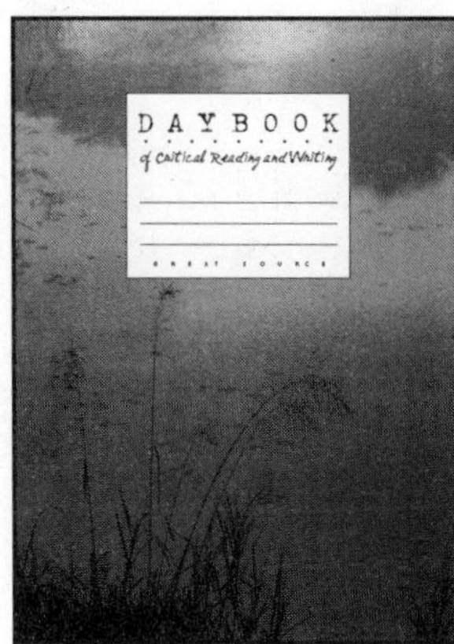

WEEK 21
Lesson 1

Read for Enjoyment

For use with *Reader's Handbook* pages 408–413

Goals

In this lesson, students read a poem for enjoyment, noting how it sounds and their personal responses to it.

Teaching Focus

Background

The imagery, figurative language, and symbolism in poems, as well as poets' use of idiosyncratic formats and punctuation, can intimidate some students. This is especially true if students expect to grasp all the nuances of a poem in one reading! This unit emphasizes that poems can—and indeed should—be read more than once.

Instruction

As a class, talk about features of poetry that set it apart from other forms of writing. Students might note the layout and punctuation of poems or their use of images and symbols. Ask whether these features make it easy or difficult for students to read and understand poetry. Point out that one way to get more out of poems is to read them multiple times. Explain that each reading can help peel back a different layer, leading to new insight into the poem's meaning and appreciation for its craft.

Teaching Approach

Use of the Handbook

Have students read pages 408–412 of the handbook on their own. Review as a class the Reading Plan on page 411 and the strategy of Close Reading on page 412. Make sure students understand the purpose of reading a poem multiple times. Then have students turn to page 413 to prepare for a first reading of "Winter Poem." Remind students to read through the poem slowly, just for pleasure, without analyzing or evaluating it.

Extend the Handbook

To emphasize appreciation and enjoyment of poetry, invite pairs to read "Winter Poem" aloud. As one partner reads, have the other partner listen and jot down thoughts about how the poem sounds and any responses or thoughts it evokes. Then have partners switch roles.

Assessment

Ask students:

- What is the purpose of reading a poem more than once?
- What do you like most about reading poems? What do you like least about poetry?

WEEK 21
Lesson 2

Read for Meaning

For use with *Reader's Handbook* page 414

Goals

In this lesson, students deepen their understanding of a poem's meaning by examining its images and language.

Teaching Focus

Background

Some students find poems puzzling, mysterious, or just plain frustrating to read. These students may not realize that the same reading strategies they use when reading stories or novels can be used to explore the meaning of poetry. In this lesson, students will use the strategy of close reading to lead them deeper into the meaning of Nikki Giovanni's "Winter Poem."

Instruction

Engage students in a discussion about their experiences reading poetry: What clues do students use to unlock the meaning of a poem? Point out that one way to deepen understanding is to examine and reflect on the poem's language and images. Explain to students that during their second reading of "Winter Poem," they will explore key words and images to discover what the poem is trying to say.

Teaching Approach

Use of the Handbook

Have student volunteers read aloud page 414 in the handbook. Discuss how students can use a Double-entry Journal to reflect on a poem's meaning. Then review with students the strategy of close reading. Have students reread "Winter Poem," this time noting words or lines that create strong images. Invite students to reflect on the images in a Double-entry Journal.

Extend the Handbook

Organize students into groups to prepare a choral reading of "Winter Poem." Remind them that they need not recite the whole poem as a group: some lines may be spoken individually, some in pairs, and some chorally. Encourage students to use tempo and inflection to express the poem's meaning. Then invite groups to perform their choral readings for the whole class.

Assessment

Ask students:

- What do you think Nikki Giovanni is trying to say in "Winter Poem"?
- What strategy can you use to discover the meaning of poetry?
- How will you use what you learned in this lesson the next time you read a poem?

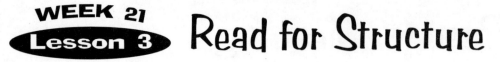

WEEK 21
Lesson 3

Read for Structure

For use with *Reader's Handbook* pages 415–416

Goals

In this lesson, students examine the role structure plays in poetry.

Teaching Focus

Background

The structure of a poem includes its typography, punctuation, and layout on the page. It also encompasses the use of repetition, rhyme, rhythm, and other poetic patterns. Reading for structure is essential because in many poems, structure also shapes meaning.

Instruction

Explain that the structure of a poem determines both what it looks like on the page and how it sounds when read aloud. Invite students to recite familiar nursery rhymes, limericks, or short poems they know. Record two or three examples on the board, and explore their structure with students. Introduce terms such as *stanza, rhyme,* and *meter* into the discussion where appropriate.

Teaching Approach

Use of the Handbook

Have students read pages 415–416 in the handbook. Then, as a class, talk about how poems are organized. Examine with students the analogy that compares the "construction" of a poem to a house being built. Make sure students understand why "Winter Poem" is an example of free verse. (For more information on free verse, see page 451 of the *Reader's Handbook*.)

Extend the Handbook

Invite students to try their hands at writing free verse. First have them choose a subject, then use a Web to brainstorm related words, images, and ideas. Remind them that free verse has no regular rhyme scheme, rhythm, or form. Students can model their verses after "Winter Poem" if they like.

For more practice, see pages 154–163 of the *Student Applications Book 7*.

Assessment

Ask students:

- What are some features of poetic structure?
- Why is Nikki Giovanni's "Winter Poem" an example of free verse?
- Why is it important to understand the structure of a poem?

WEEK 21 Lesson 4 Read for Feeling

For use with *Reader's Handbook* pages 417–421

Goals

In this lesson, students note their own responses and reactions to a final reading of "Winter Poem."

Teaching Focus

Background

In this lesson, students will revisit "Winter Poem" in order to reflect on the poem's mood and tone. A final rereading will also provide students with the opportunity to note their own connections, responses, and reactions to the poem.

Instruction

Review with students the purposes for reading introduced in each of the previous lessons (reading for enjoyment, reading for meaning, and reading for structure). Can students think of any other purposes for reading a poem? Point out that poets often try to create a particular *feeling* in readers. Explain that they do this through the poem's mood, tone, and language. (If students need a review of *mood* and *tone,* refer them to "Elements of Poetry," pages 456 and 468.)

Teaching Approach

Use of the Handbook

Have students read pages 417–421 in the handbook. Then ask students to reread "Winter Poem." Encourage them to note any feelings, connections, and reactions the poem evokes. Come together as a class to discuss the mood and tone of "Winter Poem." Then invite students to share personal responses to the poem with the class. Were students' responses influenced by the mood and tone of "Winter Poem"? Discuss.

Extend the Handbook

Provide poetry anthologies for students to browse through. *A Jar of Tiny Stars* (edited by Bernice Cullinan) and *I, Too, Sing America: Three Centuries of African-American Poetry* (compiled by Catherine Clinton) are good resources for middle-grade poetry. Invite students to choose a poem they like. Then, in small groups, have students read aloud favorite lines or stanzas from the poems they selected. Encourage students to explain why the lines they selected are meaningful to them or important to the poem.

Assessment

Ask students:

- How do poets create feelings or emotion in their readers?
- How has this unit changed the way you read or think about poetry? Explain.

WEEK 22 Lesson 5 Strategy: Close Reading

For use with *Reader's Handbook* pages 422–423

Goals

In this lesson, students learn how to use the strategy of close reading to explore the language of poetry.

Teaching Focus

Background

Because poems tend to be shorter than other forms of fiction, poets use language economically. The strategy of close reading is particularly useful for reading poetry because each word in a poem carries a lot of weight. Close reading can help readers "zoom in" on words in a poem and examine how they work, look, and sound together.

Instruction

Discuss with students the strategy of close reading. Remind students that close reading involves going word by word and line by line through a text. Discuss why students think this strategy might be useful for exploring the language of poems.

Teaching Approach

Use of the Handbook

Have student volunteers read through the information and goals on page 422 of the handbook. Then read aloud the poem "Words" on page 423. As you read, encourage students to reflect on the poet's language, noting interesting words, striking images, or unusual phrases. Explain to students that throughout this unit, they will use the strategy of close reading to explore the language of poetry in more depth. If necessary, review the information on close reading at the bottom of page 423.

Extend the Handbook

Have students reread the poem that they used in the previous lesson. Encourage them to use a Double-entry Journal to note their reactions to words or images in the poem they find striking or appealing.

For more practice, see pages 164–165 of the *Student Applications Book 7.*

Assessment

Ask students:

- How do you know what kinds of words and phrases to focus on when reading poetry?
- Why is close reading a useful strategy for looking at the language of poetry?

WEEK 22
Lesson 6

Key Words and Connotation

For use with *Reader's Handbook* pages 424–426

Goals

In this lesson, students explore the denotations and connotations of key words in a poem.

Teaching Focus

Background

After an initial reading of "Words," students may be confused by some of the author's language, for example, the use of the word *squander* in line 2 and *wrought* in line 9. An examination of the denotations and connotations of key words will help clarify these lines for students and lead to a deeper understanding of the poem's overall meaning.

Instruction

Reproduce the poem "Words" on an overhead transparency or on chart paper. Invite students to read aloud one line of the poem at a time. After each line, stop and reflect: Which words stand out? Are there words that are confusing or unfamiliar? What words do students think are important? Mark the poem to reflect students' responses. Then discuss as a class what students discovered from their close reading of the poem.

Teaching Approach

Use of the Handbook

Have students read about key words on page 424 of the *Reader's Handbook*. Ask students to compare the words highlighted in the example with the class's marked version of the poem (above). Then ask students to continue reading pages 425–426 of the handbook to learn about the connotation and denotation of words. Build understanding of connotations associated with the word *squander.* Lead students to see how the connotions of this word help them understand the speaker's point that we use words carelessly. For more information on Connotation and Denotation, see page 279 of the handbook.

Extend the Handbook

Have students return to the poems they have been using in the unit or choose a new one. Invite them to identify key words in the poems. Then have them consider whether any of these words have interesting or important connotations. Have students share findings in small groups.

Assessment

Ask students:

- Why is it important to focus on key words when reading poetry?
- What is the difference between a word's connotation and its denotation?
- Why do poets use words that have connotations?

WEEK 22 Lesson 7 Figurative Language

For use with *Reader's Handbook* pages 427–428

Goals

In this lesson, students learn about figurative language and its role in poetry.

Teaching Focus

Background

One way that poets add richness to their writing without adding a lot of additional words is through the use of similes and metaphors. In this lesson, students will examine these two forms of figurative language to see why they play an important role in so many poems.

Instruction

Write the following examples of figurative language on the board:

The old oak stands as tall and proud as a warrior.
The willow dances, a graceful ballerina.

Lead students to see that both examples of figurative language use a comparison to create an image in the reader's mind. Point out that the first example is a simile, because it uses the comparative word *as*; the second comparison, which uses no connective word, is a metaphor. Discuss with students how similes and metaphors help readers look at familiar objects or concepts in new ways.

Teaching Approach

Use of the Handbook

Have students read the bottom of page 426. Then come together as a class to discuss the example of figurative language on page 427. What does it add to the poem? What picture or image does this metaphor create in students' minds? Invite students to draw a sketch of what they see. (If students need more information on figurative language, simile, or metaphor, refer them to pages 450, 464, and 455 of the *Reader's Handbook*.)

Extend the Handbook

Have students return to the poems they have been working with. This time, ask them to concentrate on the poet's use of figurative language. Encourage students to identify examples of similes or metaphors. Have students present examples of each to the class.

Assessment

Ask students:

- How are similes and metaphors alike? How are they different?
- Why do poets use similes and metaphors in their writing?

Imagery

For use with *Reader's Handbook* pages 427–429

Goals

In this lesson, students expand their understanding of the use of imagery in poetry.

Teaching Focus

Background

Like metaphors and similes, imagery can help readers create pictures in their minds. Poets often rely on imagery to evoke thoughts and feelings related to the five senses. Recognizing the characteristics of imagery and its purposes will enable students to deepen their understanding and appreciation of poetry.

Instruction

Work with students to brainstorm the purposes of poetry. Help students understand that poems are often used to express emotions or ideas; one way poets can convey these feelings or ideas is through their use of imagery. Explain that *imagery* is language that appeals to the five senses—touch, taste, smell, sound, and sight.

Teaching Approach

Use of the Handbook

Read the paragraph on imagery at the bottom of page 427. Then ask a student to read aloud the second stanza from "Words" (top of page 428). Talk about Murray's use of imagery. To what sense or senses does the poet appeal? Which image is most vivid to students? How does the poem make them feel? Explain that students' prior knowledge and experience with an image will determine what emotions the image evokes.

Extend the Handbook

Ask students to look for examples of imagery in the poems they have been working with throughout this unit. Have students conclude the unit by working with a partner to reflect on the poems they have explored. Students may wish to try one or two of the activities on page 429 (see "Tips for Working with a Partner").

For more practice, see pages 164–165 of the *Student Applications Book 7*.

Assessment

Ask students:

- Why do poets use imagery?
- How does your prior knowledge and experience affect your understanding of an image?
- How did this unit affect your understanding of poetry?

Reading a Play

For use with *Reader's Handbook* pages 472–488

Daily Lessons	**Summary***
Lesson 1 **Drama:** **Before Reading**	Build background about drama by having students compare and contrast plays with other forms of fiction.
Lesson 2 **Drama:** **During Reading**	Help students use During Reading strategies to explore character and plot in a dramatic work. Read aloud lines from a play to deepen understanding of characters.
Lesson 3 **Drama:** **How Plays Are Organized**	Explore structural elements of plays, including acts, scenes, and the use of flashback. Contrast the organization of plays with the organization of novels.
Lesson 4 **Drama:** **After Reading**	Discuss with students strategies to use after reading drama. Have students reflect on the meaning of a play in their journals.

*Use these notes to help you teach a mini-lesson or to teach a briefer, shorter version of the lessons for more proficient students.

Lesson Resources

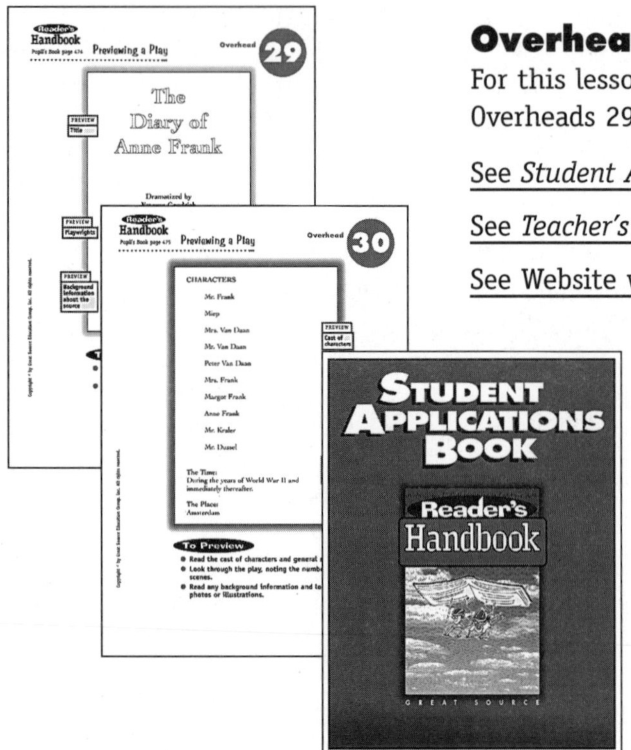

Overheads

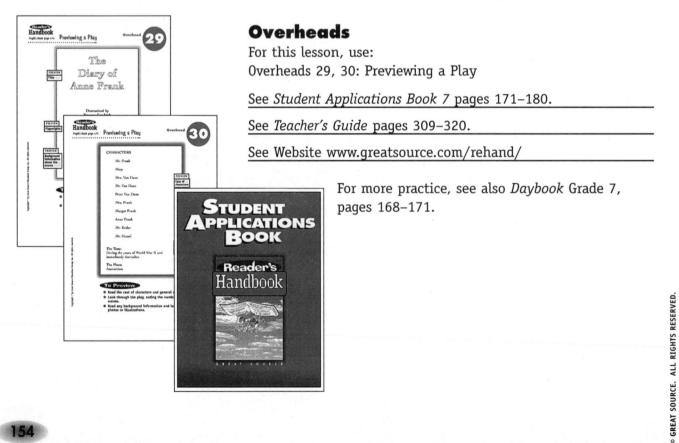

For this lesson, use:

Overheads 29, 30: Previewing a Play

See *Student Applications Book 7* pages 171–180.

See *Teacher's Guide* pages 309–320.

See Website www.greatsource.com/rehand/

For more practice, see also *Daybook* Grade 7, pages 168–171.

Elements of Drama

For use with *Reader's Handbook* pages 502–511

Daily Lessons	**Summary***
Lesson 5 **Dialogue and Monologue**	Build an understanding of the importance of language in a play. Help students explore dialogue and monologue in *The Diary of Anne Frank.*
Lesson 6 **Setting**	Discuss and examine setting in plays. Invite students to visualize a scene from a play and sketch its setting.
Lesson 7 **Stage Directions**	Build an understanding of the function of stage directions in a play. Have students work in groups to develop brief scripts that include stage directions.
Lesson 8 **Theme**	Explore the importance of theme in dramatic works. Use graphic organizers to identify and understand theme.

*Use these notes to help you teach a mini-lesson or to teach a briefer, shorter version of the lessons for more proficient students.

Lesson Resources

See *Teacher's Guide* pages 331–338.

See Website www.greatsource.com/rehand/

WEEK 23 Lesson 1 Drama: Before Reading

For use with *Reader's Handbook* pages 472–476

Goals

In this introductory lesson, students build an understanding of plays by comparing and contrasting drama with other genres.

Teaching Focus

Background

This unit offers students the opportunity to build on what they know about reading fiction as they explore the genre of drama. First students will examine the way familiar story elements, such as character, plot, and theme, function in a dramatic text. Then students will expand their understanding as they learn about the structure and features that are unique to drama.

Instruction

Work with students to compare drama with other forms of fiction. How is reading a play similar to and different from reading a short story or a novel? Help students identify the elements these genres have in common; for example, character, plot, setting, and theme. Then build background about the distinctive characteristics of plays, including lines, acts, scenes, and stage directions. Lead students to see that plays contain these elements because they are meant to be performed, not just read.

Teaching Approach

Use of the Handbook

Have students read pages 472–476 in the handbook to prepare for reading a play. Ask students to compare their purposes for reading drama to their purposes for reading other types of fiction. Then have students preview the play, and discuss what they learn about *The Diary of Anne Frank* from its opening pages. Build background as necessary about World War II and Nazi Germany prior to reading *The Diary of Anne Frank.*

Extend the Handbook

In their journals, ask students to reflect on the experiences they have had seeing, performing, or reading plays. Do they enjoy plays? Why or why not? Then encourage students to set their own goals and purposes for reading this unit. What do they hope to learn about drama?

Assessment

Ask students:

- How is drama similar to other forms of fiction?
- In what ways is drama different from other forms of fiction?

WEEK 23
Lesson 2

Drama: During Reading

For use with *Reader's Handbook* pages 477–483

Goals

In this lesson, students use During Reading strategies to understand the elements of drama.

Teaching Focus

Background

Drama offers students a new context in which to utilize what they know about the steps in the reading process. In this lesson, students will use During Reading strategies to facilitate understanding of the characters and plot in a play. Students will also explore the opportunities drama presents for developing and practicing oral language skills.

Instruction

Ask students how they learn about characters when reading short stories or novels. Explain that when reading drama, readers do not have access to descriptive details or to characters' inner thoughts. Instead, playwrights develop both characters and plot mainly through the dialogue between characters. Point out that one good way to keep track of the characters and action in a play is to use graphic organizers.

Teaching Approach

Use of the Handbook

Have students review their purposes for reading *The Diary of Anne Frank*. As they read the excerpt from the play on pages 478–480, ask them to pay close attention to how the authors develop characters and advance the action of the play. Then invite students to examine the scene-by-scene Summary Notes on page 482 and the Character Map on page 483. (*Theme* will be explored in Lesson 8 of this two-week unit on drama.)

Extend the Handbook

Organize the class into groups of three. Ask students to take the roles of Mr. Frank, Miep, and Anne as they read aloud the excerpt from *The Diary of Anne Frank* on pages 478–480. Encourage students to use their voices to express characters' thoughts and feelings.

Assessment

Ask students:

- What techniques do playwrights use to develop characters?
- How do playwrights develop plot?
- How can graphic organizers help you read drama?

WEEK 23 Lesson 3 How Plays Are Organized

For use with *Reader's Handbook* page 484

Goals

In this lesson, students develop an understanding of acts, scenes, and other structural elements of plays.

Teaching Focus

Background

Students who are unfamiliar with the structure of a script may find it difficult to follow the action when reading plays. A basic understanding of acts, scenes, and the use of flashback will help students keep track of the changes in time and place that occur in *The Diary of Anne Frank* and in other dramatic works.

Instruction

Begin by asking students why they think most novels are divided into chapters. Then have students compare the structure of a novel to the structure of a play. Lead them to see that the acts and scenes in plays serve the same function that chapters serve in novels: Acts and scenes break up the action and advance the plot by signaling a change in time or place. (If students need more background on Acts and Scenes, see "Elements of Drama," page 503.)

Teaching Approach

Use of the Handbook

Have a volunteer read aloud the first paragraph on page 484. Then invite students to examine the scene breakdown for *The Diary of Anne Frank.* Lead students to see that each new act or scene in the play marks the passage of time. Point out that not all of the action in the play moves forward chronologically; in fact, the play comes full circle, beginning and ending in November 1945. Take this opportunity to review and discuss flashback with students. (For more information on flashbacks, see page 372 of the handbook.) Conclude by walking students through the Plot Diagram for *The Diary of Anne Frank.*

Extend the Handbook

For additional practice, have students examine the structure of the play on pages 171–180 in the *Student Applications Book 7.*

Assessment

Ask students:

- What is the purpose of acts and scenes in plays?
- What function does a flashback serve in a play?
- How is the structure of a play similar to that of a novel? How is it different?

WEEK 23 Lesson 4 Drama: After Reading

For use with *Reader's Handbook* pages 486–488

Goals

In this lesson, students utilize After Reading strategies to deepen understanding of a dramatic work.

Teaching Focus

Background

As with other genres, students need to take the time after reading drama to return to their original purposes and reflect on learning. In this lesson, students revisit the excerpt from *The Diary of Anne Frank* and use the strategies of visualizing and thinking aloud to reflect on the meaning of the play.

Instruction

Review the After Reading stage of the reading process with students. (See pages 35–36 of the *Reader's Handbook* for more information.) Point out that reflecting on a play after reading can help students clarify what the play is all about, remember key ideas, and relate its themes to their own lives. Take time to answer any questions students have about *The Diary of Anne Frank* or about reading drama in general.

Teaching Approach

Use of the Handbook

Have student volunteers read aloud pages 486–488 of the *Reader's Handbook*. Use the Looking Back Checklist to check students' understanding of Scene I of *The Diary of Anne Frank*. Review with students the strategies of visualizing and thinking aloud (p. 487). Then have students read page 488 independently. Sum up by asking students to compare what they do after reading a play to what they do after reading a short story or novel. How are the steps in the After Reading process similar for drama and other forms of fiction?

Extend the Handbook

Invite students to reflect in their journals on a key idea or passage from *The Diary of Anne Frank*. First ask students to describe the idea or passage in their own words. Then have them write about why that part of the play was important or meaningful to them.

Assessment

Ask students:

- What is the purpose of visualizing and thinking aloud after reading drama?
- How will you use what you've learned in this unit the next time you read drama? What questions do you still have about reading plays?

WEEK 24
Lesson 5

Dialogue and Monologue

For use with *Reader's Handbook* pages 505–506

Goals

In this lesson, students examine dialogues and monologues to learn about the language of plays.

Teaching Focus

Background

Character, plot, and theme are developed and explored through a play's language—its conversation and speeches. Understanding a play's language is therefore critical to understanding its meaning. In this lesson, students will enhance their understanding of drama through an examination of dialogue and monologue.

Instruction

Discuss with students why it is important to pay attention to language when reading plays. Have students revisit the excerpt from *The Diary of Anne Frank* on pages 479–480. Guide students as they reflect on the play's language. What mood or feeling is communicated through the excerpt's language? What does the dialogue between Miep and Mr. Frank reveal about each of these characters? How would students describe the play's language: Is it conversational or formal, old-fashioned or contemporary?

Teaching Approach

Use of the Handbook

Read and discuss as a class the description and definition of *dialogue* on page 505 of the handbook. Call attention to the speech tags and make sure students understand their function. Ask two students to read aloud the example of dialogue on page 505. Repeat the same steps to familiarize students with *monologue* on page 506. Have students identify examples of monologue in *The Diary of Anne Frank.*

Extend the Handbook

Continue exploring the language of plays by having students annotate the excerpt from *The Diary of Anne Frank* (pages 478–480). First ask students to indicate how the play's dialogue should be spoken (for example, *sadly, coldly, impatiently*). Then have them jot down ideas about what the body postures, gestures, and facial expressions of the characters might look like as they speak their lines.

Assessment

Ask students:

- What is the difference between a dialogue and a monologue?
- What can you learn from studying the language in a play?

Setting

For use with *Reader's Handbook* page 509

Goals

In this lesson, students examine different elements of setting in dramatic works.

Teaching Focus

Background

When drama is performed, the audience views the action and the characters on the stage. The audience can see another important element of the drama as well— its setting. Scenery, costumes, lighting, and props are all used to reveal the time and place of a play. When reading drama, however, students need to visualize these important elements of the play's setting.

Instruction

Establish that students have a general understanding of setting. Then ask them to reflect on plays they have seen: How did they learn about setting, or the play's time and place? Students may note that the backdrop, scenery, and program notes of a play provide clues to its setting. Expand students' understanding of dramatic settings by asking them what costumes, lighting, and props in a play can reveal about its setting.

Teaching Approach

Use of the Handbook

Have students read page 509 of the handbook. Reinforce learning by examining general and immediate setting in *The Diary of Anne Frank*. Point out that the general setting of the play is World War II Amsterdam (see excerpt on page 475). The play's immediate setting is the Franks' hiding place on the top floor of a warehouse (see excerpt on page 478). Explain that in many dramas, the immediate setting changes several times throughout the course of the play.

Extend the Handbook

Have students return to the description of setting at the beginning of Act One, Scene I of *The Diary of Anne Frank* (page 478). Ask them to close their eyes and visualize the Franks' hiding place. Then have students sketch the hiding place as they imagined it in their minds.

Assessment

Ask students:

- What is the difference between a play's general setting and its immediate setting?
- How are time and place revealed in a play?

WEEK 24 Lesson 7 Stage Directions

For use with *Reader's Handbook* page 510

Goals

In this lesson, students examine the importance of stage directions in drama.

Teaching Focus

Background

Playwrights include stage directions to guide the actors and set the scene. Directors, actors, and others involved in staging a play use the stage directions to decide how scenes should be read and what they should look like. Readers of dramatic texts also use stage directions to imagine the action of the play and visualize its setting.

Instruction

Ask students to reread the stage directions (printed in italics) for *The Diary of Anne Frank* on pages 478–480. Then ask students whether the stage directions helped them "see" the play in their minds. Explain that stage directions guide the actors and action in a drama: They indicate how characters should look, act, move, and speak. Stage directions also help set the scene by describing what props are needed and how the stage should look.

Teaching Approach

Use of the Handbook

Ask volunteers to read the description and definition of *stage directions* on page 510 of the handbook. Then review the example and discuss the stage directions with students. What additional information do the stage directions in the example provide? Why is this information important?

Extend the Handbook

Have students look through the classroom library to find dialogue-rich scenes in novels or stories. Invite students to work in small groups to develop the scenes into short scripts. First, students need to rewrite the scene so that it consists only of dialogue between characters. Then have them add stage directions to show how the characters should look, sound, and move. Students might also use stage directions to indicate what the setting and stage should look like in the scene.

Assessment

Ask students:

- Why are stage directions important when performing a play?
- How can you use stage directions to get the most out of reading a play?

WEEK 24 Lesson 8 Theme

For use with *Reader's Handbook* pages 489–494

Goals

In this lesson, students develop an understanding of theme and its importance in works of drama.

Teaching Focus

Background

When reading drama, students need to go beyond the literal level of the text. At their deepest level, many dramatic works explore universal themes of struggle, conflict, hope, and the resiliency of the human spirit. Identifying and examining these themes in plays will lead students to a deeper understanding and appreciation of their meaning.

Instruction

Review what students know about *theme.* Remind students that a theme is the message or point that the author explores though the story and its characters. Invite students to practice coming up with theme statements for a familiar children's story, such as *The Three Little Pigs.* Lead students to see that while there are different ways of interpreting the theme of a story or play, all theme statements need to be supported by the text.

Teaching Approach

Use of the Handbook

Have students read about theme on pages 489–494. You may want to copy the three-step plan for understanding theme on the board so students can use it as a reference. Then explore with students how they can use a Double-entry Journal or a Topic and Theme Organizer to identify the theme of a dramatic work. Conclude by discussing how to write a clear and useful theme statement.

Extend the Handbook

Invite students to reflect on the theme of a movie they have seen. (Point out that classic or dramatic films are the best options for exploring theme.) First have students review the list of common topics for themes (page 490). Then ask them to create a Double-entry Journal or Topic and Theme Organizer to explore the "big ideas" of the movie. Finally, ask students to come up with a theme statement that expresses the movie's message.

Assessment

Ask students:

- How can you use graphic organizers to explore the themes of a dramatic work?
- What is a theme statement?
- Why is it important to identify the theme of a play?

Reading a Website

For use with *Reader's Handbook* pages 514–526

Daily Lessons	**Summary***
Lesson 1 **Before Reading a Website**	Help students set a purpose, preview, and plan before reading a website.
Lesson 2 **Reading a Website Critically**	Build background about websites and why it is important to to read them critically. Discuss critical reading strategies students can use when reading websites.
Lesson 3 **How Websites Are Organized**	Build an understanding of the structure of websites. Have students compare the organization of books and websites.
Lesson 4 **Evaluating Internet Sources**	Explore with students After Reading strategies for evaluating Internet sources. Ask students to evaluate a website using a checklist.

*Use these notes to help you teach a mini-lesson or to teach a briefer, shorter version of the lessons for more proficient students.

Lesson Resources

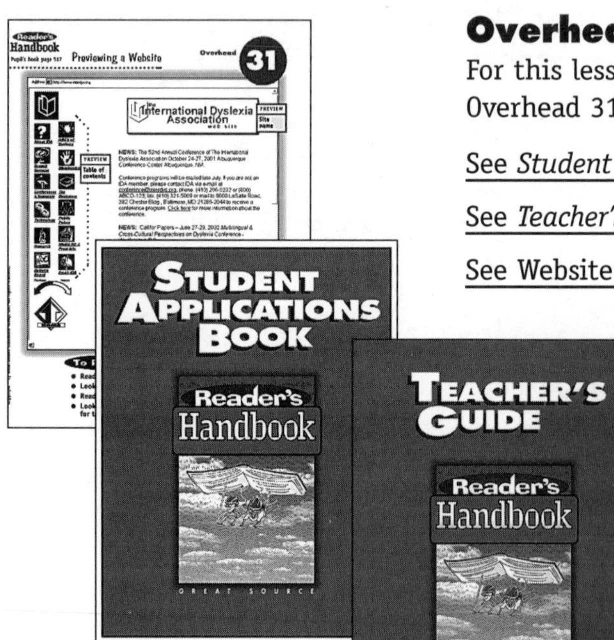

Overheads

For this lesson, use:
Overhead 31: Previewing a Website

See *Student Applications Book 7* pages 186–193.

See *Teacher's Guide* pages 340–351.

See Website www.greatsource.com/rehand/

Elements of the Internet

For use with *Reader's Handbook* pages 527–535

Daily Lessons	**Summary***
Lesson 5 **The World Wide Web**	Build background about the World Wide Web. Introduce terminology such as *home page, web page*, and *URL*.
Lesson 6 **Using Search Engines**	Build an understanding of search engines and explore strategies for searching the Internet more effectively.
Lesson 7 **Following Links**	Discuss the purpose links serve on websites. Have students follow a website's links to learn more about a topic.
Lesson 8 **Exploring Email**	Help students learn about the basic functions and features of email.

*Use these notes to help you teach a mini-lesson or to teach a briefer, shorter version of the lessons for more proficient students.

Lesson Resources

See *Teacher's Guide* pages 352–357.

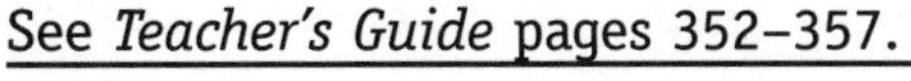

See Website www.greatsource.com/rehand/

WEEK 25 Lesson 1 Before Reading a Website

For use with *Reader's Handbook* pages 513–518

Goals

In this lesson, students discuss the importance of setting a purpose, previewing, and planning before reading a website.

Teaching Focus

Background

The Internet can be an amazing tool if students know how to use it. Because of the vast amount of information available on the Internet, however, students can easily lose track of time—and their purposes—when "surfing the Web." Setting a purpose, previewing, and planning prior to reading a website will help students use this resource more effectively.

Instruction

Access students' prior knowledge about the Internet and websites by asking questions such as the following: How much time do you spend on the Internet? What websites do you visit most often? What are your purposes for using the World Wide Web? Discuss different purposes and strategies for using the Web. Explain that in this unit students will learn how to use the reading process to read websites more effectively and to get more out of the time they spend on the World Wide Web.

Teaching Approach

Use of the Handbook

Have students read pages 514–516 in the handbook. Discuss the unit goals with the class, as well as any additional objectives students might have for reading this unit on websites. Stress the importance of setting a purpose when looking for information on the Web. Then preview as a class the sample home page on page 517. Call students' attention to key features, such as links and the main menu. Then have students read the information under "Plan" on page 518.

Extend the Handbook

Provide students with a list of websites to explore. (The sites can be tied to the classroom curriculum or to topics of general interest to students.) Invite students working in small groups to preview one of the websites. Have each group begin a learning log related to their website. In their logs, ask them to jot down notes in response to each of the items on the preview checklist (see page 516).

Assessment

Ask students:

- Why is it important to set a purpose before reading a website?
- What do you hope to learn about reading websites from this unit?

WEEK 25
Lesson 2

Reading a Website Critically

For use with *Reader's Handbook* pages 518–523

Goals

In this lesson, students explore strategies for reading websites critically.

Teaching Focus

Background

The amount of information on the Web is almost unlimited; unfortunately, not all of that information is accurate or reliable. Because the Web is unregulated, it is particularly important for students to read websites *actively*. In this lesson, students will learn how to read critically in order to judge the credibility, appropriateness, and usefulness of information they encounter on the Web.

Instruction

Explain to students that anyone who has access to the Internet can create a website. Moreover, the World Wide Web is too large for any one person or group to control. Ask students: What are some of the pros and cons of having an Internet that is not controlled? Lead students to see that because the Web is unregulated, it is important to read websites critically. When students look up information on websites, they need to make active judgements about the quality and reliability of what they read.

Teaching Approach

Use of the Handbook

Ask a student volunteer to read aloud the information on reading critically at the bottom of page 518. As a class, read and discuss the strategies for reading critically on page 519. Emphasize the importance of evaluating both the information presented on websites and the URL, or source, of the site. Then have students read pages 520–523 on their own. Discuss how keeping their purposes in mind and taking notes can help students read a website actively and critically.

Extend the Handbook

Have students return to the websites they previewed in the previous lesson. In their learning logs, ask each group to create a Website Profiler for the site. Then encourage students to use the critical reading strategies they learned in this lesson as they continue to explore the website.

Assessment

Ask students:

- What tools can you use to read a website critically?
- Why is it important to read actively when reading websites?

WEEK 25
Lesson 3

How Websites Are Organized

For use with *Reader's Handbook* page 522

Goals

In this lesson, students learn about the organization of websites in order to use these resources more effectively.

Teaching Focus

Background

Websites allow users to follow links, move back and forth, and jump from one page or resource to another. For those who are accustomed to the sequential page-by-page process of reading a book, reading a website can be confusing. Understanding how websites are organized will help students navigate sites and keep track of the information on them more effectively.

Instruction

Write the following definition on the board: *Navigate (verb): to move or travel through to steer a course.* Discuss with students how reading a website is like "navigating." Then help students compare the sequential, page-by-page organization of books to the organization of websites. Lead students to see that one of the main differences is that links on a website allow the user to jump from one document or part of the site to another.

Teaching Approach

Use of the Handbook

Have student volunteers read aloud the information under "How Websites Are Organized" on page 522 of the *Reader's Handbook*. Take time to discuss the sketches comparing the organization of a website with the organization of a book. Then talk about factors that make websites easy or difficult to read. Students may note that they enjoy reading sites with interesting or creative graphics. On the other hand, they may point out that too many graphics on a site can take a long time to download and slow connections.

Extend the Handbook

Ask students to examine the organization of the website they have been using throughout the unit. First have them create a sketch to illustrate its organization. Then invite them to describe and critique the websites' organization in their logs: Was the site easy or difficult to navigate? Were the links interesting and useful? Did the site have any special features?

Assessment

Ask students:

- How is the organization of websites different from that of books?
- How does knowing the organization of a website help you read it?

WEEK 25 Lesson 4 Evaluating Internet Sources

For use with *Reader's Handbook* page 524–526

Goals

In this lesson, students learn to use the reading strategy of skimming to evaluate Internet sources.

Teaching Focus

Background

The Internet has become the foremost source of information in the world. In Lesson 2 of this unit, students learned that in order to get the most out of this resource, it is important to read websites critically. This lesson builds on the previous one by helping students use the rereading strategy of skimming to evaluate websites and the information they contain.

Instruction

Review with students the importance of reading websites critically. Have students discuss whether they've ever encountered misinformation or unreliable sources on the Web. Explain that students can use questions such as the following to evaluate the reliability of a website: Is the information on the website consistent with what students already know or with information from other sources? Is the site up-to-date and accurate? Is the source of the information a reputable individual, group, or organization? Lead students to see that using the Internet effectively involves making judgments about what they read.

Teaching Approach

Use of the Handbook

Have students read pages 524–526 of the *Reader's Handbook*. Discuss each of the five steps for evaluating Internet sources on page 525. Ask students which of these steps they already use when reading websites. Lead them to see that all of these steps are important in order to evaluate sources thoroughly.

Extend the Handbook

Have groups evaluate the information presented on the websites they have been using throughout this unit. Ask them to use the checklist on page 525 to evaluate the site's reliability. Students can note their responses to the five points in their logs.

Assessment

Ask students:

- Why is it important to take time after visiting a website to reread and reflect?
- How does skimming help you to evaluate the information on a website?

WEEK 26 Lesson 5 The World Wide Web

For use with *Reader's Handbook* pages 534–535

Goals

In this lesson, students examine the World Wide Web and its features.

Teaching Focus

Background

The World Wide Web (also called the Web or WWW) refers to a system of computers around the world that are linked and can share files. Web pages can include text, graphics, and multimedia features such as animation, sound, and video. In this lesson, students will build their general understanding of the Web and how to use it. In the lessons that follow, students will learn about specific tools and features of the Web, such as search engines, links, and email.

Instruction

Find out what students know about the World Wide Web. Point out that connecting to the Web requires a computer, an Internet server, and a browser (for more information on Browsers, see page 529 of the handbook). These three elements allow users to connect to the huge database of information on the Web, as well as to all the other computers connected to the network, or the Internet. Explore with students why the World Wide Web is such a useful information and communications tool.

Teaching Approach

Use of the Handbook

Work with students to analyze the sample home page on page 534 of the *Reader's Handbook*. Point out its key features, such as the pull-down menu and hypertext. Then read aloud the description of the World Wide Web on page 535. Discuss specialized vocabulary, including *home page*, *web page*, and *URL*.

Extend the Handbook

Have students continue using logs (see Lessons 1–4) to assess their knowledge of the World Wide Web: How comfortable are they using the Web? What aspect of the Web are students most familiar with? What do they find confusing about it?

Assessment

Ask students:

- What is the World Wide Web?
- What would you like to learn about the Web from this unit? Explain your answer.

WEEK 26 Lesson 6 Using Search Engines

For use with *Reader's Handbook* page 533

Goals

In this lesson, students learn strategies that will enable them to use search engines more effectively.

Teaching Focus

Background

There are hundreds of millions of web pages on the Internet, and more are added every day. One of the most effective means of exploring this vast information system is through search engines. In this lesson, students will learn how to use search engines to find and keep track of the many resources available on the World Wide Web.

Instruction

Begin by asking students what resources they use to find information on the Internet. Explain that search engines are programs that can scan the huge database of the World Wide Web in seconds. Explore what students know about search engines and which search engines, if any, they currently use. Point out that there are specific techniques for using search engines that can help students utilize them more effectively.

Teaching Approach

Use of the Handbook

Walk students through the key components of Google's search engine home page on page 533. Then have students read aloud the description and definition of *search engine*. Point out that finding what you want on the Internet can be time consuming if the search is not narrow enough. Review as a class strategies for using search engines effectively. For example, point out that words that must be searched for together should be enclosed in quotation marks.

Extend the Handbook

Have students practice using a search engine, such as www.google.com or www.yahoo.com, to explore a topic of their choosing. Encourage students to choose their search criteria carefully and to use the strategies discussed in this lesson to narrow their field of results. Ask students to note the addresses of one or two of the sites to explore later in this unit.

Assessment

Ask students:

- What is the purpose of a search engine?
- What strategies can help you use search engines effectively?

WEEK 26 Lesson 7 Following Links

For use with *Reader's Handbook* page 532

Goals

In this lesson, students will learn what links are and how to use them.

Teaching Focus

Background

Links (addresses inserted into hypertext documents) are part of what distinguishes the Web from all other information systems. Links enable users to jump from one page or resource on the Web to another. Because moving from link to link can be confusing, strategies such as setting purposes and taking notes will help students organize and track their movement through websites.

Instruction

Find out what students know about links on websites. Read aloud the definition of *link* on page 532 of the handbook. Point out that links are usually underlined or appear in a second color. Lead students to see that links enable web users to connect or move from one web page to another, related, web page with a click of the mouse. Explain that this is called "following" a link.

Teaching Approach

Use of the Handbook

Have a student volunteer read the description of *link* on page 532 of the *Reader's Handbook*. If necessary, explain that hypertext refers to data that contains links to other data. Then discuss the analogy between links and the use of cross-referencing in books. Because jumping from link to link can be confusing (and just plain distracting), discuss the importance of setting a purpose for reading websites and keeping track of where you've been and where you need to go.

Extend the Handbook

Invite students to explore one of the sites they located using a search engine (see Lesson 6). Ask students to jot down questions they have about the site and its topic. Then have students search for the answers to their questions by exploring the site and following its links. Ask them to track their movement through the site: How many different links did students click on before finding answers to their questions?

Assessment

Ask students:

- What are links and how do you use them?
- How can you tell if something on a website is a link?

WEEK 26
Lesson 8

Exploring Email

For use with *Reader's Handbook* pages 530–531

Goals

In this lesson, students explore the characteristics of email and its uses.

Teaching Focus

Background

The Internet is both an information system and a communications network. The most popular way to communicate on the Internet is via email, short for *electronic mail*. Because email follows a standard format, it is easy to use. In this lesson, students will examine the features and function of this popular form of communication.

Instruction

Assess what students know about the basic functions of email, such as reading, saving, printing, and replying to email messages. Then discuss the protocol for composing and sending email. Make sure students understand the importance of filling in the email header completely and accurately. Then briefly review email protocol with students. For example, remind them that they should avoid using unnecessary capital letters, boldface, and underlined type in email.

Teaching Approach

Use of the Handbook

Begin by reading aloud the definition of email on page 531. Then walk students through the sample email on page 530. Have students identify the standard parts of an email, including the header, body, and the address. Have student volunteers read the information on email and chat rooms. Discuss why it is important that students not give out personal information or make arrangements to meet people through the Web.

Extend the Handbook

Have students extend their knowledge of email by finding out about the use of acronyms and smileys (also called *emoticons*) in email. Point out that this form of "messaging," which is unique to the Internet, consists of abbreviations, symbols, and punctuation. Invite students to create glossaries for this special form of email terminology.

Assessment

Ask students:

- What are the standard parts of an email?
- Compare email and regular (post office) mail. What are some of the similarities and differences?
- What are some precautions you should take when sending email or using chat rooms?

Reading Graphics

For use with *Reader's Handbook* pages 538–547

Daily Lessons	**Summary***
Lesson 1 **Before Reading a Graphic**	Build background about reading graphics. Work with students to set a purpose, preview, and plan before reading a graphic.
Lesson 2 **Strategy for Graphics: Paraphrase**	Review the strategy of paraphrasing. Have students use a Double-entry Journal to paraphrase the information in a graphic.
Lesson 3 **How Graphics Are Organized**	Help students explore the organization and features of graphics.
Lesson 4 **Drawing Conclusions from Graphics**	Build an understanding of After Reading strategies students can use to analyze the information in graphic sources.

*Use these notes to help you teach a mini-lesson or to teach a briefer, shorter version of the lessons for more proficient students.

Lesson Resources

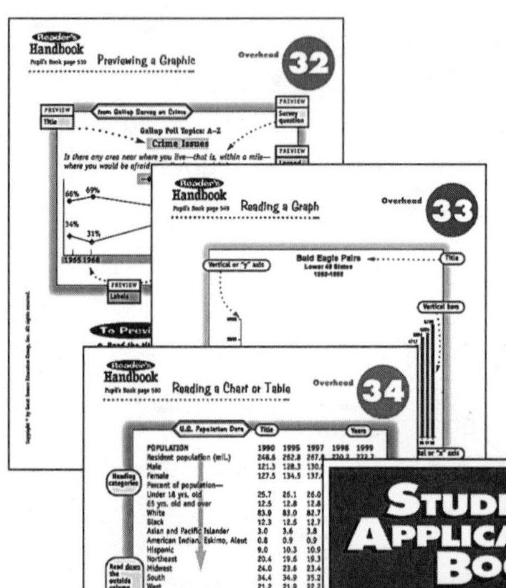

Overheads

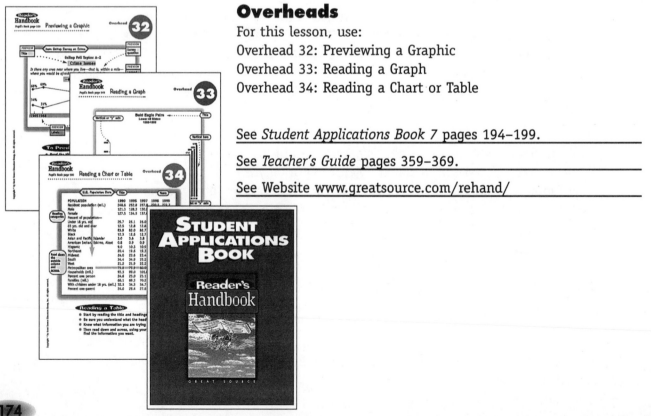

For this lesson, use:
Overhead 32: Previewing a Graphic
Overhead 33: Reading a Graph
Overhead 34: Reading a Chart or Table

See *Student Applications Book 7* pages 194–199.

See *Teacher's Guide* pages 359–369.

See Website www.greatsource.com/rehand/

Elements of Graphics

For use with *Reader's Handbook* pages 548–561

Daily Lessons	**Summary***
Lesson 5 **Reading Graphs**	Build background about bar graphs and line graphs. Explore the characteristics and purposes of these two common types of graphs.
Lesson 6 **Reading Pie Charts**	Develop understanding of how to read a pie chart. Have students create a pie chart based on data they collect.
Lesson 7 **Reading Tables**	Explore data presented in tables. Discuss strategies for reading and understanding tables.
Lesson 8 **Reading Timelines**	Discuss with students the purposes and characteristics of timelines. Have students create timelines representing a sequence of events in their own lives.

*Use these notes to help you teach a mini-lesson or to teach a briefer, shorter version of the lessons for more proficient students.

Lesson Resources

See *Teacher's Guide* pages 370–377.

See Website www.greatsource.com/rehand/

Before Reading a Graphic

For use with *Reader's Handbook* pages 538–540

Goals

In this lesson, students learn how to apply Before Reading strategies to graphics.

Teaching Focus

Background

Graphics are used in texts to present important information in an alternative format. The ability to interpret information presented graphically is critical when reading in content areas such as math, science, and social studies. The lessons in this unit will provide students with specific techniques for understanding and evaluating the graphics they encounter when reading.

Instruction

Ask students to thumb through their textbooks to find examples of graphics. Record common types of graphics students find, such as graphs, tables, and charts. Then examine one or two of these graphics as a class. Call attention to key features of graphics. Discuss why the author chose to use one type of graphic rather than another. Explain that in this unit, students will learn more about the different types of graphics, their purposes, and how to read them.

Teaching Approach

Use of the Handbook

Have students read page 538 to learn about the goals of this unit and how to set a purpose for reading graphics. Preview the graphic on page 539 as a class. Model strategies for previewing by thinking aloud as you examine the graphic's title, legend, and labels. Then go over the five-step plan for reading a graphic on page 540 of the handbook.

Extend the Handbook

Provide students with a variety of graphics to explore throughout this unit. Good sources for graphics online include the Gallup Poll (www.gallup.com) and the U.S. Census Bureau (www.census.gov). Ask students to work in pairs to set a purpose, preview, and plan for reading one of the graphics.

Assessment

Ask students:

- What are some common types of graphics? What are the key parts of these graphics?
- How can you use Before Reading strategies to prepare for reading a graphic?

WEEK 27
Lesson 2

Strategy for Graphics: Paraphrase

For use with *Reader's Handbook* pages 539–541, 544

Goals

In this lesson, students use the strategy of paraphrasing to enhance their understanding of the information in graphics.

Teaching Focus

Background

Paraphrasing requires students to read actively. When students paraphrase a graphic, they extract key information and restate it in their own words. This process facilitates both understanding and recall of important information presented in the graphic.

Instruction

Review what students know about paraphrasing. If necessary, remind students that to paraphrase something means to put it in their own words. Point out that paraphrasing is a learning tool they can use with many kinds of texts and in all subject areas. Ask students why paraphrasing might be a useful strategy to use when reading graphics. Lead them to see that paraphrasing can help them understand and remember key information in a graphic.

Teaching Approach

Use of the Handbook

Have students read the information on paraphrasing on pages 540–541. Then have students create a chart with the following headings: Title, My Paraphrase, My Thoughts, Connections. Have students fill in the chart as they paraphrase the graphic on page 539 of the handbook. Then invite students to compare their paraphrases with the sample Paraphrase Chart on page 544. (For more information on paraphrasing, see pages 650–651 of the handbook.)

Extend the Handbook

Have pairs return to the graphic they selected in the previous lesson. Ask them to work together to paraphrase the information in the graphic. Students can use a Double-entry Journal or some other format of their own choosing to restate key information in the graphic.

For additional practice, see pages 194–199 of the *Student Applications Book 7*.

Assessment

Ask students:

- What kind of information does a paraphrase include?
- How can you use paraphrasing to understand the information in a graphic?

WEEK 27 Lesson 3 How Graphics Are Organized

For use with *Reader's Handbook* pages 542–543

Goals

In this lesson, students examine key parts of graphics.

Teaching Focus

Background

Many students have a tendency to glance over graphics quickly. However, to get the most out of graphics, students need to take the time to read them, paying attention to key components. In this lesson, students learn about the importance of features such as axes and legends when reading graphics.

Instruction

Ask students to find examples of graphics in their science or social studies textbooks. Discuss and compare the graphics. Lead students to see that while graphics come in many different formats, they share certain features. Some common features include titles, units, legends, scales, and axes. Explain that learning more about these features and how to use them will help students interpret the information in graphics.

Teaching Approach

Use of the Handbook

Build understanding of how graphics are organized by having students read the information on pages 542–543 of the handbook. Then examine the graphic on page 542 as a class. Invite student volunteers to point out the graphic's title, axes, and legend. Lead students to see that there are two units of measurement in this graphic—years and percent of people.

Extend the Handbook

Ask student pairs to examine the organization of the graphic they have been using throughout the unit. Have them note its title, axes, and legend. Then ask them to identify the units and/or scale the graphic uses. Encourage partners to discuss how focusing on these features enhanced their understanding of the information in the graphic.

Assessment

Ask students:

- Why is it important to take the time to examine elements of graphics, such as legends, units, and scale?
- How does knowing the organization of a graphic help you understand the information in it?

WEEK 27
Lesson 4

Drawing Conclusions from Graphics

For use with *Reader's Handbook* pages 544–547

Goals

In this lesson, students learn how to draw conclusions and read critically to get the most out of graphic sources.

Teaching Focus

Background

Once students can paraphrase the factual information in a graphic, they need to evaluate that information and see what conclusions they can draw from it. In this lesson, students will take their learning a step further as they reflect on and analyze the data presented in graphics.

Instruction

Ask students to reflect on how and why they draw conclusions when reading. Point out that readers can draw conclusions from graphic sources as well. Explain that just as more than one conclusion can be drawn from a passage in a book, different conclusions can be drawn from the data in a graphic. Tell students that in this unit they will learn how to get more out of graphics by reading critically and drawing conclusions.

Teaching Approach

Use of the Handbook

Ask students to review After Reading strategies to use with graphics on pages 544–545 of the handbook. Discuss the importance of reading graphics critically before drawing conclusions from the data. Then have students cover the right-hand column of the example on page 546 with a sheet of paper. Ask them to practice drawing conclusions by responding to the four questions on this page. When they're finished, have students uncover the sample responses and compare their own responses to them. Discuss as a class the different conclusions that can be drawn.

Extend the Handbook

Have students work with partners to apply After Reading strategies to the graphic they have been working with. Then have partners reflect on their learning in this unit. Do students feel more comfortable reading graphics than they did previously? Why or why not? What questions do students still have about graphics?

Assessment

Ask students:

- What can you learn from reading graphics critically?
- Why is it important to draw conclusions from graphic sources?

WEEK 28 Lesson 5 Reading Graphs

For use with *Reader's Handbook* pages 549 and 554

Goals

In this lesson, students learn about bar graphs, line graphs, and the purposes of each.

Teaching Focus

Background

In this unit, students will expand their understanding of graphics by focusing on four common types: graphs, pie charts, tables, and timelines. Bar graphs and line graphs will be explored first. Students will compare and contrast the two graphics to learn what type of information they contain and how to read them effectively.

Instruction

Do a quick poll on a topic of interest to students. For example, you might compare the number of hours students spent on homework each day in third, fifth, and seventh grades. Plot student responses on the board, first using a bar graph, and then a line graph. Then compare the two graphs: How are they similar? How are they different? Which graphic is easier for students to read?

Teaching Approach

Use of the Handbook

Have students read about bar graphs on page 549 and line graphs on page 554. Come together as a class to compare the descriptions and definitions of each. Then examine the examples provided. First have students identify the axes, units, and scale of each graphic. Lead students to see that in bar graphs, the height of each bar shows quantity or amount; in line graphs, the slant of the line shows rate of change. Both types of graphics are useful for seeing relative values, amounts, and changes over time.

Extend the Handbook

Have students look through social studies, science, or math textbooks for examples of line graphs and bar graphs. Ask them to explore one of the graphics using the steps suggested on page 549 of the handbook. Make sure students take the time to write down in their own words what the graphic shows.

Assessment

Ask students:

- What techniques can you use for reading graphs?
- How are bar graphs and line graphs alike?
- How are bar graphs and line graphs different?

WEEK 28 Lesson 6 Reading Pie Charts

For use with *Reader's Handbook* page 558

Goals

In this lesson, students learn about pie charts and strategies for reading them.

Teaching Focus

Background

In pie charts, the fraction of a circle taken by each piece of "pie" indicates what fraction of the whole it represents. Pie charts are useful for showing how things are distributed. To read and understand pie charts, students need to have a basic understanding of fractions and percentages.

Instruction

As in the previous lesson, create a simple pie chart for a topic relevant to students' lives. For example, you might ask students to rank five CDs or TV shows. Then use a pie chart to show how students' preferences are distributed. Ask students to reflect on whether another graphic, such as a bar graph or a line graph, could be used to represent this data. What is the advantage of using a pie chart? Discuss.

Teaching Approach

Use of the Handbook

Have student volunteers read aloud the information on pie charts on page 558. As a class, use the strategies described to interpret the pie chart. Ask students what conclusions they can draw about the diet of nesting bald eagles based on the graphic. What information does the pie chart leave out?

Extend the Handbook

Have students work in small groups to gather data from a textbook or nonfiction book. Then have students present their findings to the rest of the class in the form of a pie chart. Does the data they chose fit the pie chart format? Why or why not?

Assessment

Ask students:

- What is the purpose of a pie chart?
- What techniques can you use to better understand pie charts?

Reading Tables

For use with *Reader's Handbook* pages 559–560

Goals

In this lesson, students explore the characteristics of tables and discuss strategies for reading them.

Teaching Focus

Background

Students have probably encountered tables numerous times, not only in their reading, but in their day-to-day lives. In this lesson, students will examine a variety of tables and learn why these graphics are so commonly used to organize and summarize information. Students will also learn techniques they can use to locate and read information in tables.

Instruction

Provide students with examples of simple tables, such as a multiplication table, the box scores from the sports section, and the nutritional information from a cereal box. Ask students what these tables have in common. Lead students to see that although each table contains very different information, the basic structure (consisting of columns and rows) of all three tables is the same.

Teaching Approach

Use of the Handbook

Have students examine the tables and read the information on pages 559 and 560 of the handbook. Walk students through the six steps for reading a table. Model how to find specific information by using your finger or a ruler to move down rows and across columns. Then discuss why tables are useful tools for summarizing and organizing data and information.

Extend the Handbook

Provide students with several newspapers. Have students skim the newspapers to find examples of tables. (Students might also look for examples of other graphics they've learned about in this unit.) Have students gather in small groups to discuss and compare the information in the graphics they found. Challenge each group to come up with a list of things they learned from one of the graphics.

Assessment

Ask students:

- What distinguishes tables from other types of graphics you've learned about?
- What strategies can you use to read tables effectively?

WEEK 28 Lesson 8 Reading Timelines

For use with *Reader's Handbook* page 561

Goals

In this lesson, students examine the characteristics and purposes of timelines.

Teaching Focus

Background

Timelines are useful for presenting information that has a clear sequential pattern. Timelines show the order in which key events occur. Closer examination of timelines can reveal additional information as well, such as how a series of events leads to a final outcome.

Instruction

Explain to students that timelines show a series of events in sequential order. Have students brainstorm topics of interest that could be organized in this way. Use one of the ideas generated by students to create a sample timeline on the board. Then discuss the timeline, including its format (vertical or horizontal), use of labels to indicate time spans, and the importance of including concise summaries of key events.

Teaching Approach

Use of the Handbook

Have a student volunteer read aloud the top of page 561 of the *Reader's Handbook*. Discuss the timeline ("Rebellion of the Thirteen Colonies") with students, calling attention to its subject and organization. Encourage students to try to identify relationships between the events on the timeline. Then have students finish reading page 561 independently.

Extend the Handbook

Have students create timelines representing a series of events in their own lives. Students might wish to create a timeline covering a specific time period (for example, "The Year I Turned Twelve"). Alternatively, students can create a timeline that examines a series of events leading up to an outcome (for example, "The Season My Baseball Team Made It to the Playoffs"). Invite student volunteers to share their completed timelines with the class.

Assessment

Ask students:

- Compare two of the graphics you learned about in this unit: What is the purpose of each?
- How will you use what you learned in this unit the next time you encounter a graphic in your reading?

Reading Tests and Test Questions

For use with *Reader's Handbook* pages 563–579

Daily Lessons	**Summary***
Lesson 1 **Before Taking a Test**	Work with students to explore how they can use Before Reading strategies to prepare for taking a test.
Lesson 2 **Test-Taking Strategy: Skimming**	Discuss with students the strategy of skimming. Build understanding of how this strategy can be applied in a test-taking situation.
Lesson 3 **Analyzing Test Questions**	Discuss the importance of analyzing test questions. Help students identify different types of test questions.
Lesson 4 **After Reading a Test**	Review the strategies of visualizing and thinking aloud. Have students apply the strategies as they work through challenging test questions.

*Use these notes to help you teach a mini-lesson or to teach a briefer, shorter version of the lessons for more proficient students.

Lesson Resources

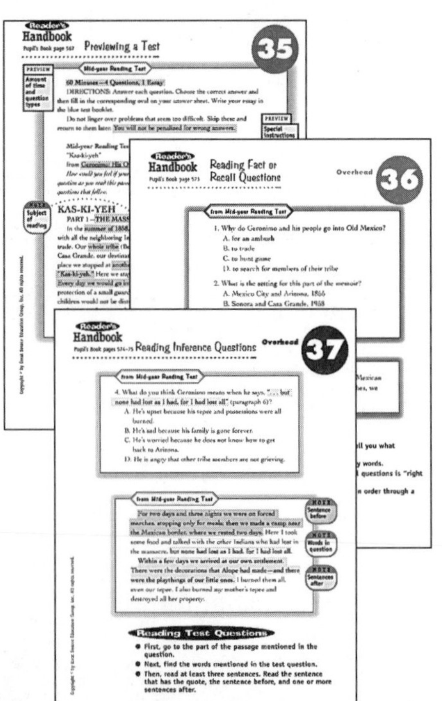

Overheads

For this lesson, use:

Overhead 35: Previewing a Test
Overhead 36: Reading Fact or Recall Questions
Overhead 37: Reading Inference Questions

See *Student Applications Book 7* pages 200–206.

See *Teacher's Guide* pages 379–388.

See Website www.greatsource.com/rehand/

Focus on Essay Tests

For use with *Reader's Handbook* pages 580–583

Daily Lessons	**Summary***
Lesson 1 **Reading Essay Questions**	Explore strategies to use when preparing for and taking essay tests. Have students practice reading and analyzing essay questions.
Lesson 2 **Planning Your Answer**	Discuss the importance of planning before writing an essay. Introduce graphic organizers that will help students plan essay responses.
Lesson 3 **Answering Essay Questions**	Review general strategies for writing effective essays. Ask students to generate an essay in response to a prompt.
Lesson 4 **After Answering Essay Questions**	Discuss with students why it is important to review their written work on essay tests. Develop a checklist students can use to evaluate essays.

*Use these notes to help you teach a mini-lesson or to teach a briefer, shorter version of the lessons for more proficient students.

Lesson Resources

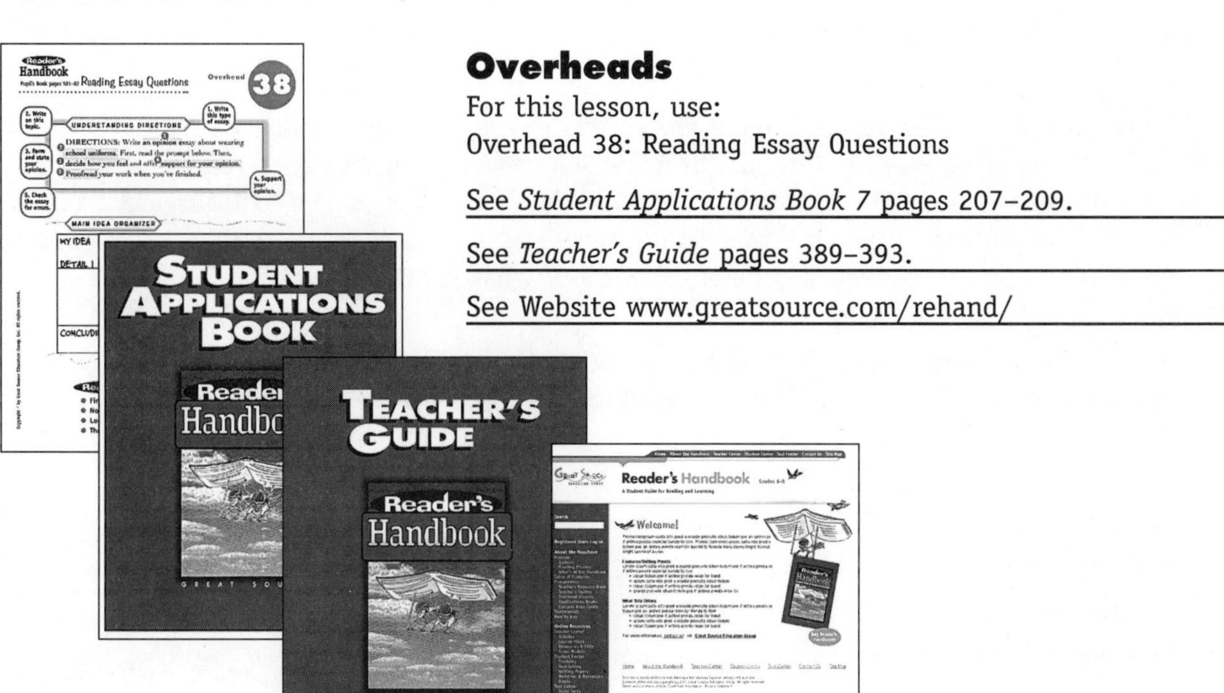

Overheads

For this lesson, use:

Overhead 38: Reading Essay Questions

See *Student Applications Book 7* pages 207–209.

See *Teacher's Guide* pages 389–393.

See Website www.greatsource.com/rehand/

WEEK 29
Lesson 1

Before Taking a Test

For use with *Reader's Handbook* pages 564–570

Goals

In this lesson, students learn how to use Before Reading strategies to prepare for a test.

Teaching Focus

Background

Most students recognize that taking the time to study class notes, their textbooks, and vocabulary will significantly improve their test performance. They may be interested to learn that there are other general strategies that can help them become more successful test-takers as well. In this lesson, students will learn how to apply Before Reading strategies (set a purpose, preview, and plan) to a test-taking situation.

Instruction

Ask students how they prepare for tests. After discussing students' responses, point out that part of being prepared for a test involves knowing what to expect. Help students brainstorm a checklist of questions that will help them prepare for tests. Possible questions include: What kind of material will be covered? Will the test be timed? What kinds of questions will the test include (e.g., multiple choice, short answer, essay)? Lead students to see that using the steps in the Before Reading process can help them find the answers to these questions.

Teaching Approach

Use of the Handbook

Have students read pages 564–565 of the *Reader's Handbook* independently. As a class, compare the Preview Checklist on page 566 to the checklist generated by students above. Work with students to preview the test on pages 567–570. Discuss why it is important to take the time to preview. Lead students to see that previewing gives test-takers a general overview of what is on the test.

Extend the Handbook

Have students return to the test on pages 567–570 of the handbook. Ask them to "prepare" for the test by responding to each of the items on the preview checklist (page 566). Then encourage students to jot down two or three other key pieces of information they learned from previewing this test.

Assessment

Ask students:

- What strategies can help you prepare for a test?
- What do you hope to learn about taking tests from this unit?

WEEK 29
Lesson 2

Test-Taking Strategy: Skimming

For use with *Reader's Handbook* pages 567–571

Goals

In this lesson, students utilize the reading strategy of skimming to identify important information on tests.

Teaching Focus

Background

Once students have read the questions on a test, they need to identify key sentences and passages that contain the answers. With this purpose in mind, students can skim to locate information quickly. Because skimming enables students to "screen out" irrelevant details and information, it saves time and leads to more efficient test-taking.

Instruction

Find out what students know about the strategy of skimming. Remind students that skimming involves quickly glancing through a text. Ask students how and why they use this strategy during reading. Then ask: How do you think skimming can help you answer the questions on a test? Discuss students' responses.

Teaching Approach

Use of the Handbook

Ask a student volunteer to read aloud the information on skimming when reading a test (page 571 of the *Reader's Handbook*). If necessary, have students review general information on skimming (see pages 656–657 of the handbook.) Work with students to compare and contrast the following processes: skimming for general ideas, skimming for specific information, and skimming on tests.

Extend the Handbook

Have students review the test questions on pages 569–570 of the handbook. Then ask them to return to the sample test and skim to find key information related to the questions. Encourage students to use sticky notes or some other method to highlight the sentences or passages that contain the relevant information or details.

Assessment

Ask students:

- What is the purpose of skimming a test?
- What is the difference between skimming for general ideas and skimming when reading a test? Explain.

WEEK 29 Lesson 3 Analyzing Test Questions

For use with *Reader's Handbook* pages 572–576

Goals

In this lesson, students learn how to analyze different types of test questions.

Teaching Focus

Background

In this lesson, students will review the two main types of questions they are likely to encounter on tests. The first type (fact or recall questions) tests students' ability to locate key information. The second type (inference or conclusion questions) requires students to synthesize, analyze, or integrate ideas. Students generally find the second type, which requires higher-order thinking, more challenging.

Instruction

Have student volunteers define the words *fact, recall, inference,* and *conclusion.* Build understanding of how these terms can be applied to different types of test questions. Point out that with fact questions, students can find the answers right in the text or passage. Inference questions, however, require students to reflect on or extend the information provided. Revisit the five test questions on pages 569–570. Ask students to identify which are fact/recall questions and which are inference/conclusion questions.

Teaching Approach

Use of the Handbook

Have students read pages 572–574 in the handbook. Ask a student volunteer to briefly summarize the section on fact/recall test questions. Ask another volunteer to summarize the information on inference/conclusion questions. Compare the strategies for answering fact or recall questions with those for reading inference or conclusion questions. Then have students continue reading through page 576.

Extend the Handbook

Ask students to revisit the sample test on pages 567–570 and apply the techniques discussed in this section to it. Encourage students to use the strategies to answer at least one fact/recall question and one inference/conclusion question. Come together as a class and discuss how these techniques affected students' understanding of the material.

For more practice, see pages 200–206 of the *Student Applications Book 7.*

Assessment

Ask students:

- What are the two main types of test questions?
- How can analyzing a test question help you answer it correctly?

WEEK 29 Lesson 4 After Reading a Test

For use with *Reader's Handbook* pages 576–579

Goals

In this lesson, students examine the role visualizing and thinking aloud play in answering test questions successfully.

Teaching Focus

Background

Students need to utilize their time on tests wisely. It's important to save time at the end of a test to review work, check answers, and address any remaining questions. This is particularly true for students who opt for the strategy of "answering the easy ones first." In this lesson, students will learn how to review their work at the end of a test and revisit challenging questions with some new strategies.

Instruction

Discuss with students what they do when they encounter difficult questions on tests: Do they skip over them? Do they keep working until they figure out the answer? Do they guess? Point out that it is beneficial for students to avoid spending too much time on any one question; then, students can use the time remaining at the end of the test to revisit tough questions. Explain that there are strategies students can rely on to help them return to challenging questions and answer them correctly.

Teaching Approach

Use of the Handbook

Have students read the information under "Pause and Reflect" and "Reread" on pages 576–577 of the *Reader's Handbook*. Then walk students through the sample on pages 577–578. Model the strategies of thinking aloud and visualizing as you work through the sample. Then discuss why these two strategies are helpful when revisiting difficult test questions. Have students finish reading this section on their own.

Extend the Handbook

Have students work with partners to practice the After Reading strategies discussed in this lesson. Ask pairs to revisit one of the more challenging test questions on pages 569–570 of the handbook. Invite partners to practice visualizing and thinking aloud as they work through the question.

Assessment

Ask students:

- Why is it important to apply After Reading strategies in a test-taking situation?
- How can you use the strategies of thinking aloud and visualizing to answer difficult test questions?

WEEK 30 Lesson 1 Reading Essay Questions

For use with *Reader's Handbook* pages 580–581

Goals

In this lesson, students learn to read and analyze essay questions for key information.

Teaching Focus

Background

Essay tests require students to utilize reading, thinking, and writing skills. This lesson will emphasize the importance of taking the time to read and analyze essay questions carefully before writing. The lessons that follow will provide students with strategies for planning, writing, and reviewing their responses to essay questions on tests.

Instruction

Ask students how essay questions are different from other types of test questions. Students might note characteristics such as the following: Essay questions take longer; they are answered in sentences or paragraphs; they include the student's own thoughts and ideas (as well as facts or details). Students might also note that they find essay questions difficult or that they dislike this type of test. If so, explore the reasons for this. Then point out that there are strategies students can use to prepare for and improve their performance on essay tests.

Teaching Approach

Use of the Handbook

Have students read pages 580–581 in the handbook. Come together as a class to review the purpose of previewing before answering an essay question. Have a student volunteer read aloud the sample instructions on page 581. Emphasize the importance of reading questions carefully. Then invite volunteers to identify key details in the sample instructions (for example, the type of essay, the essay's topic, and the essay's organization).

Extend the Handbook

For additional practice, see pages 207–209 of the *Student Applications Book 7.*

Assessment

Ask students:

- Why should you take the time to read an essay question carefully before answering it?
- Do you find taking essay tests easy or difficult? If so, what might you do to make them easier for you?

WEEK 30 Lesson 2 Planning Your Answer

For use with *Reader's Handbook* page 582

Goals

In this lesson, students learn how to plan before writing an essay.

Teaching Focus

Background

There are a variety of techniques that will help students prepare for and take essay tests. Although students may feel pressed for time in a test situation, they need to take a few minutes to gather their thoughts and organize ideas before responding to an essay question. Taking the time to think *before* writing will improve the overall quality of students' essays and improve their test performance.

Instruction

Ask student volunteers to share what they do before writing an essay for class. List their ideas on the board. Point out that on an essay test, students have a limited amount of time. Ask students how they could adapt the prewriting process to a test-taking situation. Lead students to see the importance of planning, even if only briefly, before responding to questions on an essay test.

Teaching Approach

Use of the Handbook

Have students read page 582 of the *Reader's Handbook* on their own. Walk through the Main Idea Organizer as a class. Point out that this is one way of organizing ideas before writing an essay. Brainstorm other methods students can use to plan responses to essay questions. Outlines, Summary Notes, and Webs are all good tools students can use to plan and organize essays.

Extend the Handbook

What are students' opinions on the issue of school uniforms? Ask students to reflect on the prompt provided on page 581 of the handbook. Then have students create an Outline, a Web, or a Main Idea Organizer as a framework for organizing their thoughts on this topic.

For more practice, see pages 207–209 of the *Student Applications Book 7*.

Assessment

Ask students:

- Why is it useful to plan before writing a response to an essay question?
- What strategies can you use to help you plan your answers to essay questions?

WEEK 30
Lesson 3

Answering Essay Questions

For use with *Reader's Handbook* pages 582

Goals

In this lesson, students explore strategies for answering essay questions.

Teaching Focus

Background

Essay tests are very different from other types of tests. The process of answering an essay question requires students to process information, perceive relationships, synthesize ideas, and present thinking in a clear and organized manner. In this lesson, students will learn specific strategies that will help them write more effective essays and boost their scores on essay tests.

Instruction

Ask student volunteers to share techniques they currently use when writing essays. Record students' ideas on the board. Help students determine which techniques would be useful in a testing situation. For example, while revisions can (and should) be made on essay tests, there is generally not enough time for students to draft and rewrite an entire essay. Point out that in this lesson, students will review and develop a checklist of specific techniques they can use to improve their performance on essay tests.

Teaching Approach

Use of the Handbook

Work with students to develop a checklist of techniques for essay tests. Discuss the importance of beginning with a clear opinion statement. (Remind students that statements that include words such as *all, never, best,* and *worst* are difficult to support.) Then review other techniques for writing essays, such as supporting an opinion with facts and details, sticking to the topic, and ending with a concluding statement. Discuss the importance of each step on the checklist.

Extend the Handbook

Have students use the techniques they learned in this lesson to write a brief essay in response to the prompt on page 581 of the handbook. Students may want to begin by reviewing the graphic organizers they created in Lesson 2 of this unit. Ask students to share and compare their completed essays in small groups.

Assessment

Ask students:

- What techniques can you use to improve your performance on essay tests?
- Which techniques do you think will be most helpful to you? Explain your choice.

WEEK 30
Lesson 4

After Answering Essay Questions

For use with *Reader's Handbook* pages 583

Goals

In this lesson, students examine strategies for reviewing their work on essay tests.

Teaching Focus

Background

As with other types of tests, it is important for students to check their work after completing an essay test. Many students do not leave enough time to review their responses on essay tests for errors and to make necessary revisions. In this lesson, students will explore the importance of this final step in the process that will help them answer essay tests questions effectively.

Instruction

Review with students what they have learned about essay tests. Then emphasize the importance of applying After Reading steps to essay tests. Review steps such as *reflect* and *reread*. Invite the class to brainstorm how they might use these steps to review and improve their performance on essay tests.

Teaching Approach

Use of the Handbook

Have student volunteers read the information on page 583 of the handbook. As a class, invite students to use what they know about writing essays to expand the list of questions on this page. For example, students might include ideas such as:

- Does the introductory statement take a clear position on the question?
- Are examples or details provided to clarify and support each point?
- Does the essay include transitions?
- Is the argument persuasive?

Extend the Handbook

Have students return to the essays they wrote in the previous lesson. Ask them to review their work, using the questions on page 583 of the handbook and those generated by the class as a guide. Then have students revise their essays as necessary to meet all of the criteria set by the class.

Assessment

Ask students:

- What steps can you apply to review and revise your work on essay tests?
- What is the most important thing you learned about essay tests from reading this unit? Explain your answer.

Focus on Math Tests

For use with *Reader's Handbook* pages 593–597

Daily Lessons	**Summary***
Lesson 1 **Reading Math Tests: An Overview**	Help students build background about and activate prior knowledge of math tests. Have students set goals for reading.
Lesson 2 **Before Taking Math Tests**	Work with students to develop their understanding of strategies they can use before taking math tests.
Lesson 3 **Reading Math Tests**	Examine with students During Reading steps to use when reading challenging problems on math tests.
Lesson 4 **Solving Problems Involving Graphics**	Work with students to examine techniques for solving problems on math tests that involve graphics, including figures, graphs, charts, and drawings.

*Use these notes to help you teach a mini-lesson or to teach a briefer, shorter version of the lessons for more proficient students.

Lesson Resources

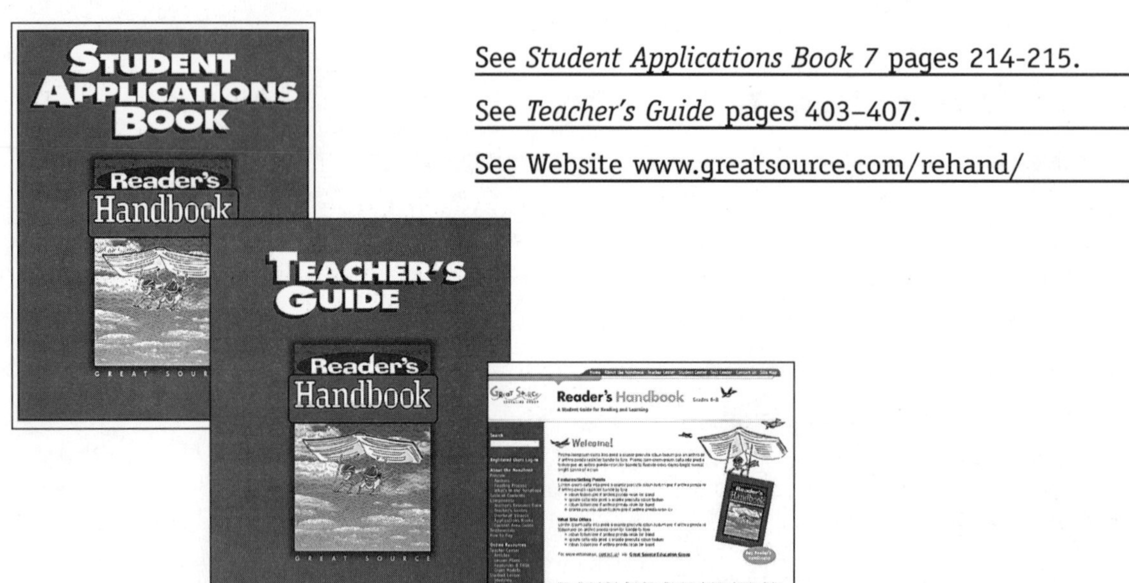

See *Student Applications Book 7* pages 214-215.

See *Teacher's Guide* pages 403–407.

See Website www.greatsource.com/rehand/

Focus on Science Tests

For use with *Reader's Handbook* pages 598–605

Daily Lessons	**Summary***
Lesson 1 **Reading Science Tests: An Overview**	Work with students to build background about and activate prior knowledge of science tests.
Lesson 2 **Before Reading Science Tests**	Help students examine Before Reading steps they can use to help them prepare for science tests.
Lesson 3 **Reading Science Tests**	Build students' understanding of techniques for reading science test questions involving charts or tables.
Lesson 4 **Reading Science Tests (continued)**	Have students explore techniques for reading diagrams and graphs on science tests.

*Use these notes to help you teach a mini-lesson or to teach a briefer, shorter version of the lessons for more proficient students.

Lesson Resources

See *Student Applications Book 7* pages 216–217

See *Teacher's Guide* pages 408–412.

See Website www.greatsource.com/rehand/

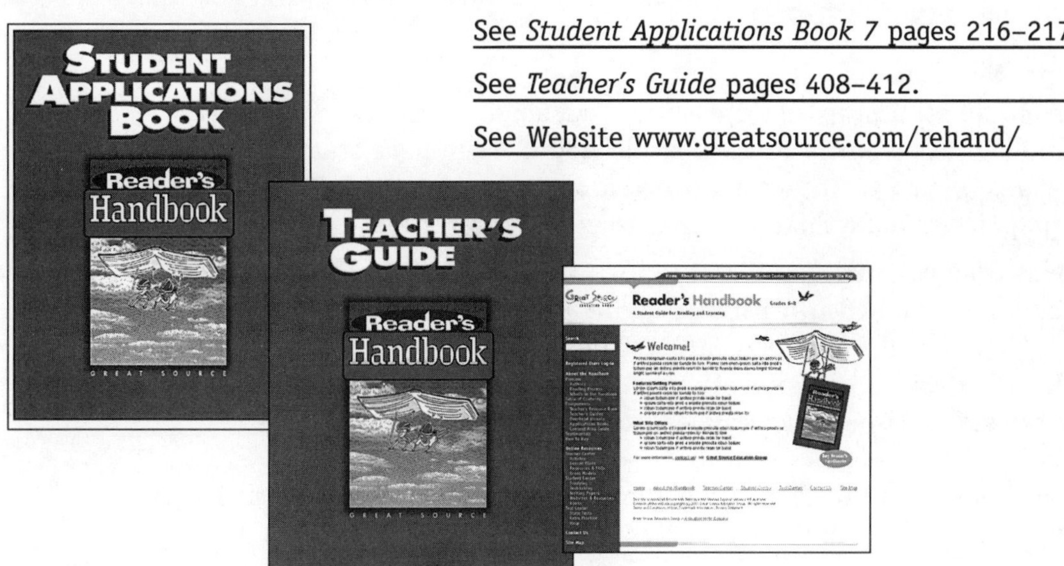

WEEK 31
Lesson 1

Reading Math Tests: An Overview

For use with *Reader's Handbook* pages 593–597

Goals

In this lesson, students build background about and activate prior knowledge of math tests.

Teaching Focus

Background

Throughout the *Reader's Handbook*, students learn how to utilize reading methods to prepare for, read, and reflect on different texts. In this unit, students will apply these tools and strategies to reading math tests. Reviewing active reading methods will help students understand and retain the steps in the reading process.

Instruction

Ask students what they know about math tests. How do they study for math tests? Do they expect to find mostly multiple-choice questions, word problems, or equations? Discuss what students do before and after taking a math test. Then compare math tests to other content area tests. Explain that in this section, students will learn additional techniques for taking math tests effectively.

Teaching Approach

Use of the Handbook

Invite students to set a purpose for reading. They might write their purposes in their reading journals or share them in small groups. Then have students preview pages 593–597. Remind them to skim the section, paying particular attention to headings, graphics, and anything else that they find interesting.

Extend the Handbook

Have students reflect on their math test-taking ability in their journals. Questions to consider, "How would I rate my math test-taking skills? What would I like to improve about my ability to take math tests? What is my biggest strength when taking math tests? What are my weaknesses?"

Encourage students to think about what they do before, during, and after taking math tests as they reflect on these questions. After completing the activity, have students return to their purposes for reading this section and modify them as necessary, based on their reflections.

Assessment

Ask students:

- What do you hope to learn from this section of the handbook?
- What did you gain from previewing this section?

WEEK 31
Lesson 2

Before Taking Math Tests

For use with *Reader's Handbook* pages 593–594

Goals

In this lesson, students develop understanding of steps to apply before taking math tests.

Teaching Focus

Background

In large part, what students do before taking a math test, or any test for that matter, determines their success. Applying the familiar Before Reading steps will help students prepare for math tests effectively.

Instruction

Review what students do before taking a math test. Write their ideas on the board. Ask student volunteers to share what they learned about this stage of the math test-taking process from their preview. Talk about how students might apply the Before Reading steps of setting a purpose, previewing, and planning to take math tests.

Teaching Approach

Use of the Handbook

Have a student volunteer read aloud the top of page 593 of the *Reader's Handbook*. Compare the list of goals to students' own goals for reading this section. Work through the rest of page 593 with the class. Discuss steps for remembering mathematical formulas and other information needed for math tests. Continue reading the top of page 594. Talk about the purpose for dividing a math test into two parts.

Extend the Handbook

Gather copies of math tests for students to work with throughout this section. Have students preview a test, using the system described on page 594. Remind them to star the easier questions.

For additional practice, see pages 214–215 of the *Student Applications Book 7*.

Assessment

Ask students:

- How do the prereading steps described in the handbook differ from what you do currently to prepare for a math test? Which approach do you think is more effective? Explain.
- How would you explain the purpose of Before Reading steps to a new student in the class?

WEEK 31
Lesson 3

Reading Math Tests

For use with *Reader's Handbook* pages 594-596

Goals

In this lesson, students learn techniques to use when reading challenging problems on a math test.

Teaching Focus

Background

The types of questions on math tests vary from straight numerical problems to lengthy word problems. Having a repertoire of techniques on hand will enable students to tackle different kinds of problems they encounter more effectively. This lesson concentrates on methods for answering the more challenging problems found on math tests.

Instruction

Ask students to reflect on what they do currently when they take a math test. Do they have a method for answering the questions? How effective are they at tackling difficult problems? Invite volunteers to share their techniques. Then ask students how they might use what they've learned about the During Reading stage of the reading process when they take math tests.

Teaching Approach

Use of the Handbook

Read aloud or have a student volunteer read aloud the first paragraph under During Reading on page 594 of the *Reader's Handbook*. Discuss the purpose of answering the starred (easier) problems first. Then divide the class into four groups. Have each group read and discuss one of the following techniques: Eliminating Wrong Answers (page 594), Estimating the Answer (page 595), Visualizing the Answer (page 595), and Trying Easier Choices First (page 596). Invite groups to present their technique to the class. Encourage groups to demonstrate the technique by thinking aloud as they apply it to a sample problem.

Extend the Handbook

Encourage students to apply the technique described in the handbook as they work through problems in their math textbooks. Have them reflect on the process: Which techniques most effective? Which do students already use? Do those techniques students use change depending on the type or difficulty of the problem?

Assessment

Ask students:

- Describe the four techniques discussed in this section. How would you decide which one to apply first when faced with a challenging math problem?
- Has exploring these During Reading techniques changed the way you will read math tests? Why or why not?

WEEK 31
Lesson 4

Solving Problems Involving Graphics

For use with *Reader's Handbook* pages 596–597

Goals

In this lesson, students learn strategies for solving problems on math tests that involve graphics, including figures, graphs, charts, and drawings.

Teaching Focus

Background

Many students are intimidated by math problems involving graphics. Arming students with specific strategies for working through these types of problems will increase both their self-confidence and their ability to answer this type of math test question successfully.

Instruction

Ask students what types of math questions they find easy and what types they find more challenging. Point out that many students find problems involving graphics, such as figures and graphs, intimidating, even though these might actually be simple problems to solve. Explain that in this lesson students will learn a four-step plan that will help them tackle these types of problems and reduce their anxiety when they encounter them.

Teaching Approach

Use of the Handbook

Have students work in small groups to read and discuss the steps for solving problems involving graphics on pages 596–597 of the *Reader's Handbook*. Encourage groups to talk about the purpose of each step and what they think of this plan overall. Have each group summarize their discussion for the rest of the class.

Extend the Handbook

Have students apply the strategies discussed in this and the previous lesson to the math test that they have been using throughout the unit. Encourage students to reflect on the process in their reading journals. Questions they might consider: Which strategy worked best for me? How did the four-step plan help me solve problems involving graphics? Do these types of problems intimidate me? If so, will using this plan help ease my concerns? Why or why not?

Assessment

Ask students:

- Describe the four-step plan for solving problems involving graphics.
- How has this unit changed the way you read or think about taking math tests? Explain.

WEEK 32 Lesson 1 Reading Science Tests: An Overview

For use with *Reader's Handbook* pages 598–605

Goals

In this lesson, students build background about and activate prior knowledge of science tests.

Teaching Focus

Background

Many of the strategies proficient test-takers rely on are discussed in other sections of the handbook. Understanding specialized vocabulary (Week 34), strategies for answering essay questions (Week 30), and other general test-taking techniques foster student success across the curriculum. This unit, however, concentrates on more specific strategies for reading science tests.

Instruction

Ask students to reflect on what they know about science tests. What sort of questions do they expect to find on a science test? How are science tests similar to other content area tests? How are they different? What strategies do they use when they read a science test? Explain that in this unit students will explore a variety of strategies that will help them read and take science tests more effectively.

Teaching Approach

Use of the Handbook

Read aloud or have a student volunteer read aloud the section goals on page 598 of the *Reader's Handbook*. Walk through the three goals of the section, and then invite students to brainstorm and write down their own goals for reading. Have students work in pairs to preview the remainder of the section (pages 598–605). As a class, discuss what students learned about science tests and this section of the handbook from previewing.

Extend the Handbook

Invite students to think about their past experiences taking science tests. How well did they do? Did they perform as well as they could have? If not, what could they do to improve their performance? Invite students to review their goals for reading and modify them as needed, based on their reflections.

Assessment

Ask students:

- What strategies do you use currently before, during, and after reading science tests? How effective are they?
- What is your main purpose for reading this section of the handbook? Explain.

WEEK 32 Lesson 2 Before Reading Science Tests

For use with *Reader's Handbook* pages 598–599

Goals

In this lesson, students explore Before Reading strategies they can use to help them prepare for a science test.

Teaching Focus

Background

As with all content area tests, the time to prepare for a test is not the night before, but rather every day. But even students who study daily will benefit from this lesson that offers practical tips for preparing for a science test. Students will review strategies such as skimming their textbook for key terms and previewing the test before starting it.

Instruction

Discuss what students do before taking a science test. How do they prepare for the test? What strategies do they use? Invite volunteers to share their techniques with the rest of the class. Explain that in this lesson students will learn four tips for preparing to take science tests.

Teaching Approach

Use of the Handbook

Have students work in pairs to read pages 598–599 of the *Reader's Handbook*. Encourage pairs to discuss each tip as they read, focusing on its purpose. Come together as a class and discuss the reading. Answer any questions students have about the tips; then discuss how these tips can help them prepare for a science test.

Extend the Handbook

Divide the class into four groups. Assign each group one of the Before Reading tips. Either individually or as a group, have students apply the tip to a chapter from their science textbook (tips 1–3), or a sample science test (tip 4). After completing the activity, ask students to discuss how well the tip worked for them.

For additional practice, see pages 216–217 of the *Student Applications Book 7*.

Assessment

Ask students:

- Which tip do you think is the most helpful? Explain your choice.
- What is the point of previewing a science test? How can previewing help you read a science test effectively?

WEEK 32 Lesson 3 Reading Science Tests

For use with *Reader's Handbook* pages 600–601

Goals

In this lesson, students learn strategies for reading science test questions involving charts or tables.

Teaching Focus

Background

Test questions involving graphics, such as charts and tables, can look overwhelming at first. In order to answer the question correctly, students need to understand the information presented in the graphic. This lesson offers specific techniques for reading and interpreting science test questions involving charts and tables.

Instruction

Review with students the various types of questions they would expect to see on a science test (see Lesson 1). Lead students to see that often science tests include tables, charts, and other kinds of graphics. Review strategies for reading graphics. (See pages 538–561 of the *Reader's Handbook* for more information on reading graphics.) Invite students to share strategies they use currently when they come across a table or chart on a science test. Explain that in this lesson they will learn a three-step technique for reading charts and tables on science tests.

Teaching Approach

Use of the Handbook

Read aloud or have a student volunteer read aloud the information on the top of page 600 of the *Reader's Handbook*. Then walk through the three steps for reading a chart or table at the bottom of this page. Think aloud as you work through the sample chart on page 601. Focus your think-aloud on how you use the three steps from page 600 to help you read the chart and answer the question correctly. Invite student volunteers to think aloud as they work through the sample table at the bottom on page 601. Discuss the effectiveness of the three steps for reading charts and graphs on science tests.

Extend the Handbook

Have students work in pairs to apply these steps to questions on one of the science tests they used in Lesson 2. Ask pairs to take turns thinking aloud as they read the chart or graph. Encourage pairs to talk about how using these techniques increased their understanding.

Assessment

Ask students:

- Describe the three-step technique for reading charts and tables on science tests.
- Has this lesson changed the way you will approach science test questions involving charts and tables? Why or why not?

WEEK 32 Lesson 4 Reading Science Tests (continued)

For use with *Reader's Handbook* pages 602–605

Goals

In this lesson, students explore techniques for reading diagrams and graphs on science tests.

Teaching Focus

Background

Like charts and tables, diagrams and graphs are often found on science tests. The three-step plan outlined in this section will foster students success when they encounter test questions involving these types of graphics. (See pages 538–561 of the *Reader's Handbook* for more information on reading graphics.)

Instruction

Review the tips for reading charts and tables on science tests explored in the previous lesson. Explain that in this lesson students will explore similar techniques for reading diagrams and graphs. Invite students to share strategies they use currently for reading diagrams and graphs on science tests. How are the strategies similar? How are they different?

Teaching Approach

Use of the Handbook

Walk students through the steps for reading a diagram on page 602 of the *Reader's Handbook*. Think aloud as you explore the sample test questions and diagram on the bottom of page 602. Repeat this procedure with the information on how to read a graph on page 603. Scaffold students' learning by asking them to work through the sample bar graph question on their own. Encourage them to jot down their thoughts as they work, using your think-aloud as a guide. Conclude by having students read the rest of the section (pages 604–605) on their own.

Extend the Handbook

For additional practice reading science tests, have students work through pages 216–217 of the *Student Applications Book 7*.

Assessment

Ask students:

- Did you meet your goals for reading this section of the handbook? Why or why not?
- What is the most surprising thing you learned from this section of the handbook? Explain.

Improving Vocabulary

For use with *Reader's Handbook* pages 608–620

Daily Lessons	**Summary***
Lesson 1 **Learning New Words**	Work with students to learn strategies for expanding their vocabulary. Have students reflect on their vocabulary-building strategies.
Lesson 2 **Boosting Vocabulary**	Have students learn and play word games and other activities for building vocabulary.
Lesson 3 **Context Clues**	Examine strategies for using context clues to help students unlock the meaning of unfamiliar words.
Lesson 4 **Context Clues (continued)**	Continue exploring strategies for using context clues to determine word meaning.

*Use these notes to help you teach a mini-lesson or to teach a briefer, shorter version of the lessons for more proficient students.

Lesson Resources

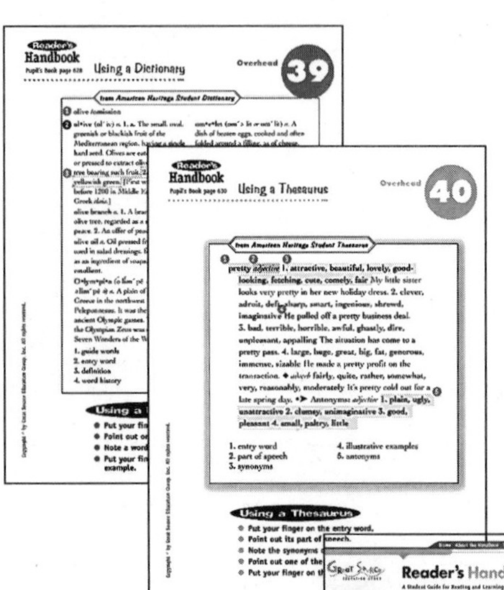

Overheads

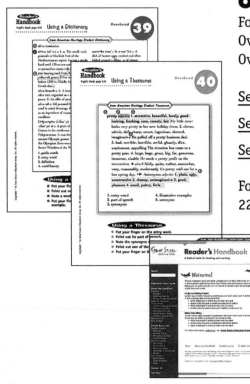

For this lesson, use:
Overhead 39: Using a Dictionary
Overhead 40: Using a Thesaurus

See *Student Applications Book 7* pages 218–223.

See *Teacher's Guide* pages 414–428.

See Website www.greatsource.com/rehand/

For more practice, see also *Sourcebook* Grade 7, pages 220–229, 230–238; *Daybook* Grade 7, pages 195–196.

Improving Vocabulary (continued)

For use with *Reader's Handbook* pages 621–639

Daily Lessons	**Summary***
Lesson 5 **Understanding Roots, Prefixes, and Suffixes**	Review and expand students' understanding of how to use word parts to determine the meaning of unfamiliar words.
Lesson 6 **Reading Dictionaries and Thesauruses**	Work with students to expand their understanding of how to use dictionaries and thesauruses effectively. Have students create a slang dictionary.
Lesson 7 **Understanding Specialized Terms**	Help students learn strategies for determining the meaning of specialized terms.
Lesson 8 **Understanding Analogies**	Work with students to explore strategies for reading and understanding analogies. Have students work in pairs to create their own analogies.

*Use these notes to help you teach a mini-lesson or to teach a briefer, shorter version of the lessons for more proficient students.

Lesson Resources

Overheads

For this lesson, use:
Overhead 39: Using a Dictionary
Overhead 40: Using a Thesaurus

See *Student Applications Book 7* pages 218–223.

See *Teacher's Guide* pages 414–428.

See Website www.greatsource.com/rehand/

For more practice, see also *Sourcebook* Grade 7, pages 220–229, 230–238; *Daybook* Grade 7, pages 195–196.

WEEK 33 Lesson 1 Learning New Words

For use with *Reader's Handbook* pages 608–613

Goals

In this lesson, students learn strategies for expanding their vocabulary.

Teaching Focus

Background

Readers with a variety of strategies for learning new words are better able to construct meaning from text and to articulate that meaning. In this unit, students will learn strategies that will help them actively determine the meaning of unfamiliar words. Explicit instruction will help students become stronger, more independent readers.

Instruction

Discuss with students the advantages of having a large vocabulary. How would students describe the relationship between vocabulary and reading comprehension? Point out that a large vocabulary makes reading comprehension much easier, since readers can focus on the meaning of entire passages rather than the meaning of individual words. Ask students to describe what they do when they come across an unfamiliar word. List their strategies on the board. Explain that in this lesson they will learn a variety of other strategies for learning new words.

Teaching Approach

Use of the Handbook

Have students explore strategies for improving their vocabulary by reading and discussing pages 608–613 of the *Reader's Handbook* in small groups. Have groups apply these strategies by choosing unfamiliar words from a content area textbook and recording them in their journals, using the information in the handbook as a guide. After completing the activity, invite groups to discuss how the strategies affected their understanding of the unfamiliar words. Have groups summarize their discussion for the rest of the class.

Extend the Handbook

Have students reflect on their vocabulary-building strategies in their journals. Questions to consider: What do I do when I come across an unfamiliar word? What strategies do I have at my disposal for unlocking the word's meaning? How effective are my strategies? What would I like to improve about my vocabulary-building abilities?

Assessment

Ask students:

- What do you hope to learn from this section of the handbook?
- What did you gain from reading this section?

WEEK 33 Lesson 2 Boosting Vocabulary

For use with *Reader's Handbook* pages 613–614

Goals

In this lesson, students learn word games and other activities for building vocabulary.

Teaching Focus

Background

Developing vocabulary involves not only decoding words, but also conceptualizing their meaning. Vocabulary development is a lifelong process. Word-building strategies can also be fun: word games, scavenger hunts, and simply reading for pleasure help improve vocabulary.

Instruction

Explain to students that in this lesson they will learn about activities that can help them improve their vocabulary. Invite students to predict what these activities might be. List their predictions on the board. Ask students if they would be surprised to know that the number one way to enrich their vocabulary is to read for fun. Invite students to read this section to find out more about this and other ways they can boost their vocabulary.

Teaching Approach

Use of the Handbook

Divide the class into four groups. Assign each group one of the four vocabulary-enriching activities on pages 613–614 of the *Reader's Handbook*. Ask groups to "teach" their activity to the rest of the class. As a class, discuss the four activities. How effective do students think these activities are for increasing vocabulary? Challenge students to think of additional activities that might boost vocabulary, and add them to the list.

Extend the Handbook

Invite students to work in small groups to invent a vocabulary booster word game. Have groups choose five or six vocabulary words from a current content area textbook or class novel, and then create a vocabulary booster word game for them. Games could be modified versions of existing word games or something completely inventive. Invite groups to share (and play) their games with one another.

For additional practice, see pages 220–221 of the *Student Applications Book 7*.

Assessment

Ask students:

- Are you surprised that reading for fun is the number one way to boost your vocabulary? Why or why not?
- How will you use this lesson to help you boost your vocabulary?

WEEK 33 Lesson 3 Context Clues

For use with *Reader's Handbook* pages 615–618

Goals

In this lesson, students learn strategies for using context clues to help them unlock the meaning of unfamiliar words.

Teaching Focus

Background

Fluent readers have a repertoire of strategies for making informed predictions about the meaning of unfamiliar words; most of these strategies involve the use of context clues. The next two lessons in this unit introduce a variety of contextual strategies students can use to help get a sense of an unknown word's meaning.

Instruction

Write the phrase *Context Clues* on the board. Ask students if they have ever heard this phrase. If so, invite student volunteers to define it. If not, explain that context clues are hints in the text that give readers a sense of what an unfamiliar word means. Point out that in this and the next lesson students will learn eight strategies for using context clues to unlock the meaning of unfamiliar words.

Teaching Approach

Use of the Handbook

Read aloud or have student volunteers read aloud page 615 of the *Reader's Handbook* for general information on context clues. Think aloud as you read the excerpt from *Lyddie* on the bottom of page 615. Focus your think-aloud on how you use context clues to figure out the meaning of *impeccable*. Have students read the top of page 616 for more information on using context clues. Then have students work in pairs to read about the first four kinds of context clues (pages 616–618). Have pairs take turns thinking aloud as they use context clues to figure out the meaning of unfamiliar words in the samples.

Extend the Handbook

Have pairs look through textbooks, novels, or other reading material for examples of the four kinds of context clues described in this lesson: definition or synonym, concrete examples, contrast clues, and description clues. Challenge pairs to find at least one example of each kind.

Assessment

Ask students:

- How can context clues help you determine the meaning of unfamiliar words?
- Describe the four kinds of context clues described in this section.

WEEK 33 Lesson 4 Context Clues (continued)

For use with *Reader's Handbook* pages 618–620

Goals

In this lesson, students explore four more kinds of context clues to determine the meaning of unfamiliar words.

Teaching Focus

Background

This lesson continues the instruction begun in Lesson 3 on the importance of using context clues to unlock the meaning of unfamiliar words. Recognizing the various types of context clues and learning techniques for using them encourage students to become active participants in the meaning-making process.

Instruction

Review the four kinds of context clues students learned about in Lesson 3. Discuss how understanding the different kinds of context clues can help students use them to determine the meaning of an unknown word. Explain that in this lesson students will learn four more kinds of context clues. Do students have any predictions about what these kinds might be?

Teaching Approach

Use of the Handbook

Divide the class into four groups. Assign each group one of the following: Words or Phrases That Modify (page 618), Conjunctions Showing Relationships and Connecting Ideas (page 619), Repeating Words (page 619), and Unstated or Implied Meanings (page 620). Ask each group to explain their context clue to the rest of the class. Challenge groups to include an example sentence containing their context clue type in their presentation.

Extend the Handbook

For additional practice using the eight kinds of context clues discussed in this section of the *Reader's Handbook*, have students choose eight vocabulary words from a content area textbook. Ask students to write eight sentences; each sentence should include a vocabulary word and one of the eight kinds of context clues. Invite students to exchange sentences with a partner and think aloud as they use the context clues to try to determine the meaning of the vocabulary word.

Assessment

Ask students:

- Describe the four kinds of context clues described in this section of the handbook.
- How will you apply what you have learned about context clues the next time you come across an unfamiliar word?

WEEK 34
Lesson 5

Understanding Roots, Prefixes, and Suffixes

For use with *Reader's Handbook* pages 621–625

Goals

In this lesson, students review and expand their understanding of how to use word parts to determine the meaning of unfamiliar words.

Teaching Focus

Background

Understanding word parts (roots, prefixes, and suffixes) is another tool for developing a rich vocabulary. With a basic understanding of word parts, structural analysis can be a powerful addition to students' vocabulary-building repertoire.

Instruction

List the following word parts on the board: *-ful, un-, port*. Discuss with students what these word parts mean. Work with students to brainstorm words containing these word parts. List their ideas on the board. Lead students to see that by knowing the meaning of roots like *port*, prefixes like *un-*, and suffixes like *–ful*, students can figure out the meaning of any number of words.

Teaching Approach

Use of the Handbook

Have students meet in small groups to work through pages 621–623 of the *Reader's Handbook*. Challenge groups to add more words to the examples found in this section. Conclude the lesson by having students read pages 624–625 independently.

Extend the Handbook

For more help learning root words, prefixes, suffixes, have students 1) collect roots and related words (page 624), or 2) play the game Concentration (page 625). Encourage students to reflect on how well the activity helped them learn and remember word parts.

For more practice, see pages 218–223 of the *Student Applications Book 7*.

Assessment

Ask students:

- How can breaking a word into roots, prefixes, and suffixes, help you determine its meaning?
- Which strategy discussed in this section do you think will be the most useful to you? Explain your choice.

WEEK 34
Lesson 6

Reading Dictionaries and Thesauruses

For use with *Reader's Handbook* pages 626–630

Goals

In this lesson, students expand their understanding of how to use dictionaries and thesauruses effectively.

Teaching Focus

Background

Dictionaries and thesauruses can be powerful resources for helping students expand their vocabulary, but only if students know how to use them correctly. Use this lesson to reinforce students' understanding of how to use these reference sources to get the most out of their reading.

Instruction

Remind students that when the meaning of a word is critical to understanding, context clues and structural analysis may not be enough. Point out that dictionaries can help clarify meaning and check accuracy of predictions based on structural and contextual clues. Ask student volunteers to brainstorm common features of dictionaries, such as how entry words are spelled and pronounced.

Teaching Approach

Use of the Handbook

Have students read more about dictionaries on pages 626–629 of the handbook on their own. Come together as a class and work through the information on thesauruses, a reference source students might be less familiar with than dictionaries. Point out the key parts of a thesaurus entry at the bottom of page 630. Talk about the similarities and differences between a dictionary and a thesaurus.

Extend the Handbook

Work with students to create a class slang dictionary. To begin, have students choose a slang term that they would like to include in the dictionary. Ask students to write a dictionary entry for their word, using the information in the handbook as a guide. Invite students to share their entries. If students chose the same term, have them compare their entries. Did both students define the term in the same way?

Assessment

Ask students:

- How would you explain to a younger student when to use a dictionary and when to use a thesaurus?
- What did you learn about dictionaries or thesauruses from reading this section of the handbook?

WEEK 34
Lesson 7

Understanding Specialized Terms

For use with *Reader's Handbook* pages 631–634

Goals

In this lesson, students learn strategies for determining the meaning of specialized vocabulary.

Teaching Focus

Background

Many of the strategies described throughout this section, including structural and contextual clues, can provide some assistance in determining the meaning of specialized terms. But because so much of the terminology in content area reading will be unfamiliar to students, specific strategies for unlocking their meaning will help students construct meaning from the text.

Instruction

Write the following sports on the board: hockey, soccer, and basketball. Ask volunteers to provide examples of language related to each sport, for example, checking, goalie, and zone defense. List students' ideas under the appropriate heading. Point out that school subjects also have their own special vocabularies. Talk about some of the terminology students have learned over the years from reading science, math, or social studies texts.

Teaching Approach

Use of the Handbook

Divide the class into four groups. Assign each group one of the following strategies for understanding specialized terms: Record Key Terms (pages 631–632), Get Savvy about Textbooks (page 632), Use Webs and Concept Maps (page 633), Learn Specialized Terms (page 634). Have each group present its strategy to the rest of the class.

Extend the Handbook

Have students create a Concept Map to connect specialized terms from a current chapter in a science or social studies textbook. After completing the Concept Map, ask students to reflect on the activity. Did creating the Concept Map help them understand the specialized terms from the chapter? Why or why not?

Assessment

Ask students:

- What are some strategies you currently use to figure out the meaning of specialized terms?
- How will this lesson help you read content area textbooks?

WEEK 34
Lesson 8

Understanding Analogies

For use with *Reader's Handbook* pages 636–639

Goals

In this lesson, students explore techniques for understanding analogies.

Teaching Focus

Background

Strengthening students' proficiency in understanding analogies boosts vocabulary. It also fosters critical reading skills. Use this section of the *Reader's Handbook* to introduce and reinforce strategies for reading analogies successfully.

Instruction

Write the following on the board: *teacher : school :: doctor : hospital*. Ask a student volunteer to explain the relationships being compared. Point out that this is an example of an analogy. Discuss with students what they know about analogies. Explain that by improving their ability to understand analogies, students can boost both their vocabulary power and their logical thinking skills.

Teaching Approach

Use of the Handbook

Walk students through the information on analogies at the bottom of page 636. Then think aloud as you work through the first few types of analogies on page 637. Finish this page by having student volunteers answer the remaining analogies, using your think-aloud as a guide. Scaffold the learning by having students work in small groups to examine the analogies on pages 638–639.

Extend the Handbook

Challenge pairs of students to create their own analogies. Remind pairs to model their analogies on the types described on pages 637–639. Have pairs choose one or two analogies to share with the class.

Assessment

Ask students:

- How would you rate your ability to read and understand analogies? What might you do to improve your ability?
- What is the most important thing you learned from this section of the handbook? Explain.

The Reader's Almanac

For use with *Reader's Handbook* pages 640–692

Daily Lessons	**Summary***
Lesson 1 **The Reader's Almanac: An Overview**	Work with students to explore the Reader's Almanac. Have students assess their proficiency with the strategies and reading tools found in the Almanac.
Lesson 2 **Close Reading**	Help students review and expand their understanding of the strategy of close reading. Have students apply the strategy to a text of their choice.
Lesson 3 **Outlining**	Reinforce students' understanding of outlining as a strategy for organizing information in nonfiction texts.
Lesson 4 **Paraphrasing**	Review and expand students' understanding of the uses and purpose of paraphrasing. Compare the strategies of summarizing and paraphrasing.

*Use these notes to help you teach a mini-lesson or to teach a briefer, shorter version of the lessons for more proficient students.

Lesson Resources

See *Teacher's Guide* pages 429–478.

See Website www.greatsource.com/rehand/

The Reader's Almanac (continued)

For use with *Reader's Handbook* pages 652–663

Daily Lessons	**Summary***
Lesson 5 **Questioning the Author**	Help students review and extend their understanding of the strategy of questioning the author. Have students apply the strategy to a text of their choice.
Lesson 6 **Reading Critically**	Work with students to enhance understanding of the steps involved in reading critically.
Lesson 7 **Using Graphic Organizers**	Review with students the various graphic organizers available to help readers keep track of information and organize their thoughts.
Lesson 8 **The *Reader's Handbook*: A Review**	Work with students to review and reflect on their learning throughout their work in the *Reader's Handbook*.

*Use these notes to help you teach a mini-lesson or to teach a briefer, shorter version of the lessons for more proficient students.

Lesson Resources

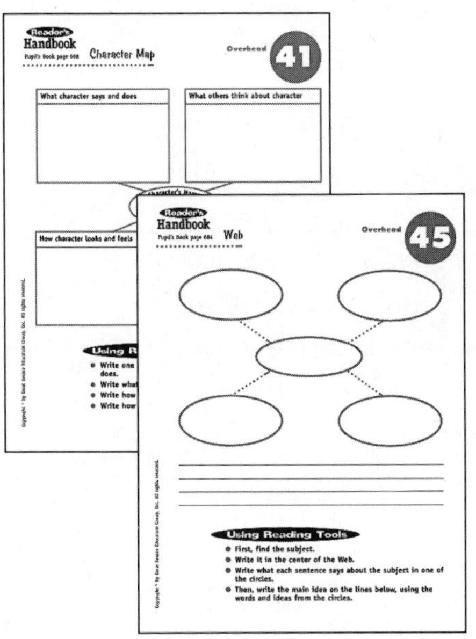

Overheads

For this lesson, use: Overheads 41 and 45

See *Teacher's Guide* pages 429–478.

See Website www.greatsource.com/rehand/

WEEK 35
Lesson 1

The Reader's Almanac: An Overview

For use with *Reader's Handbook* pages 640–692

Goals

In this lesson, students explore the Reader's Almanac and expand their understanding of how to use this resource.

Teaching Focus

Background

Most likely, students have already used the Reader's Almanac section of the handbook by now. Every strategy and reading tool described here has been referenced throughout the handbook. Use this section, then, as an overall review of active reading strategies and as a means of student self-assessment.

Instruction

Ask students to describe the Reader's Almanac without looking in their handbooks. How is it organized? What kinds of information can they find in it? Talk about students' use of the Almanac. Have they used it as a resource throughout the year? How has it changed the way they read? Finally, discuss the purpose of the Almanac. Help students see that the Reader's Almanac can be used as a reference to locate information about the reading strategies and tools in the handbook.

Teaching Approach

Use of the Handbook

Ask students to look at page 640 to identify the three main parts of the Almanac. Then read aloud the introduction to the Strategy Handbook on page 641. Ask students to mark each of the twelve key strategies, using a + for those that they understand completely, a * for those they understand reasonably well, and a – those for they need to work on. Read aloud the introduction to the Reading Tools section on page 666. Have students use similar markings as they read through the list of reading tools. Then have students review and make note of the variety of word parts listed on pages 685–692.

Extend the Handbook

Have students meet in small groups to discuss what they hope to learn from exploring the Reader's Almanac. Invite groups to summarize their findings for the rest of the class.

Assessment

Ask students:

- What part of the Almanac are you most familiar with? What part of the Almanac could you benefit from exploring more?
- Describe the purpose of the Almanac.

WEEK 35 Lesson 2 Close Reading

For use with *Reader's Handbook* pages 642–643, 671

Goals

In this lesson, students review and expand their understanding of how and when to use the strategy of close reading.

Teaching Focus

Background

Close reading is an excellent strategy for helping readers construct meaning from short passages where every word carries weight. The strategy of close reading was introduced and reinforced earlier in the handbook. Help students use this lesson to assess their understanding of close reading and to develop a plan for using the strategy to increase comprehension as needed.

Instruction

Review with students what they know about close reading. Invite them to skim the handbook to note sections in which the strategy was discussed. Before reading the information on close reading in the Almanac, encourage students to reflect on their current understanding of the strategy. Are they satisfied with their ability to use the strategy? What, if any, aspects of the strategy need clarification?

Teaching Approach

Use of the Handbook

Read aloud the description of close reading on page 642 of the handbook. Walk students through the steps for using the strategy. Help clarify the steps by thinking aloud as you perform a close reading on a poem or short excerpt. Have students find out more about Double-entry Journals by reading page 671 of the handbook. Discuss why a Double-entry Journal is a good reading tool to use with close reading. Invite students to share other tools they might use for close reading.

Extend the Handbook

Have students apply the strategy of close reading to a short passage of their choice. Remind them to follow the steps outlined on pages 642–643. After completing the activity, have students use their journals to reflect on the strategy. Questions to consider: How would I rate my understanding of close reading? What part of the strategy do I need to work on? What can I do to improve my ability to use this strategy effectively?

Assessment

Ask students:

- How do you decide when to use close reading as a strategy for reading or rereading a text?
- What is the purpose of close reading?

Outlining

For use with *Reader's Handbook* pages 648–649, 675

Goals

In this lesson, students reinforce their understanding of outlining as a strategy for organizing information in nonfiction texts.

Teaching Focus

Background

Outlining is a key reading strategy for keeping track of information in nonfiction texts. By separating information into topics and subtopics, outlining not only highlights key information but also helps the reader distinguish between main ideas and details.

Instruction

Discuss students' use of outlining as a reading or rereading strategy. Invite student volunteers to share their experiences using outlining. Did outlining help them keep track of information? Why or why not? Explain that in this lesson students will review the steps involved in outlining effectively.

Teaching Approach

Use of the Handbook

Walk students through the sample Outline on page 648 of the *Reader's Handbook*. Compare it to the Outline framework on page 675. Discuss the differences between topics and subtopics. How can students determine what is a topic, or main idea, and what is a subtopic, or supporting detail? After discussing outlining in general, have students read page 649 independently.

Extend the Handbook

Outlining is a particularly useful strategy for organizing information in textbooks. Have students create an Outline of a content area textbook chapter, using the samples in the handbook as guides. Have students choose either a Topic or Sentence Outline, depending on which framework they think will help them retain the information most successfully.

Assessment

Ask students:

- What is the difference between a Topic and a Sentence Outline? How do you decide which to use?
- How would you rate your ability to use outlining as a reading or rereading strategy? What could you do to improve your ability to outline effectively?

WEEK 35 Lesson 4 Paraphrasing

For use with *Reader's Handbook* pages 650–651, 676

Goals

In this lesson, students review and expand their understanding of the uses and purposes of paraphrasing.

Teaching Focus

Background

With the abundance of both online and print reference sources available to students, the ability to paraphrase becomes increasingly important. Paraphrasing involves two main skills: 1) the ability to understand what is read and 2) the ability to restate the information in the reader's own words. It is in this second step that students often stumble. While this lesson focuses on using graphics to paraphrase, you can expand it to include a review of paraphrasing in general.

Instruction

Explain that in this lesson students will review the strategy of paraphrasing. Ask students to reflect on what they have learned about paraphrasing throughout their work in the handbook. Questions they might ask themselves: What do I do when I paraphrase? How often do I use this strategy? How effective am I at using it? What parts of the strategy do I need to work on? How can I use this section to fine-tune my paraphrasing ability?

Teaching Approach

Use of the Handbook

Have students work through the information on paraphrasing on pages 650–651 independently. Encourage them to use their reflections (see above) to help them focus their reading. Discuss with students how the Paraphrase Chart can help them organize their thoughts. Clarify the use of this reading tool by having students explore the Paraphrase Chart framework on page 676 and compare it with the sample on page 651.

Extend the Handbook

Extend students' understanding of paraphrasing by asking them to rewrite a passage from a nonfiction text in their own words. Encourage them to follow the steps listed on pages 650–651. After completing the activity, have students look over their reflections (see above) and modify them based on any new understanding they gained from this lesson.

Assessment

Ask students:

- What do readers gain from paraphrasing?
- Describe a Paraphrase Chart. What does it look like? How does it help you paraphrase?

WEEK 36 Lesson 5 Questioning the Author

For use with *Reader's Handbook* pages 652–653

Goals

In this lesson, students review and expand their understanding of the reading strategy of questioning the author.

Teaching Focus

Background

Questioning the author incorporates a variety of reading strategies: first, readers must read actively and ask appropriate questions; second, they need to infer and draw conclusions based on information in the text; finally readers must evaluate the author's purpose and how well it was met. A breakdown of comprehension at any of these steps will limit students' ability to use the strategy effectively.

Instruction

Discuss what students know about the reading strategy of questioning the author. Invite students to skim the handbook for examples of the strategy in action (see pages 185, 240). Explain that the strategy can be broken down into a number of other reading strategies, such as asking questions, making inferences and drawing conclusions, and evaluating the author's purpose and how well it was met. Ask students to reflect on how well they use either the overall strategy of questioning the author or these substrategies. Encourage students to use their reflections to help them set a purpose for reading this section.

Teaching Approach

Use of the Handbook

Walk students through the information on questioning the author on pages 652–653 of the handbook. Discuss the list of questions on page 652 and encourage students to add to them. Point out that the questions will change depending on both the reader's purpose and the nature of the text itself. Invite students to skim the Reading Tools section of the handbook to find graphic organizers, such as an Inference Chart (page 672), which will help them use the strategy effectively.

Extend the Handbook

Have students apply the strategy of questioning the author to a text of their choice. Remind them to follow the steps as outlined on pages 652–653 and to use any graphic organizer that will enable them to use the strategy more effectively. Have students revisit their purposes for reading and reflect on how well they were able to meet their purposes.

Assessment

Ask students:

- What are the steps involved in questioning the author?
- What kinds of texts would you choose to use this strategy? Explain.

WEEK 36 Lesson 6 Reading Critically

For use with *Reader's Handbook* pages 654–655

Goals

In this lesson, students enhance their understanding of the steps involved in reading critically.

Teaching Focus

Background

Reading critically enables the reader to move beyond the literal meaning of the text to gain a deeper understanding of the material. Critical readers are strategic, active readers who understand the necessity of evaluating information rather than accepting what they read at face value.

Instruction

Create a Concept Web for the strategy of critical reading. Invite students to brainstorm ideas related to the strategy and add them to the Web. Use the Concept Web as a basis for a discussion of the strategy. What does it mean to read critically? Why should students read critically? Explain that in this lesson, students will review the steps involved in becoming critical readers.

Teaching Approach

Use of the Handbook

Read aloud or have a student volunteer read aloud the description of reading critically on page 654 of the *Reader's Handbook*. Then walk students through the three steps for using the strategy effectively. Have students skim the Reading Tools section of the Almanac for graphic organizers that might help them follow these steps more effectively, such as an Inference Chart or a Viewpoint and Evidence Organizer.

Extend the Handbook

Have students apply the strategy of reading critically to a text of their choice. Encourage them to follow the steps described on pages 654–655 and use one or more graphic organizers to help them organize their thinking. After completing the activity, ask students to reflect on how effective the strategy was for deepening their understanding of the text.

Assessment

Ask students:

- What does it take to be a critical reader?
- Why is reading critically important?

WEEK 36
Lesson 7

Using Graphic Organizers

For use with *Reader's Handbook* pages 662–663

Goals

In this lesson, students review and expand their understanding of the various graphic organizers available to help readers keep track of information and organize their thinking.

Teaching Focus

Background

Students have used graphic organizers to keep track of information and organize their thinking throughout their work with the handbook. Use this lesson 1) to review students' general understanding of the uses and purposes of graphic organizers and 2) as a means of assessing students' familiarity with the graphics listed in the Reading Tools section of the Almanac.

Instruction

Work with students to brainstorm a list of graphic organizers with which they are familiar. Write the headings *Fiction* and *Nonfiction* on the board, and list students' ideas underneath one or both of the headings. Review the purposes of graphic organizers in general. Then ask students to reflect on their own experiences using graphic organizers. Which do they use most often? Do they tend to use graphic organizers more with nonfiction or fiction? Why?

Teaching Approach

Use of the Handbook

Have students review the information on using graphic organizers on pages 662–663. Then ask students to skim the Reading Tools section of the Almanac, paying particular attention to those they marked with a – in Lesson 1. Encourage students to create a plan for mastering these organizers.

Extend the Handbook

To help students practice working with graphic organizers, ask them to choose one from the Reading Tools section and apply it to a text of their choosing. Remind them to be sure the organizer fits the text (for example, a Character Map with a piece of fiction, or a Viewpoint and Evidence Organizer with a persuasive piece).

Assessment

Ask students:

- How has your use of graphic organizers changed since using the *Reader's Handbook*?
- Since you began using the graphic organizers described in the handbook, have you noticed a change in your ability to organize information? Explain.

WEEK 36
Lesson 8

The *Reader's Handbook*: A Review

For use with the *Reader's Handbook* as a whole

Goals

In this lesson, students review and reflect on their learning throughout their work in the *Reader's Handbook*.

Teaching Focus

Background

At the beginning of students' work in the handbook, they explored the goals of the handbook and their own goals for reading. Use this last lesson as a means for students to review what they have learned and reflect on how well they have met their original purposes for reading the handbook.

Instruction

Hold a class discussion about what students learned from using the *Reader's Handbook*. Encourage students to skim through the Table of Contents to help them review the various reading strategies explored in the handbook. Explain that in this lesson students will pause and reflect on their learning, just as they have been taught to do after reading other texts and genres.

Teaching Approach

Use of the Handbook

Have students meet in small groups to review and discuss the goals of the *Reader's Handbook* on pages 14–15. How effective do groups think the handbook was at helping them meet these goals? Invite each group to summarize their discussion for the rest of the class.

Extend the Handbook

Invite students to review their own list of reading goals set forth at the beginning of their work in the handbook. Have them use their journals to reflect on how effectively they met these goals. Then ask them to assess their overall learning in the handbook.

Assessment

Ask students:

- How has working with the *Reader's Handbook* changed the way you view the reading process?
- What is the most important thing you learned from using the handbook? Explain your choice.

Lessons Index